COCO CHANEL

COCO CHANEL

Her Life, Her Secrets

MARCEL HAEDRICH

Translated from the French by
Charles Lam Markmann

With Illustrations

Little, Brown and Company · Boston · Toronto

For Andrée — if not the creation,
the creator.

With thanks to my friend
Hervé Mille. Without him, without
his help, this book could not have been written.

*Chanel created a feminine character
such as Paris had never before
known.*

MAURICE SACHS

COCO CHANEL

"Those on Whom Legends Are Built
Are Their Legends"

I first met Coco Chanel in 1958. She was seventy-five years old — a prodigy beatified. And triumphant: she had imposed her style on the whole world. Because she had succeeded in everything in her life, I urged her to describe her victories into the tape recorder. She murmured into the microphone: "I don't even know whether I've been happy."

She would say: "Every day I simplify something because every day I learn something." She would say: "When I can no longer create anything, I'll be done for." She would say: "There goes a woman who knows all the things that can be taught and none of the things that cannot be taught." She would say: "Youth is something very new: twenty years ago no one mentioned it." She said too: "Only truth has no frontiers." And this: "There is only one thing about which I am still curious: death."

From the flood of her talk I sifted the nuggets — though not all of them. She spoke rapidly, and I had to become accustomed to her muted voice. I thought she was overly made up, aggressively made up, with too-red lips, oversized and overblackened eyebrows, harshly dyed hair. That was my first impression of her: an almost outrageously done-up old lady who talked endlessly. She was two years older than my mother. That thought occurred to me as I was asking myself: what are *you*, the Alsatian of Alsatians, doing here at Coco Chanel's? She intimidated me. I opened my ears. To enter her presence was to step into a monologue.

I opened my eyes as well. I was in the presence of a national monument: how does one examine the Eiffel Tower? My own mental image of Coco Chanel had been conventional. I knew that she had been very beautiful. I knew that a celebrity of *la Belle Epoque* had discovered her in Moulins, a cavalry garrison, and brought her to Paris, where she proceeded to liberate womankind from corsets; and that she had created a fashion "look" and a famous perfume; and that the Duke of Westminster had covered her with jewels (eight yards of pearls, shovelfuls of emeralds and diamonds); and that she had launched the little black dress, short hair, costume jewelry, et cetera.

Coco Chanel! In her drawing room I was in Ali Baba's cave with the treasures of Golconda — calamander screens, mother of pearl, ebony, ivory, deer and lions, gold and crystal, masks, a wall of rare books, spheres, magic, the scent of tuberoses. It was Byzantium and the imperial palace of China, Ptolemy's Egypt, and, in the mirrors above the fireplace, reflections of Greece with a fourth-century Aphrodite side by side with a fantastic raging wild boar, a meteorite that had fallen from the sky on Mongolia thousands of years ago — everything agglomerated and conglomerated, mingled and mangled, ordered into a disorder magnificently made harmonious by Coco's taste. It was sumptuous — too much for me. Could anyone live in this? Sleep, make love on that couch? I had asked myself the same questions in the Borgias' apartments in the Vatican: could anyone really breathe, eat, drink, kiss in such magnificence? Against that setting? Did the Pope keep his biretta on when his barber was shaving him? Coco never removed her hat on her visits to herself in the Chanel Museum.

That day (my notes begin with the date of 1 August 1959) the hat was a flat, broad-brimmed straw, with a large jewel pinned at the front. Coco was wearing a suit cut from a very light, almost white material with a vague hint of pale gold. She tugged at her jacket, and all the time she was talking she never stopped smoking.

"When all this brouhaha is over, I am going to change several of the models," she said.

Accompanied by Hervé Mille, I had just seen a Saturday showing of her collection for store buyers. At that time I was editor in chief of *Marie-Claire*,* but I paid virtually no attention to fashion, since I was convinced that I knew nothing about it; and besides it did not interest me. For this part of the magazine we had our ladies, fascinating creatures at once innocent and perverse, smooth-tongued and ruthless, grandees of a Spain of their own because they could say "Christian" when they meant Dior or Bérard, "Jacques" when they meant Fath, "Pierre" for Balmain ("that darling Pierre is redoing his pretty Madame"). At the sight of all of them in congress to inspect a collection, those ladies of the fashion press, one could not help wondering about fashion. And yet they served it, like the Vestals who tended the fires on the altars of Rome, with equal devotion and conviction, and often as chaste as the Vestals — though not from faith but from necessity — and therefore edgy and irritable in their perfume and the body armor that was still worn at that time. They lived on diets and knew virtually no mode of counting but the calorie. When they were derelict they could not, like the Vestals, be buried alive.

"A philosophy of fashion?" Coco said. "I don't understand: that doesn't mean anything. A fashion for the young? That is a pleonasm: there is no fashion for the old. What does a 'young

* A "women's magazine" with a huge circulation in France. Translator.

style' mean? Dressing like a little girl? Nothing could be more stupid, nothing could make one look older. People confuse everything. Sometimes fashion is idiotic; when it is, it is forgotten. It is forgotten, too, when it is not pretty. I'd like to ask the dress trade a question: 'What is fashion? Explain it to me.' Not one would give me a decent answer. And I couldn't give you one either. Fashion in a country's style should reflect the way people live, the way people dress in that country. Here everyone does everything he can to prevent Frenchwomen from dressing the way one dresses in France. The trade wants to sell abroad, that's all the dressmakers think of, and since they think they're very important . . ."

What follows is not said simply to shock: she made me think back to Premier Mossadegh of Iran, for a variety of reasons, and primarily because I felt as astonished at finding myself in her home, in her luxurious drawing room, as I had been in Teheran when I entered Mossadegh's monastic cell with its whitewashed walls decorated only with a steel-banded wristwatch hung from a nail driven into the wall above the night table.

In Teheran a revolution was taking place. The Paris newspapers splashed across eight columns the news that blood was flowing in the streets. What was flowing more than anything was vodka with lime, down the gullets of journalists gathered from everywhere in the world. It was summer and the heat was abominable.

Mossadegh explained to me — in French — the essential meaning of the oil crisis. At first I understood him no better than I understood Mademoiselle Chanel. He did not speak so rapidly as she, but like her, he was rich in digressions. One felt that he had left oil far behind when he was reciting a Zoroastrian poem on the conflict between light and darkness. He told me quite simply what was going on: a more equitable distribution of the world's wealth, no longer by way of demoralizing handouts from the West but through a rise in the prices of crude oil and the other raw materials that the West was buying from the Third World.

Politics, which is antithetical to realism, can be practical only when merged with the morality of its time: this makes it possible for the greatest number of people to live together. This was the profound truth that Mossadegh taught me as I listened at his bedside, happy and proud to have been chosen out of two hundred colleagues to receive his truth.

Chanel confronted me with the same problem as Mossadegh: to find the gold in the torrent of her words. As she spoke, she impaled one with her look like an insect on a pin: *Are you listening? Do you understand me? This is no mere noise that comes from my bleeding lips. I have a great deal to say. No one listens to me attentively enough. People think I talk in order to fill the silence of my life. You, Alsatian, you seem able to pay attention. Sit beside me. From now on we shall be friends.*

Is there such a gap between fashion and oil? Each is a closed circle in which money seeks triumphs at the expense of morality.

"When one is the editor of a fashion publication, one cannot tolerate bad taste," Mademoiselle Chanel said. We were getting to the meat of my first talk with her. It had been brought about by Hervé Mille, one of her oldest friends, who since Coco's comeback in the rue Cambon had been constantly doing battle on her behalf.

Can you imagine the Aga Khan — not the current one but the old one, the fat one — coming down off the scale on which each year his weight was matched in diamonds and upbraiding his followers for having done him out of ten or twenty carats of the two hundred–odd pounds of diamonds to which he was entitled?

That was how *la Grande Mademoiselle* was behaving. Her new winter collection was a success; still, below the surface of the compliments — expected yet despised, necessary yet ineffectual — she sensed with some irritation that there were certain reservations about the inevitable Chanel suit. *Who are these scribblers buzzing in my ears?* She who never asked for anything was always amazed, when she was given everything, that it was so little.

The day before, at the first showing of the collection, she had seen the novelist Edmonde Charles-Roux, who was then editor in chief of the French edition of *Vogue,* wearing "something horrible." This meant, obviously, something from another designer.

"Why are you wearing that, Edmonde?"

"It was given to me."

"One more reason for not wearing it."

Her wit and her smile made her young again. She had very pretty, well-rounded knees, which she invariably covered with two folds of her skirt, one on top of the other, with her hands over them.

"If I were a fashion editor," she said to me, "I should dress with the utmost care when I was going to a collection." Her eyes, black beads spangled with gold, were saying: *If you were a woman and covering my collection, you'd wear a Chanel, wouldn't you?*

A servant brought some flowers. Who had sent them? She glanced at the card and made a face: Richard Avedon, the well-known American photographer. "What an ass," she said, twisting her mouth in a moue. She had the flowers taken into another room, which she called the cemetery: "It's for flowers that come from people I don't like."

There were some flowers in her drawing room, however. "Those are flowers from people I like. Those I keep even when they fade."

Why this banishment to the "cemetery" for Avedon? He had done a picture story for *Harper's Bazaar,* with a text by Truman Capote, photographing clothes chosen and worn by Audrey Hepburn. In America, Paris fashions were still news: magazines competed intensely with one another in covering them.

Commission Truman Capote for that? They must really have

money, I thought. But Coco cared nothing for the writer's reputation; what irritated her was the actress. How could she tolerate her clothes being shown by Audrey Hepburn, who had always been dressed by Givenchy? "Why did they have to get a foreigner for it?" she grumbled. "Are there no pretty women in France?"

My eyes were dazzled by the wonders created for the winter — suits in tweeds as light as eiderdown, astonishingly romantic evening gowns, black velvet, lace. Every model had a dozen new touches. Coco's gowns, as the film director François Reichenbach has observed, are like the music of the masters. They always offer one what one expects, with an extra surprise.

Twice a year *Marie-Claire* published the edicts of the fashion dictators, analyzing them in meticulous detail that with the passage of time becomes quite touching: round necks, broad shoulders, high waists, emphasized bosoms, knee-length skirts, straight coats, dresses on the bias, who knows what else? All this was uttered by our ladies, and conformity must follow on pain of being out of fashion — what misery, what ignominy for a woman. Elegance depended on a hem. Even in 1959, however, only four years after Chanel's comeback, it was clear that none of this made sense anymore: the Chanel look had killed that kind of fashion.

Who was aware of what was happening? The most ignorant of all were the couturiers.

Mademoiselle Chanel pretended to despise them. Nevertheless, this peremptory empress who acted so very sure of herself was the embodiment of anxiety. She must have spent her life trembling on her tightrope, across a void that she herself had created. The longer I knew her the more and the better I wanted to know her. She seemed more pathetic with every visit, often even pitiable, poisoned by a secret that she no longer remembered.

"I've had no time for living," she said. "No one's ever understood this. I don't even know whether I've been very happy. I've

wept a great deal, more than most people do. I've been very unhappy in the middle of great love affairs." And this was followed
by a splendid observation that one barely had time to snatch out
of the torrent: "Great loves too must be endured."

She was growing used to me. She talked to me with great freedom: "I remember only that I've been miserable in a life that
from the outside seemed magnificent," she confided to me the
third or fourth time I saw her.

"I've always been under pressure," she said, "first of all because I've never wanted to give up the House of Chanel, which is
the only thing that's mine, in which no one else has had any part,
the only place where I've felt truly happy. There no one could
ever get under my skin. Everything I've tried has been a success.
When I needed money I had only to ask for it. All I saw was
smiles. No one would have dared to be unpleasant with me."

One forgot her age. One let oneself yield to her imploring
eyes. Within a pound or two her weight had not changed since
she was twenty. Why did she encourage confusion as to her age?

During our first meeting she mentioned a young American
who had just paid her a visit. She described him: narrow trousers
on long legs, a severe jacket with all three buttons buttoned.
When he was announced, his name had reminded Coco of
friends whom she had neglected — "dull people, but just the
same I'd never been displeased to see them in the United States."
Since she was alone, she ordered that the American be shown up,
as if in expiation.

She told her stories in a kind of temporal dimension. In the
time that it must have taken the young man to climb the stairs,
she denounced America to me: "a doomed country because all it
knows now is comfort; the rich buy pictures as investments and
hang them one on top of another because they can get publicity
out of it: everyone immediately knows they've bought a Renoir."

Germany, on the other hand, was discovering luxury: "I
visited German castles. You still have a footman behind your

chair. The silverware is splendid — too heavy, it's true, but this is luxury. In France everything is half measures. France is becoming too American. What a mistake to give up luxury. America is nothing but *le gadget*" — she used the American word.

Her digression was completed. The young American in the narrow trousers was now in her drawing room. Coco greeted him: "You're the son of Madame So-and-so."

"No," he replied (she quoted his words). "We have the same name, but nothing else in common."

"Well, what can I do for you?"

"Well, look, mademoiselle: there are two of us; my friend and I (*I've forgotten the friend's name,* Coco interpolated) are revolutionizing the art of the interview."

"Really?"

"Yes, mademoiselle. All we ask is three questions, because three properly chosen questions, if we get answers, can tell us all we want to know."

"That's not bad."

"Would you be willing to answer our questions, mademoiselle?"

"Please sit down, sir."

"Do you agree, then?"

"I don't know yet. I'm very busy. Make it quick."

"How old are you, mademoiselle?"

"That doesn't concern you."

"That's not an answer, mademoiselle."

"You are right, monsieur. Since I promised you a reply, I'll give you one. So I will tell you that my age varies according to the days and the people I happen to be with."

"That will do beautifully, mademoiselle."

"But wait, monsieur, I haven't finished my answer: there's a conclusion to it." (Here she turned to Hervé and me and explained: "I really was getting fed up to here, you know?" Whereupon she went back to the young American.)

"When I'm bored I feel very old, and since I'm extremely bored with you, I'm going to be a thousand years old in five minutes if you don't get the hell out of here at once."

That was the end of the young American. The two other questions that would tell everything there was to know about Coco were left filed in his head. *Good-bye, young man. Oh, in the United States, you know, such things are perfectly permissible, reporters can ask anything.*

I was diverting myself a good deal at that time with a tape recorder that had been given to me by Roswell Keller, an American artist. I had used it for an interview with Brigitte Bardot, with good results. Coco was rather reluctant. "I ramble on . . ." she said.

As I visited her more frequently, I became used to her makeup and her voice, and I listened to her more closely. One evening I found her asleep on her couch, her hat over her eyes, her skirt pulled over her knees and her hands folded on her stomach, one thumb hooked to a necklace. She was wearing tweed, not shantung anymore. Months had gone by and it was winter — February, after another collection. I had already congratulated her, and I was coming back to dine with her. From outside I had heard muted music — Wagner — and so I had gone on in, assuming that she had not heard my knock. She was sleeping. (So it was possible to sleep on that show-window couch.) There were glasses everywhere, the acid smell of champagne, butts in the ashtrays. No one had cleaned up, lest she be awakened. But before I could go out again she opened her eyes.

"Don't go," she said. She sat up, her legs under her on the couch. "You see," she murmured, "that's what fame is: solitude."

Each night as she was about to go to bed she teetered at the edge of a precipice, perhaps because she fell asleep as one has to sink into death. Everyone who had dined out with her knew the script:

"It's late, mademoiselle. Don't you think you should . . ."

She would not be listening. The guest would rise, and she would not notice. She would go on talking, arranging the edges of her skirt over her rounded knees.

"It's time to . . . Don't you think, mademoiselle . . ."

She would pour out her story or her confidence, her complaint or her recrimination. "All right," she would sigh at last, "I must go to bed. I have to work tomorrow."

She would get up, adjust her scarf, settle her hat, and sit down again. She would take her bag, open it, put things into it, take them out again, examine them — pills; eyeglasses (three pairs: one for reading, one for distance, one for movies); her cigarette holder; brand-new ten-franc notes folded in four for tips; various letters received during the day (these she would unfold, read, fold again and return to their envelopes). Step by step she would be led toward the door. When the weather was bad, her raincoat would be waiting on a chair in the lobby. The stairs would be taken with many pauses, her monologue never interrupted, and then it was the street, the brief walk to the Hotel Ritz with intermediate stops before the final one outside the hotel's revolving door — where she was apparently determined to spend the night. She showed not the slightest sign of weariness, although your legs might be about to break. It became impossible to follow her, to listen to her, to remember what she had related. One was exhausted when one left her.

In notes made on 9 February 1960 I find a confidence that she gave me at the revolving door of the Ritz: "The ice has now been broken between us. Come back, and ask me questions. I will think back about everything. I have notes, and I'll reread them."

Throughout the evening she had been confiding in the tape recorder. I was urging her to tell the story of her life. She was evasive.

"If there's one thing no one cares about it's someone's life story. If I wrote a book about my life, I'd begin it with tomorrow. I won't start out by telling you in order about my early life, my childhood and youth. First one must give one's views on the period in which one lives. It's more logical, newer, and more amusing."

Confronting her life, she reminded me of a kitten with a ball of yarn: it pulls at a strand, the ball rolls, the kitten leaps back in fright, backs off farther, studies the situation, advances again reassured, thrusts out a paw, and pulls again.

"I speak in maxims," she said; "I've written hundreds."

An American publisher was pressing her to write a book of advice for women. I objected that she had more important things to do. "No, no," she said; "I'll do the advice book, and then we'll see." After a pause she added: "I want to leave something behind."

The American publisher was offering her a large advance. "I don't need money," she said. "I'll leave plenty of it. I can't even spend what I earn."

She would order a hard-boiled egg and probe the white with her knife, cleaning it even after the shell had been removed. I would have roast chicken, and she would ask: "Do you like the drumstick? I always had it when I was little, because I had to leave the other parts for the grown-ups. Now I don't want it."

She read me some of her maxims, which, she was careful to tell me, she had written while visiting her close friend Maggie van Zuylen in New York. She had spent Sunday selecting these "from thousands of others." I did not pay too much attention to the reading, because I ascribed less importance to Coco Chanel's maxims than to her recollections. I was wrong — not so much about the maxims as about her. She was trying to show me the tone in which it would be best to write about her. That was it: she was looking for the music that would constitute the grand opera that she dreamed of leaving behind her. I realized this when the tape recorder re-created the scene, the memory of which had begun to blur but revived at once with a clarity that underlined too late the importance of what at that moment Coco was giving me of the essence of herself. Here then are some of the maxims of Mademoiselle Chanel as she read them that night:

Happiness consists in bringing one's thoughts to realization.

One can pursue thought after life in order to realize it in death.

Material things aside, we need not advice but approval.

For those who understand nothing about art, beauty's name is poetry.

As she reread these observations and scribbled them into an old notebook to furnish out the void of a Sunday, she must have felt a moment almost of self-pity. How good the things she had written were; how little anyone cared about understanding her; who knew that this fire too was alive in her? When she read these things out to Hervé Mille, his brother Gérard, and me, she was no longer so certain of having written something eternal. (And yet there was no stinting of praise.) She went on faster and faster, not looking at us:

One must be alert against those who have wit but little judgment. We are surrounded by them.

Was it for our benefit that she was turning skeptic? The next maxim was an observation about herself:

Undoubtedly I have faults and weaknesses, but it is what is best in me, my desire for justice and truth, that has vexed my friends and aroused their anger.

And this too dealt with herself:

Of necessity, superiority isolates one. It compels one to choose one's friendships and one's relationships.

Why? One might have put the question to her, who said: "I'd rather dine with a bum who amuses me than with rich people who bore me." Indeed, I can almost see her raising her head, after she had read us this maxim, as I listen to her saying (thanks to the tape recorder): "I must have been extremely fed up with America when I wrote that."

She read another aloud:

> *The greatest flattery that one person can offer another is carnal pleasure, and only carnal pleasure, because reason has no share in it and there can be no question of merit, and because it is addressed not to the character of the person but to the person himself.*

"Not bad," she commented. "Now and then I write things that amaze even me."

I found her more convincing when she gave us what had come spontaneously, when she showered us with her instinctive truths and did not concern herself with polishing their form. "One grows used to ugliness but never to slovenliness. Slovenliness in a woman means being neither perfumed nor washed. I am very fond of perfume. I like women who are well turned out and perfumed. It's degrading when they smell of slovenliness."

And yet was it not right to admire the literary effort that she imposed on herself out of sheer self-respect?

> *A saint in human society is no more useful than a saint in the desert. If the saints who live in the desert are useless, those who live in human society are often dangerous.*

> *Fear of God preserves from sin those who have no desire for it or who are in no position to commit it.*

> *The glories of divine mercy hearten even criminals, who have reason to hope that they will share in it with the rest.*

She turned to us for counsel after she had read these three maxims. "What was I thinking of when I wrote those?" Before we could reply, however, she was reading again, starting with this, which she emphasized with a laugh:

My friends, there are no friends.

And, by way of conclusion:

Since everything is in our heads, we had better not lose them.

"There," she said: "that's what I wrote on the last page of my notebook. I must surely have been with someone who annoyed me. I pretended to be taking notes."

Our approval and our compliments, however, gave her no reassurance: "I spent my Sunday tearing up bits of paper. I've made myself absolutely sick for this little bit of work that everyone thinks is worthless."

The rebuke was aimed at me. *Everyone* meant me, as I see ten years later: because I was making her tell the story of her life. But not necessarily me. By now I knew her well enough to appreciate the difficulties of such a task. She had tried before, beginning with Louise de Vilmorin, then working with Gaston Bonheur, Georges Kessel, Michel Déon, and many others. She spared none of them when she talked of them to me, and I had no trouble making the mental transposition and imagining what she would say of me after another attempt at literary collaboration had collapsed. Nevertheless I should have recognized that it would require something more than inexhaustible patience to tell Coco's story with Coco.

What is the truth of any life? A birth certificate? Dates? Baptismal, vaccination certificates? She said: *Those on whom legends are built* are *their legends.*

That was why she devoted so much care to the construction of the Chanel myth, even at the cost of creating enormous confusion: *I am no longer what I was. I will remain what I have become.*

Why not? It was a moving resolve, and one, moreover, that we permit to others, to the eminences whom we automatically set up in certain conventional fields: scholars, field marshals, politicians.

Chanel: a Chanel creation — that alone is what she was, born of herself, shaped by her own hands, in her own clay. Chanel: nothing else, and in any event nothing less.

Are you wearing your Chanel? Who else has given his name to a suit? After the Chanel look came the Chanel hemline. The caprices of fashion have ordained that henceforth what is reasonable and dignified shall be and shall remain synonymous with Chanel. Chanel has come to mean modesty, taste, proportion. The Chanel is a classic: people wil go on making Chanels.

"When my wife wears your clothes I feel comfortable," President Georges Pompidou of France confided to Mademoiselle Chanel one evening when she was dining at the Elysée Palace.

She departed from us with the certainty that she had become a way of life: this was confirmed to her in the Madeleine, her last stop in Paris, with incense and holy water.

As for the rest, for her life . . . When Hervé Mille first met her in 1935 and talked to her about the early *Marie-Claire*, which had made a dramatic start with a press run of almost a million copies, she said: "Chanel customers read the very expensive magazines, *Vogue, Harper's Bazaar.* These magazines are our publicity. The popular magazines with mass circulation are better: they create our legend. When my customers come to me, they like to cross the threshold of some magic place; they feel a satisfaction that is perhaps a trace vulgar but that delights them: they are privileged characters who are incorporated into our legend. For them this is a far greater pleasure than ordering another suit. Legend," Coco summed up, "is the consecration of fame."

To embroider her own she became Penelope. Each night she undid what she had made that day, and each day she started over, unwearyingly. Toward what truth was she faring? And with whom to share it?

"I Was My Family's Little Prisoner"

*Was it because I was an Alsatian as she was an Auvergnat,
and both of us were born poor? The ice was broken between us.
She told me of her rather harsh childhood: the death of her
mother when she was six; her rejection by her father, who left
her to make a new life for himself in America; her strict aunts;
her First Communion; ordering her first dress.*

One of the many reporters, chiefly Americans, who asked her the
most intimate question of all — her age — was Ernest Hauser of
the *Saturday Evening Post.* He got no answer. Her age? She did
not know what he meant. Somewhat thrown off by this silence,
which he could not interpret, Hauser tried his second question:
"Where were you born?" After all, he must have thought, once
he knew her birthplace it would be a simple matter to check the
records there.

"I was born on a journey," she told him. And this is how she
told it to me:

"My father was not there. That poor woman, my mother, had

to go looking for him. It's a sad story, and very boring — I've heard it so many times . . .

"My mother was always unwell. What with the clothes of that time, I suppose, no one could see that she was about to have a baby. Some people helped her — they were very kind: they took her into their home and sent for a doctor. My mother didn't want to stay there.

" 'You can get another train tomorrow,' the people said, to soothe her. 'You'll find your husband tomorrow.'

"But the doctor realized that my mother wasn't ill at all. 'She's about to have a baby,' he said.

"At that point the people who had been so nice to her were furious. They wanted to throw her out. The doctor insisted they take care of her. They took her to a hospital, where I was born. One of the hospital nuns was my godmother."

Coco was a sickly child at first. There was some question whether she would survive. It seemed wise to baptize her at once, in one of those emergency rites for which a priest need not be present. What name to give her? Her mother apparently had not thought about it. Perhaps she was not making a very quick recovery from her delivery (the convalescence was in fact quite difficult).

Coco said:

"The nun who took care of me was called Gabrielle Bonheur. Since she didn't have much imagination, she gave me her Christian name and her surname, so I was baptized Gabrielle Bonheur Chanel. I knew nothing of this for a long time. There was never any occasion to check my baptismal certificate. During the war I sent for all my documents because one was always afraid of the worst. As for my First Communion, they knew me. The priest who taught me the catechism wasn't going to ask for my baptismal certificate."

Except for the lack of a date of birth, this story fitted in with what was already known. All this occurred on 19 August 1883 in

Saumur, as everyone knows now: every newspaper in the world published the date in her obituary.

I have seen the birth certificate issued to Mademoiselle Chanel by the town hall in Saumur. Her father's name is given as Henri Chasnel, with an *s* that has since vanished.* Her mother's maiden name was Eugénie Jeanne Devolles. The year of birth is shown as 1893, but the 9 is unskillfully inked in in green over the black of the second 8, which is still discernible.

What did her parents do for a livelihood? They were trades-people, according to the Saumur certificate, and they lived in Saumur. Coco said: "My father's people were Southerners, from somewhere around Béziers. They were not regular shopkeepers: they speculated on wines. One year they'd make a lot of money, the next they'd starve. My family lost everything the same year as Pierre Reverdy's." (Reverdy was a poet she liked. She would have liked to see his talent widely recognized; he was actually little known. She ranked him above Cocteau, whom she disliked for having overshadowed Reverdy.)

"They bought the wine on the spot. If they bought it for two francs and sold it for three, it was a big day. And if they paid three and sold for one, it was the end of the world. That year there was so much wine that it was being thrown away. An ocean of it! I was a child but I heard the talk: 'It's terrible, there's too much, we'll all starve. No one can stay in such a region, it's starvation,' my grandmother said. 'Let's move along.' All this was said with a laugh, the way people do in the South. And everyone was perfectly happy all the same."

Her parents' occupation was listed as trade. Accuracy requires a correction: they were peddlers, itinerants, wandering from town to town, from market to fair, always on the road. There were many such traders at that time: second-class tradesmen who had no fixed premises. Sometimes they vanished without

---

* Actually, there was a clerical error. There was no *s* in her father's name. See page 40. M.H.

leaving any address. A rolling stone gathers no moss, the proverb says. Proverbs still have a certain worth.

"My father was a very young man," Coco said. *"I don't know what he did."* (Was he not a wine merchant in Béziers, as she had just said? Or in Nîmes, like Reverdy's people?) "It's hard to remember things at the age of six. You have a father and you love him very much, and you think he's perfectly all right." She added: "He wasn't perfectly all right, that's all."

Later she said: "My father was mortally afraid people would call me Gaby [the "right" diminutive for Gabrielle]. He used to call me Little Coco until something better should come along. He didn't like Gabrielle at all; it hadn't been his choice. And he was right. Soon the 'Little' drifted away and I was simply Coco. It was awful, and I'd have loved to get rid of it, but I never will."

Here then, from Mademoiselle Chanel's own mouth, is the official version of the transformation of Gabrielle into Coco. She remembered that she had been miserable being called Gabrielle by the aunts who took her in, when she was six, after her mother's death.

"I wasn't easy," she said. "Once, entering the room where my aunts were, I slammed the door shut behind me with my foot.

" 'Gabrielle,' one of my aunts said, 'go out of the room and come in again properly, without banging the door.'

"I obeyed. I went out, came back in again, but couldn't shut the door. I broke into sobs.

" 'Why are you crying so hard, Gabrielle?' one of my aunts asked. She couldn't understand why I was so miserable. 'I didn't scold you so harshly.'

"And I said: 'I'm not crying because you scolded me; I'm crying because everyone calls me Gabrielle here. At home I was called Coco.' "

She added: "If anyone had told me before the war that I'd be Coco Chanel to the whole world, I'd have laughed. Mademoiselle Chanel had four thousand employees, and the richest man in England loved her. And now I'm Coco Chanel. Coco! Nevertheless, it isn't my name. My friends can call me that. People stop me in the street: 'Are you really Coco Chanel?' When I give autographs, I write 'Coco Chanel.' On a train to Lausanne a couple of weeks ago the whole car paraded past me. In my own premises I'm called 'mademoiselle'; that goes without saying. I certainly don't want to be called Coco in the House of Chanel."

She was anything but displeased by being called Coco in a street in Amiens when she was driving to Holland to meet her friend Maggie van Zuylen at the castle of Haar. It was after Suez: there were many shortages and much social unrest. Her Cadillac was stopped by a group of strikers, one of whom thrust his head in an open window and demanded ferociously: "Where did you get all your money?"

A woman yanked him back. "Let her alone! Don't you know who that is? That's Coco Chanel! She worked for her money."

She told me about her parents' marriage. "My mother had a brother, and that wretch gave his only sister to my father. They'd become pals in the army. He told my father: 'I have a charming sister, I think you'll like her.' My father, who was a very dashing type, went to see the girl after he got out of the army. He was on his way home, walking, and he and his friend went part of the way together, stopping at his friend's house. And there my father married his pal's sister, and of course he ruined her. All this I found out by listening at closed doors."

Her father had done his army service in the Lyon area. He could have taken a train back to his home in the South. But after all — two good friends on the road; it was like the guys in the Tour de France. What did they have by way of luggage? The clothes they wore — the gift of the Republic, which had also filled their canteens with local wine; a solid meal or two in their knapsacks — rock-hard army bread and some sardines. Hell, Auvergne wasn't too far out of the way back to Nîmes. It might have been summer. The two friends slept in the open. They lent a hand to peasants trying to get the harvest in before a storm, and in return they got a pot of soup. Marvelous — better than ratatouille. They poked each other in the ribs. Life was great — and wait till you see my sister! Coco's father's eyes gleamed with anticipation. He's my pal, his pal thought, and he's going to be my brother. This was how Coco told the story.

The fact remains that there was a railroad from Lyon to Nîmes, following the right bank of the Rhône and operated by the PLM; and the army gave free tickets to soldiers who had finished their service.

The marriage took place in accordance with the Auvergnat pal's hopes. This Chanel could be very likable when he wanted to be — he was a light-hearted, exuberant fellow, like so many Southerners. His laughter dissolved the gloom in which Coco's mother languished. *That poor Jeanne.* She died of tuberculosis.

"I was six years old," Coco said. "My aunts came. Actually, they weren't my aunts but my mother's first cousins. Families gathered like that in the country when someone died. It was an event. One went to see, to find out what had happened. One poked into everything. I realized a deal was being made to take me away. One day I was sent off to the remotest corner of the Auvergne. My aunts were good people, but absolutely without tenderness. I was not loved in their house. I got no affection. Children suffer from such things."

I got no affection. That evening, before I turned on the tape recorder, we had talked over dinner about a story in the papers: a case of babies being switched at birth in a hospital. One of them was a twin who had been separated from his brother by mistake and given to the mother of a single boy. She did not want to give up the child that had been given to her by mistake. Her blood and her heart spoke different languages: she preferred to keep the twin, to whom she had not given birth. The story inspired all kinds of sentimentalities and outcries in the press.

"That's disturbing," Coco said. "I'll adopt the little boy that no one wants. Provided no one finds out about it. I don't want it to look like a publicity stunt." And then she added: "I'll send him to the best boarding school in Switzerland. When he comes of age he'll have enough money to do whatever he wants."

I still did not know her very well. I remember my reaction: she has no heart. I soon forgot that.

"I owe a great deal to my aunts in spite of everything," she acknowledged. "Out of a kind impulse, when my mother was dying, they promised to take one of the children. It was me."

One of the children. Thus far I had heard mention only of a younger sister, Antoinette, whom Coco loved very much and who was to die tragically at the age of thirty. And yet it was impossible that she could have forgotten her elder sister, Julia-Berthe, who also died young. "No one in that family reached forty," Coco said; "I don't know how I escaped the slaughter." Julia-Berthe left a little boy named André Pallasse, and Coco assumed responsibility for him: one might say that she adopted this nephew.

"My father would have liked me to be a boy," Coco told me. She added details. "At that time my father had a mistress, who had borne him a son at about the same time I was born. I've never seen him, I don't know him. In the family, of course, there were people who knew all about it and told me about it. It's of no importance. Even I have no interest in it. Whom else could it interest?"

She said of her childhood: "People say I'm an Auvergnat. There's nothing of the Auvergnat in me — nothing, nothing. My mother was one. In that part of the world, though, I was thoroughly unhappy. I fed on sorrow and horror. I wanted to kill myself I don't know how many times. 'That poor Jeanne' — I couldn't stand hearing my mother talked about that way anymore. Like all children, I listened at closed doors. I learned that my father had ruined my mother — 'poor Jeanne.' All the same she'd married the man she loved. And having to hear people call me an orphan! They felt sorry for me. I had nothing to be pitied for — I had a father. All this was humiliating. I realized no one loved me and I was being kept out of charity. There were visits — plenty of visitors. I heard the questions put to my aunts: 'Does the little one's father still send money?' "

It was a long outcry and one of great importance, essential to remember if one wished to understand Mademoiselle Chanel. Humiliation; a mother whom people pitied; a father who did not send the money that he ought to have sent; people who whispered about these things when they came to visit. And Coco's cry of denial: "I am not an orphan! I have a father! My father made my mother happy!" These are all clues to the character of a little girl.

What were the two aunts like? It never occurred to me to ask Coco Chanel. I could *see* them: they materialized from what she narrated, wearing black, their gray, very tidy hair caught in flat headbands, their hands dry, their eyes without warmth, their faces unsmiling. They wore black shawls crossed on their bosoms, violet ribbons around their white necks: that was how I envisaged them. Coco herself never mentioned a single detail of physical appearance or clothing. Were they as old as I imagined them?

"When my father came to visit," Coco said, "my aunts did themselves up for him. He had a great deal of charm, and he told many stories. 'Don't listen to my aunts,' I said to him. 'I'm so unhappy; take me away. I swear I'm very unhappy.' "

How old was she? By now she had spent almost a year in the Auvergne with her aunts; she must have been seven; it must have been 1890. She did not say so, but one could deduce it. Now she acted the part of a little girl overjoyed to see her father again because she adored him. And at the same time a miniature woman, who saw very clearly how the two aunts, so austere and strict with her, were nothing but smiles and cordiality in the presence of her father, *a man*, someone gay and loud and strong. My aunts are going to trick him, the little girl thought; he won't believe I'm unhappy. He'll believe them, their pretense of loving me. But they don't love me! No one loves me. This was the whole desperate message that she wanted to convey to her father.

"He used his charm on me," she said. " 'You'll see,' he told me, 'soon we'll have a new house.' He told me all those loving things a father can tell his little girl. But he knew then that he was going to take off for America and that he'd never see me again."

It was painful to think of the child betrayed by the father who caressed and kissed and promised, who talked of a beautiful house bigger than her aunts', in the South and the sun, beside the sea — and who was running out on her!

"I never saw him again," she said. "He wrote sometimes. He still sent a little money — not much. That's all I know — I know he sent money and then one day no more. There was no more mention of him. He was young — not yet thirty. He'd made a new life. I understand that. He made a new family. His two daughters [what about Julia-Berthe?] were in good hands. They were being brought up. He had more children. He was right. I would have done the same thing. No one under thirty could have coped with the situation. Imagine, a widower with two daughters! [Again, what about Julia-Berthe?] He really loved me. I represented the good days, fun, happiness. When I was born everything was going well. After my sister was born my mother became very ill. She couldn't have any more children. That was why my father didn't love my sister. He was mean to her. She represented bad luck."

There she was, then, in the Auvergne, deserted by her father and dependent on her two aunts, who, she said, "had promised to bring me up but not to love me." She added: "I was my family's little prisoner." To her, life was hard in the Auvergne, "at the farthest corner of that backward province." Before living with her aunts she had known the South, gaiety, sunshine, the street, playmates and friends. There were no friends for her up there in the Auvergne. Never did she mention a school friend, another child who went to her house or took her hand in the schoolyard.

What did her aunts do? They were not peasants: Coco was very emphatic.

"My mother and my aunts came from the same place, but she was not a peasant. People like to think my mother was a peasant, and I too — peasant women in wooden shoes. I said as much the other day to a gentleman who wanted to write an article about me: 'Don't take away the *sabots* — they're such a help.' The Americans don't know what they are; and even you, my dear, in spite of being a peasant, wouldn't know how to walk in wooden shoes. I used to wear them to go out in the snow. People say I arrived in Paris in wooden shoes. I was quite good at walking in them. In winter there were pairs at the door for everyone: you left them there when you came in. There were snowdrifts as high as that [she gestured]. No one knew about skis. The winters were frightful — winters nowadays aren't what they used to be. I loved winter. I was allowed to stay in the kitchen, and we burned trees in the fireplace. In the country the kitchen is the soul of the house.

"When people came in, frozen, you filled their pockets with chestnuts, and gave them more when they went out again. Potatoes for the pigs were boiled in a big cast-iron pot hung over the fire. I wasn't allowed to go out, but whenever the door was opened I grabbed the chance to sneak out. Then I would put on the wooden shoes. If I'd gone out in ordinary shoes I'd have got my feet wet and dirtied everything in the house when I came back in. It isn't easy to walk in wooden shoes: they're huge and rigid, they don't bend at all — the wood is bad for the feet. We would put straw inside them. I'd make my way sliding and slipping into the snow. Sometimes it would be as much as a week that I didn't have my nose outside the door. One didn't go out in winter."

What did the aunts do if they were not peasants? I was given to understand that they owned farms and lived on the income from various holdings in which Coco's mother had owned a share. Someone showed Coco a run-down property, a neglected hut in a field of stubble, and said to her: "All this would still be yours [the formal "yours"] if your father hadn't ruined your mother."

Who told her that, and so coldly? There was no way of asking her the questions that crowded into my mind. But no matter: it was much better to let her follow the current of her thought. And in any case she refused to listen to people who raised such issues; she closed her ears to them because she would not suffer anyone to criticize her father, even though he had abandoned his little Coco, his favorite daughter. He will come back, she convinced herself, and we will have a very big house. She did not elaborate on these details, but it was not difficult to guess at them when she described her reaction:

"I straightened up and thought to myself: what luck that this doesn't belong to us anymore. What would I do with an old farm or other such junk? I found the whole thing abominable."

She said: "My aunts had a nice house, which in those days meant a great deal. It was very tidy. I didn't realize it then — I understood it later. When I was living there it revolted me. But if I have a certain preference for order, for comfort, for having things done right, for chests filled with linens that smell good, and gleaming floors, I owe it to my aunts. Living with them gave me that solid substance that is to be found only in the French. I didn't learn any of that out of novels or abroad."

Novels. She said: "I thought all that [her aunts' house] was awful because in my novels there was nothing but silk pillows and white-lacquered furniture. I'd have liked to do everything in white lacquer. Sleeping in an alcove made me miserable, it humiliated me. I broke off bits of wood wherever I could, thinking *what old trash this is.* I did it out of sheer wickedness, for the sake of destruction. When one considers all the things that go on in a child's head . . . I wanted to kill myself. I wouldn't want to bring up any. [That was exactly how she said it; she did not say 'I never wanted to bring up any.'] Or else I'd give them the most romantic novels — that's what one remembers most. I remember all my books, melodramas in which everything happened in a wild-eyed romanticism. I liked that, and it was a lucky thing for me that I had read all those books, because I came to Paris at a very romantic time, the time of the Ballets Russes."

I remember all my books. Chiefly she read the serialized novels of Pierre Decourcelle, whose books included *Les Deux Gosses* (*The Two Little Boys*). He was the principal source of supply for *Le Matin* and *Le Journal.*

On the same spring date every year every chest and drawer in the aunts' beautiful house was emptied, the various linens and garments were sorted out and whatever had got wrinkled was ironed. As she described this, Coco went through the motions of ironing as it was done in those days, dipping her fingertips in a bowl of water and sprinkling the material as it was about to be pressed. She recalled the blue tablets that were dropped into the rinse water to dissolve, and she said: "Now sheets smell of chlorine everywhere; at the Ritz they're changed every day, so that every night I go to sleep in the aroma of chlorine." And she sighed: "Life in the country was luxurious."

She said: "The table was always very beautifully laid in my aunts' house, and well provided. The tenant farmers didn't pay cash rent, they paid in kind — at least half of them did. A whole pig would be laid open on a board. That disgusted me. Everything connected with food disgusted me. But it also gave me a foundation of experience, so that nothing has ever amazed me.

"When I lived in England, in a luxury that one cannot even imagine anymore — the marvelous luxury of waste, where one doesn't have to save anything — well, that didn't surprise me, because I'd had that childhood in a good house where there was everything everyone needed and there was no penny pinching on food. In those days that was a big thing. The maids who came to work for my aunts changed shape as you watched them: they were totally different in a few weeks because they ate as much as they wanted, meat and whatever else they wanted.

"The house was well kept, since there were servants. In winter [always winter!] the rooms were cold, but one had whatever one needed, without stinting. Something that did really surprise me, later, in other houses, was the napkin ring. That was unknown in my aunts' house. In the end, a clean napkin at each meal is the true luxury. I'd rather not have a napkin at all than keep the one I'd just finished with and use it again. Better to give me a paper napkin — I'd prefer it. It hasn't been used, and that's better. I have encountered napkin rings in the homes of people who talked about simplicity. That kind of simplicity I don't want — I take out my handkerchief, I can't eat any more. I disgust easily. The French are so dirty."

She was eleven when she received her First Communion. "I went to confession," she said. "It was a very serious thing for me. I was convinced that the old priest in the confessional didn't know it was me speaking to him. I didn't know what to tell him. In the dictionary I'd found the adjective 'profane,' and it seemed to fit. So I said: 'Father, I have had profane thoughts.'

" 'I didn't think you were as stupid as the others,' he replied casually.

"As far as I was concerned, that was the end. The end of the confession. Does he know then who it is that's talking to him? I thought. I was furious. I hated him! Poor man. He wondered where I'd got 'profane.' He often came to our house to lunch. He was afraid of my aunts. 'They invite you,' I told him, 'but they don't like you.'

"We were very good friends. He pretended to scold me. 'You can't say such things.'

" 'I can say whatever I want,' I replied.

"My aunts wanted me to wear a cap with my white dress when I went to receive my First Communion. That was what the little peasant girls wore; I wanted a crown of paper roses, which I thought was exquisite. Most of all I didn't want to wear a cap like the peasants. I said I wouldn't make my communion if they forced me to wear one of those caps. 'It doesn't matter to me whether I make my communion,' I said.

"I got my crown of artificial roses."

So, stern as they were, the aunts had given in. Were they beginning to love Coco?

Occasionally preaching monks would come through the town — "real monks, barefoot, with a rope around the waist." They would stay with the priest. After Vespers they told the children stories about far-off places. In particular they talked about the little Chinese, who were very hungry. Coco said:

"Every year my grandfather sent me five francs for New Year's Day. That was my present. But what should I buy? The only thing I liked was mint candies, and one could get a lot of them for two sous. I bought a franc's worth, and I put the four francs remaining in my bank. But I always had to break the bank for the little Chinese! I didn't like that one bit! I didn't have any of the characteristics that are attributed to children. I was impressed by how mean people were. How could anyone ask me to break my bank for the little Chinese, whom I didn't care a damn about? I was miserable."

Her first experience with money. "I have never been interested in money," she said, "but I was concerned with independence."

She added: "If I analyze myself a little, I see immediately that my need for independence began to develop when I was still a very young girl. I heard a great deal of talk about money among my aunts' servants, who would say: 'When we have money, we'll leave.' Those girls worked like the devil. It was fascinating to watch them iron aprons, or caps — all the aprons and then all the caps. This was how they learned their trade as chambermaids. It took three years. After three years they left."

Here, it seemed, I had a clue to an understanding of *la Grande Mademoiselle:* in order to attain her independence, she must earn her own way. She had grasped this very early, listening to the whispers of the young ironers of bonnets, the poor peasant girls glad to have jobs in a good house where they could eat as much as they liked and learn a trade that would offer them rights: the right to live in their own homes, to go out, perhaps to dance, and also to love. They put money aside *to go up to town* as soon as their savings were considerable enough. But didn't they think about getting married? Didn't most of them have someone waiting for them back home? Coco never heard them talk about that; she had no recollection of it. *My need for independence began to develop when I was still a very young girl.*

"Until I was sixteen," she said, "I wore what all the girls of that period wore, a little tailored suit. That was the origin of my suits. I ought to have hated that suit, but I can't wear anything else.

"Every year, in the spring, I was given a black alpaca suit. Black because I was in mourning. And anyway that was how little girls in the provinces were dressed: either one went to a convent and wore its uniform, or else one was a girl who didn't go to the convent but was taught at home, and one wore a double-breasted suit."

Were things really so rigidified, so patterned, in the country, in the Auvergne, at that time? I found it somewhat exaggerated when I heard Coco say so, but then she was describing . . . She said:

"I should have liked a pink dress, or a sky-blue one. I was in mourning all the time. The peasant girls wore pink and blue. I envied them. I thought it was pretty — I liked it much more than what I was wearing.

"For summer they gave me a horrible leghorn hat, regardless whether it was hot or cold, with a little piece of velvet and a rose above the brim. It looked awful on me. I knew even then what suited me. For winter I had a kind of cloche, very hard, with a kind of feather on it. I was told it was an eagle's feather: I knew it was a turkey's, stiffened with paste. There was a little rubber band in the back that went under one's hair, to hold the hat in place when it was windy. I thought the whole business was very ugly. It was my uniform."

My uniform? She said: "Oh, if only I'd been allowed to dress as I pleased! The first dress I ordered, when I was fifteen, caused a scandal. It was a mauve princess dress that went up to here [the neck], with a great flounce and matching underskirt in Parma violet.

"I was fifteen, or perhaps sixteen, but I looked about twelve. The dressmaker had been instructed to make the dress according to my taste. My aunts had kept out of it. So I had chosen a clinging mauve material. With nothing for it to cling to. The dressmaker had put a bit of taffeta at the bottom, with a flounce. Parma violet underneath!"

That was how she told it and the tape recorded it. I thought it a splendid story. To me it was the source of a vocation, and I thought of the article I could write on the basis of this confidence: Coco's mauve dress, the Parma violet underskirt, a princess dress clinging to nothing.

She went on talking: "The idea of this dress had come to me from a novel in which the heroine was dressed like that, and I thought that Parma violet was ravishing. My heroine wore it on her hat. The dressmaker didn't have any more, so she put a twig of wisteria on mine. And all this was done with great mystery: my aunts were supposed to know nothing."

These were those stern aunts who did not love her. I come back to it because it cannot be disregarded.

"Well, then," Coco said, "that Sunday morning I dressed with a great deal of excitement, after a very thorough wash. Coquetry consists in being very clean.

" 'Are you sure you washed your ears?'

" 'Yes, aunt.'

" 'Did you wash your neck?'

" 'Yes, aunt.'

"I washed what I wanted to wash — no one was asking me to

undress. When I toweled myself vigorously I was a little pinker than usual.

"That day I had arranged everything very well. My aunts were waiting for me at the foot of the stairs. When I appeared at the top of the stairs, all that was said was: 'Coco, go and change. Hurry. We'll be late for Mass.' "

Poor little Coco! How could anyone not be moved by that story? She said:

"I realized I was a victim. The dress was sent back to the dressmaker and she was never called in again. She was very angry with me over it. I had told her over and over: 'Yes, certainly, it's all right with my aunts,' and she'd asked: 'Including the Parma violet underskirt?' and I'd said: 'Yes, everything.' "

And still, on reflection . . . those two aunts in their black, who one day, just like that, allowed Coco to select her own dress, when she had been wearing the same schoolgirl suits for years?

And what about the dressmaker? If she had been uncertain over Coco's choice, would she not have spoken to the aunts? Would she not have gone to their house to show them samples? Before ordering the mauve material? Would she not have discussed with the aunts the model that Coco had selected from her catalogue or the magazines that she undoubtedly got from Paris?

Coco herself raised these questions — not I, who took as gospel everything she said. But she, as a woman, felt it necessary to convince me, who had no doubts. Unless the whole thing seemed strange to her, almost unbelievable. She elaborated the details that added authenticity. She said: "Dresses in those days were awful — completely straight, with a flounce at the bottom. Underneath there were what were called street sweepers — braid. Women tucked them up. I thought they were marvelous. That was what the dressmaker had made for me."

A woman hearing all this, I suppose — a woman who knew the fashions of 1900 as Coco described them in talking about her first real dress — would have paid more attention than I did to such details as "underneath there were what were called street sweepers . . . women tucked them up."

Can one imagine a kid in a village of the Auvergne in 1898 — Coco at fifteen — ordering from her dressmaker, and without any supervision, a dress like those worn to the races by the great kept women? But why should I have been taken aback? I knew nothing about such matters.

"My aunts' reaction," Coco said, "was hardly what I wanted: 'Go and change, we'll be late for Mass.' I wept. I thought they were bad and mean. That way they had of looking down their noses at me. 'Hurry and get out of that dress, Coco.' In a normal family children are loved, and everyone would have laughed.

"My aunts didn't laugh at all. It was an outrage and I suffered by it. I didn't dare to leave the house: I was afraid of running into the dressmaker. They sent the hat with the wisteria back to her, too.

"I must admit she was a little crazy, that dressmaker. She should have realized I was only a kid.

"But what a blow to me. I'd been dreaming of that dress ever since I'd read a novel by Pierre Decourcelle."

We were back to the author of *The Two Little Boys*. Coco said:

"I met him later; he was already a very old gentleman. I said to him: 'Ah, monsieur, you cost me a very sad day, and even some sad weeks; in fact, some difficult months.'"

Once they had sent her back to her room to change for Mass, Coco's aunts never mentioned her mauve dress to her again. She observed:

"Silence is the cruelty of the provincial."

"Myth and Truth"

*So now I knew Coco's childhood as described by herself —
what she remembered of it, what she wanted to reveal of it in
the twilight of her life, what had marked her. Why, as I listened
to her bring forth her past, should I have imagined that she was
creating her own legend?*

Other tales have been told about her, notably one repeated by
Truman Capote: her father was a blacksmith not in the Auvergne but somewhere in the Basque country. A horseman
stopped at the forge because his mount had lost a shoe. Unfortunately the smith was not there. But no matter: Coco was. She
relighted the forge, she worked the bellows, the embers caught
again, the iron turned red. Coco took the horse's hoof into her
lap.

"How pretty you are!" the horseman said (he was none other
than the Duke of Westminster!). The sequel was inevitable. The
whole thing greatly amused Coco, who found it thoroughly absurd; she was forty-five when she met the duke in 1928.

According to another version, Coco's aunts were in the remount trade — that is, the army sent them its ailing or wearied horses to be brought back to health on the aunts' meadows. The advantage of this tale was that it explained how, through the military horses, Coco had been able to meet Etienne Balsan, the dazzling knight on horseback who was to take her off to Paris and society.

In the version of Louise de Vilmorin, who had begun to write a life of Chanel with Coco, the aunts managed the estate of a country gentleman or something of the sort — a lawyer, a large landowner.

But Mademoiselle Chanel herself set forth the childhood narrative that you have just read. And why cast doubt on her story? Does it not have the ring of truth? Can one not visualize the unhappy girl, betrayed by her father, taken in by aunts who were anything but loving, endeavoring in spite of all kinds of obstacles to find her own identity?

Where did I get the notion that Coco Chanel was *inventing* her childhood? That she was *confecting* a childhood for herself? Yet this was the case.

Of course not everything in her narratives was wholly plausible. Her relations with her aunts, for example. Anyone will have noted the contradictions in her story: the severity and then, for example, the excess of trust in the matter of the mauve dress. Other details become suspect as soon as doubt sets in. The uniform: those suits worn of necessity by every girl who got her education at home . . .

What is the truth? Here it is, in all its simplicity.

When Coco's mother died she left five children: two boys and three girls. Their father turned over Alphonse and Lucien to the public authorities. Thereupon he went off to his mother in Vichy with the girls — Julia-Berthe, the eldest; Coco; and Antoinette, the youngest, whose birth had accelerated his poor tubercular wife's death. And then, as they say of husbands who vanish: "I'm going out for some cigarettes."

No one ever saw him again.

And the aunts and their beautiful house? All that was Coco's invention, just like the story of her father's voyage to America. I admit that when I found out I was more than dumfounded: I was upset. And yet I knew that Coco had always dealt in fantasy. All through the years of our friendship I realized, obviously, that day after day she was endowing herself with a different life. I have a good memory. The details would change. She would alter her memories to suit her convenience. She was the Penelope of her own legend, as I remarked earlier; she undid every night what she had embroidered during the day. But what was the reason for the embroidery? What was the essential theme? Why should she have invented a childhood for herself? And an adolescence? Are not such memories the substance of our most precious roots? One embellishes them, but one does not invent them.

Coco's grandfather, an arrogant man, was from the Savoie, a Chanel without an *s*, a member (it would appear) of the family of that St.-Pierre-Marie Chanel whom Roger Peyrefitte made one of the characters in his *Les Clés de St.-Pierre* (*The Keys of St. Peter's*). But the grandfather was in no sense a saint. He was a giant, an itinerant merchant who wandered through France selling whatever he found to sell wherever he stopped. Life was luxurious when he had done well. Somewhere near Nîmes he had dazzled a Protestant beauty from a good family, Virginie Fournier, whom he married and carried off into his gypsy adventures. Ultimately they settled in Vichy, near the station. Happy in their marriage, they had a long chain of children, the links of which were added over a period of twenty years. Virginie Fournier kept her beauty throughout her life. Coco was her image — her "spitting" image, apparently.

One can picture Grandmother Virginie with her son's three daughters in her arms. Her own last child, who was called Adrienne, was barely two years older than Coco. What would she have done with the two boys if the public authorities had not taken them?

In 1914, when he had just been mobilized, Alphonse read in a newspaper that his sister Gabrielle, his elder by two years, was becoming famous! "I am leaving for the war," he wrote her, "leaving behind a wife and two children." Coco answered immediately; or more exactly, she had her aunt Adrienne answer for her because she rarely wrote letters herself: "Don't worry about a thing, my dear Alphonse, your family will lack nothing. I'll send you a package every week." Coco delegated Adrienne to go to Florac, where Alphonse's wife lived with her first two children, a boy named Yvan and a little girl who in 1914 had just made her appearance in the world, to whom in order to favor the renewed contact with Coco they had given the name of Gabrielle.

Coco would have liked to take Yvan in her charge.

"She would have sent him to England," explains Gabrielle Chanel, the niece, today. "But my mother didn't allow it — it was impossible — one doesn't *give away* one's child like that. In those days, England seemed like the other end of the world!"

For years Coco, who demonstrated a weakness for Alphonse, gave him a monthly income of three thousand francs. This was a lot of money for the years between the two wars. Alphonse had a car, like the doctor and the local deputy. There were only three in the whole area. He also had a tobacco and beverage store. Lucien got mad when he learned that his brother was a proprietor and not he. But Coco helped him, too, at his own turn.

She never wanted to see either Lucien or Alphonse. Whenever they called on her at rue Cambon, Mademoiselle was away on a trip.

How old was Coco when her grandmother put her into the convent at Moulins? That will come out when it is possible to go through the records of that religious institution.

The convent was mixed in the sense that it accepted both paying and charity pupils. The latter, obviously, were in an inferior position with regard to the more fortunate, the elect of life: separate tables in the refectory, poorer food, an unheated dormitory, chores from which the others were exempt. Not to speak of the lessons. Who would have paid for Coco? And yet *I am not an orphan!* In the story as she told it to the tape recorder, she shot out her protest whenever visitors asked her (imaginary) aunts whether "the little one's father still sends money." In reality it was at the Moulins convent that she objected: "I'm not like the others!"

Can one picture her, a rebellious girl, clenching her fists and defying the monitors, holding aloof from the other girls in their black aprons? As I have mentioned, she never mentioned a childhood friend, I never heard her speak the given name of a playmate out of her early life. Nor did she supply given names for her two (nonexistent) aunts.

"I have a father!" Coco used to scream. At the end of her life she tried so hard to persuade herself that he had preferred her above her sisters: "I was the good-luck child," she said.

Why did he not pay anything toward her support? "My father's in America!" Coco shouted.

Why America? Because that was where fortunes were made. One set out poor and humiliated, and one came back a millionaire, one's pockets full of gold nuggets, rehabilitated and triumphant. Then one dispensed justice, one settled scores and punished the wicked. That, at least, was how things happened in the serials.

But it is a hundred-to-one shot that Coco's father, Chanel the itinerant merchant, never left France. Would Mademoiselle Chanel's file be more convincing if proof of this could be adduced after dogged search through one public record after another?

Her file. I have followed many trials during my journalistic career, and always with the same interest. It goes without saying that I am not about to hale Mademoiselle Chanel into court on a charge of lying. She was not lying; she was talking to herself. As men on trial talk to themselves when the court takes over the questioning. There the emphasis is laid on their contradictions:

"You said the opposite on such and such a day, when you were first questioned." Or: "But how could you have been in Paris and Bordeaux at the same time?"

What does the defendant reply? "But that's how it was." And he bows his head, crushed at being so poorly understood, and, still more, despairing at the lack of desire to understand him. His truth is not in the facts that are thrown into his face: it is in his contradictions, in the *why* of his lies.

Why did Coco lie? And, even more basically, did she really lie?

In her aunts' house, she said, she always wore the same suit, and with complete assurance she added that in the country all the girls were dressed in the same way. "That was my uniform," she said another time. For an attentive listener the truth had been merely transposed; unmistakably she was talking about the convent, the orphanage. But no one paid attention.

And, for that matter, why not the orphanage? The legend of Coco Chanel would not have been harmed by it. What more dramatic touch than that *la Grande Mademoiselle* should have been taken in out of charity and spent her early years in a remarkably strict religious institution?

But things were not like that in the decade from 1890 to 1900. The orphanage, like the hospital, was for the poor. And poverty, when one did not resign oneself to it with the Lord's help — what a disgrace it was! The Good Lord of that age, which is not so remote, was aligned on the side of the good families that one met at Mass. Coco was marked by that ethic. The orphanage did not suit her purpose when the question of recalling it arose. How could an orphan girl have risen to the level of the Duke of Westminster?

She remembered only too well the road she had followed. In order to forget it, she elevated the starting point. Her aunts' nice house became a springboard. We shall see that she borrowed some of her details from her friend Misia Sert. She found others in the newspaper serials of Pierre Decourcelle. *If I had to bring*

up children, I'd give them the most romantic things to read —
that's what one remembers most. I remember all my books.

I looked for the story of the mauve dress in some of Decourcelle's books. I could not bring myself to reread all of them, but
when I was leafing through *Quand on aime* (*When One Loves*),
I came on this passage:

In the summer house in the garden, undressed except for a dressing
gown of mauve crêpe de Chine . . .

It was not the dress but a dressing gown, and in it Sabine:

. . . her pointed teeth sank into her lips until they bled; her breasts
heaved with the tempest of her breathing. If he had not come by now,
then he would not come at all. Was it possible that he could so fla-
grantly break his promise? Slowly the bells sounded four o'clock.

This was the prose that had so stirred Coco and in which she
dredged for her childhood. Hélène de Montlaur, the heroine of
Les Deux Gosses,

was an adorable blonde — one would almost have said a young girl:
such was the look of ingenuous innocence that her blue eyes still kept,
such was the high-colored freshness of childhood still vivid in the pink
of her lips.

Nevertheless, she found herself caught in a vast despair. Irre-
proachable in her virtue, she had given her husband a splendid
son. But, as a consequence of a fantastic series of misunderstand-
ings, her husband had convinced himself that he had been betrayed and the boy was not his. What was to be done? He lay
awake thinking in the middle of the night when . . . a burglar!
And what a robber! A looter of graves, a violator of corpses. Ramon de Montlaur, a pistol in his hand, soon had the burglar at
his mercy. He was thinking — about his revenge on his wife. It
was atrocious, as he wanted it to be. Was it too cruel? No: he
had suffered a mortal blow.

He crept to Fanfan's little bedroom. Very softly, turning the knob
with infinite precautions, he entered. The child was sleeping peace-

fully. With every pure breath his red lips quivered slightly in their unbroken smile. He must have been dreaming of heaven and the angels.

Montlaur seized him in his arms. The child awakened, somewhat frightened. Then, recognizing the man who held him, he was reassured; and, still filled with sleep, his lips thrust forward in a charming little pout, he murmured: "Kiss me, Daddy dear."

Then he let his blond head drop against Ramon's shoulder and went back to sleep.

The latter neither saw nor heard. He wrapped his prey in a blanket and carried him out of the room.

"Take this child!" he said in a muffled voice to the brutal felon who was waiting for him in another room. "Take him; take this money; and disappear forever, far away. Never return!"

"He's really handsome! I don't say it to flatter you, governor, but on my honor he looks just like you!"

"Be silent!" Ramon gasped.

To be continued in our next. One had to wait on pins and needles.

Coco read these serials during her vacations and dreamed about them the rest of the year. Her grandmother cut them out: all women kept the serials from their newspapers and traded them with their friends. That was the circulating library of the poor.

As soon as one stops regarding Coco's memories as legal tender, their serial-story side emerges with all its banalities: the wicked aunts, the fireplace big enough to burn whole trees, the endless winters, the preaching monks wandering about barefoot, the secrecy of the confessional; the dramatic effects degenerate into formulas.

If, like her elder sister, Julia-Berthe, Coco had borne a child to a peasant at eighteen, or if she had married a railroad worker, like her aunt Julia, with whom she spent part of her vacation at Varennes-sur-Allier, or if she had become a shopkeeper in Moulins, she would have forgotten her stories; but in her unique life, whatever out of the ordinary happened to her was naturally linked to her adolescent fantasies, flushed out with mauve, with

noble names, with trembling women created by Pierre Decourcelle or some other hack.

Did she know that she was making up stories? And for whom?
For herself? For others? Others asked for nothing and knew
nothing.

Here a necessary digression. Coco Chanel was a sleepwalker.
"They found me in the hotel corridor last night, leaning over the
stair rail," she said. Or: "I walked out into the garden in my
nightgown, and it was way below freezing. I woke up in a sweat.
I couldn't go another step. Before I could go back to bed, I had
to cover the bed with my coats and dresses so I could be really
warm."

During one episode of somnambulism she cut her bathrobe
into a suit, to the lapel of which she attached a gardenia, her
favorite flower, cut with a scissors from a hand towel, which was
also white. Her maid discovered this masterpiece carefully laid
flat on the carpet of her little drawing room at the Ritz, between
her bedroom and her bathroom, while Mademoiselle Chanel lay
sleeping soundly and very quietly in her bed.

"I need more and more sleep," she insisted. Occasionally she
ordered dinner served to her in bed: porridge. "I adore it," she
declared.

Even if they were less spectacular than Coco made them seem,
her attacks of somnambulism did endanger her. She had to be
barricaded in her bed.

Why did she not consult a doctor? A close friend, the daughter
of Professor Delay, suggested that her father psychoanalyze
Coco.

"I should go and tell my secrets to a doctor?" she said to me
with a laugh that was not devoid of mischief. "I've never even
told the truth to my priest." And she added: "Freud? What a
joke."

One must return to *I've never even told the truth to my priest.*
With that warning, Chanel's itinerary becomes clearer.

4

"I Was Flirting with Reform School"

She refused to be either orphaned or poor: that was not fitting for Chanel. But what came after the orphanage? How could a girl who had fled the orphanage manage to "go up" to Paris and become Coco Chanel? This was the mystery of the years that she elided from her legend.

MOULINS. Capital of the Allier Department, on the Allier River, population 22,000; PLM Railroad; 313 kilometers from Paris. Cabinet-making, hat factories, vinegar factories. Birthplace of Villars, Lingendes, Théodore de Banville. In 1566 Michel de l'Hospital * promulgated there his famous Moulins decree for the reformation of the judicial system.

This was the information to be found in my father's *Larousse pour tous.*

Moulins was also a cavalry garrison. It was a very old and beautiful city. Its cathedral boasted a triptych of the Nativity by

* Claude, duc de Villars (1653–1734), a famous diplomat and general, won a number of victories against German and Austrian forces. Jean de Lingendes (1580–1616) was a poet, as was Théodore de Banville (1823–1891). Michel de l'Hospital (1505[6?]–1573) was a French statesman who was a pioneer in the cause of religious toleration. Translator.

Le Maître de Moulins. Favorite strolling places were the court-yards and the old filled-in moats of the Bourbon castle, in the shadow of the tower called the Malcoiffée where prisoners used to be kept. The light-cavalry garrison was established at La Madeleine, on the other side of the river. This was a chic regi-ment, in which, in 1903, a second lieutenant was completing his tour of duty. He was Etienne Balsan — twenty-five years old, dark, a first-rate horseman, with handlebar moustaches and a skin well tanned by service in Algeria, and straight as a ramrod. The Balsans were not noble, but they were rich, and they were listed in *Le Bottin mondain* (the French *Who's Who*) and all the elegant clubs' rosters, exactly like the descendants of the old dynasties and by the same right as certain other, though rare, exalted commoners: the Lebaudys, the Says, the Hennessys.* The Balsans were industrialists, trained in the State School of Engineering or the Military Academy of Artillery and Engineer-ing. The head of the family at this time — the one who signed himself simply Balsan, without a given name — was a flier: Jacques. Another brother, Robert, went into industry. Even to-day the Balsans have longer listings in *Who's Who* than many noble families; they are as at home there, or almost, as the Rochefoucaulds or others. The Balsan who today signs without his given name — François Balsan — is at the moment exploring an unknown desert in central Asia and is generally regarded as a remarkable fellow.

In the legend of Mademoiselle Chanel, Etienne Balsan consti-tutes a fixed pole, a point of reference. It is a matter of fact that this dashing light-cavalry officer was completing his military service in Moulins in 1903.

Coco was almost twenty. One would give anything to have seen her at that age! "I was born twenty years too soon," she occasionally murmured.

---

* The Lebaudy and Say families had amassed huge fortunes in the sugar industry; the Hennessys are the cognac family. Translator.

Now and again, two or three times in a hundred years, a woman's face appears that demotes all the others and establishes new canons of beauty. Coco had no idea, when she was twenty, that she was going to create a new face for women.

"I saw myself as very different from the rest," she said. But how did she see herself? "I was told I had black eyes." She shrugged. "They're anything but black."

To me they seemed black with gold flecks. She saw in them violet, green, who knows what else? Then she mentioned her neck:

"I have an unbelievably long neck. Look how far it extends at the nape. No one has a neck as long as mine, particularly in photographs. I always hold my head high when I eat. I must be very careful of my vertebrae. My Swiss doctor tells me that everything depends on these two [the cervical vertebrae]. I massage myself, I do exercises. But it's too late to change anything now, the doctor says. All that business is very delicate."

We turned to her figure. "I don't weigh five pounds more now than I did at twenty," she told me. To Truman Capote she had said: "Cut off my head and I'm thirteen."

How old was she when she was twenty?

When Etienne Balsan, who was to carry her off to Paris, was concluding his army tour in Moulins, Coco was living in the town with her aunt Adrienne — who, it must be remembered, was only two years older than she. Adrienne was the mistress of a cavalry officer. Both girls were said to have been dressmakers. I asked Coco: "In Moulins with your Aunt Adrienne and your young sister, Antoinette . . ." But she was not listening. It was as if she had been asked: "When were you born?"

I asked her too when and in what circumstances she had, as people said in the South, gone up to Paris. She laughed defensively: "Come, now, you don't think I'm going to tell you the story of my life!"

But I was insistent: "Yes, absolutely, tell me." I promised that she could keep the tapes. "Your story must be made known; it's fascinating. You can put the finishing touches to it whenever you like, with whomever you prefer."

"Later," she said. "We'll see; we'll do it together." But, though I was not certain why, I sensed that with her, with all her "explanations," it would never be possible to understand her. Because she refused to understand herself. For it was from herself that she was hiding the truth.

It was very seldom that she would give a date for something (at least when I knew her, in her last years). Nevertheless, when she told me about her first dinner at Maxim's, she began: "It was in 1913. I was a very young girl. I'd been told that *cocottes* went there."

I made a note of the date most ingenuously (this was in May of 1965) without realizing that in 1913 she was thirty years old. I did not give any thought to placing her recollections temporally. What interested me then was the recollection in its raw state, not the truth-about-Chanel that was wrapped inside her ostensible lie. But now, in order to understand Mademoiselle Chanel, one must certainly give the lie the prominence that it deserves. A "very young girl" in 1913.

Another thing. Six or seven years after our tape-recorder evenings, during which she had described her childhood with her two (imaginary) aunts, she mentioned a trip to Paris with them when she, Coco, was fourteen. This surprised me because it in no way accorded with the idea of the aunts (whom I still believed to have been real) that I had formed. But by the time I began to write this book, it became clear to me that all that was needed was the transition from "my aunts" to "my aunt." Since I now knew that "the two aunts" had never existed, I had to conclude that the "aunt" who took Coco to Paris was Adrienne, her father's very young sister who had been brought up with her by Coco's grandmother in Vichy.

Adrienne Chanel was a beauty. She too had spent some time in the Moulins convent. Her mother was counting on marrying her off to a conveyancer in Brive. She would emerge from her mediocrity and become a lady. The white gown was ready.

Was it summer? Vacation time? Not all the pupils at the Moulins convent left at vacation time. Those whose parents did not know what to do with them stayed at the convent. Coco was to spend that summer there. She had a cousin, Julia Costier, who was younger than she and who, like her, was a boarder: her parents paid something. The father was a railroad worker and a poet, a charming man whose head was in the clouds. The mother, also named Julia, had a generous character. When she came to get her daughter, the girl said: "We must take Coco too, Mamma."

"And who else?" Her mother shrugged.

"Her little sister, Antoinette."

"For the whole vacation?" Madame Costier objected. "Daddy will be furious."

"No he won't," the girl pleaded.

So Madame Costier received permission from the mother superior to take her two Chanel nieces. Why not? No one was paying anything for their keep.

"I'm sure I'll never see Gabrielle again," the mother superior probably said to herself at the time. (Coco was always called Gabrielle in the boarding school. All her relatives called her Fifine — never Coco, as she insisted. It was through Balsan that she was to become Coco: his friends called him Rico as a result so they could have the joke of CocoRico.*)

Costier had a little house in Varennes-sur-Allier, not far from Vichy. There Adrienne visited Coco. The story is a bit fuzzy, but interesting.

"I don't want to marry the conveyancer," Adrienne sobbed.

"Then let's run away," Coco said.

"Where?"

Where could two rustic beauties go? To Paris, where, obviously, magnificent triumphs waited.

* The French rendition of the rooster's cry. Translator.

There was a holiday in Varennes-sur-Allier, with a fair and bands and the rest. Adrienne and Coco walked about with the little kids, Antoinette and Julia, without a penny even for a ride on the merry-go-round or an ice. And then a kind of miracle happened. A hawker called them: "Hey, you girls! Young ladies."

He was selling candies at a stand and had to leave because his wife had been hurt. "Take over for me," he urged the girls.

Once Adrienne and Coco were behind the counter, the stock was sold out in no time. Apparently they obtained more — I have no idea how. By the end of the afternoon, when they counted up their earnings, Adrienne and Coco discovered wealth enough to take them to Paris by train.

Without, of course, a word to Aunt Julia. One Chanel, however, was let into the secret: the youngest brother of Coco's father. He gave his niece all the money he had on him, and his blessing as well. In order not to arouse Aunt Julia's suspicions, the girls dropped their bundles of clothes out the window before they left the house. They had two bundles — no suitcases. But Adrienne, who had taken charge of the finances, decided that they could not travel third class, which still existed then; in fact, on certain lines, there was even a fourth class. She bought two second-class tickets.

"We'll travel first class," Coco decreed.

"But —"

"Wait and see."

The conductor was not to be wheedled; in addition to the difference in fare he wanted them to pay a small penalty. Forty years later Coco had not forgotten. "I told Adrienne we should have bought first class to start: it would have saved us the fine." And that, for the girls, was a huge sum when every sou counted.

What happened in Paris? That is a mystery. How did Adrienne and Coco manage? One must rely on one's imagination, and not necessarily suppose the worst. All that is known is that this invasion of Paris was not a success and that Adrienne soon went back to Vichy, taking Coco with her. The two were inseparable after that.

In Vichy the summer was far from over. There were races to distract the tourists taking the waters. And what amusement was there for the cavalry officers who had come from Moulins to ride in those races? In his story *Yvette,* Maupassant sketches the life of a pretty woman who in order to escape from poverty ("I didn't want to be a slavey," she was to tell her daughter) took an attractive house in which she entertained a series of minor Norman noblemen, local landowners, who one after another took care of her needs. This was how Maud M. — a pretty woman rather older than Adrienne and Coco — kept herself alive in Vichy. Her house was in Souvigny, and there Adrienne met an officer of an excellent family. She lived with him for several years until she met Baron de Nexon.

Adrienne, who was very beautiful, had one dream: security. She hoped to find it through the man she loved. Coco, whose dream was independence, knew already that she would achieve it only through money. Her relatives, who were somewhat frightened by her, used to say: "That one wants everything." And they anticipated the worst for her; they thought the devil was in her.

How old was she when she first gave her people reason to worry over her? Her grandmother in Vichy, for instance? Coco said: "Twelve is the age at which little girls are most strongly attracted by *that kind of thing.*"

What kind of thing? She had just seen the film *Mouchette,* in which a girl of twelve is raped by an old man. Robert Bresson, the director, had married the sister of Coco's nephew's first wife, and a kind of family relationship had developed between him and Coco.

"I told Bresson: 'Your Mouchette wasn't raped. She went to the old man's house in order to be seduced.'" Repeating to me what she had said to Bresson, she added: "Girls of twelve are terrible. Anyone can have them who uses a little subtlety. They're in the middle of changing."

All one can do is try as skillfully as possible to put together what pieces of the puzzle one has, in the hope that, if it cannot be worked out altogether, at least it will provide a general idea of the whole. This piece — Coco's observation on twelve-year-old girls — obviously becomes important when it is set next to the fear expressed previously: the danger of reform school.

The flight to Paris with Adrienne took place in 1899 or 1900: thus Coco was sixteen or seventeen. What had happened before that? Something at the convent, where the mother superior had only the most tenuous illusions as to Coco's virtue? Or during the vacation in Vichy? Did the fifteen-year-old Coco spend every night in her own bed at her grandmother's or her Aunt Julia's? One can only wonder. In those days social services did not concern themselves with difficult children. And if a girl ran off her family did not immediately call the police; the police would just have said: "Don't worry, folks; your kid'll be back when she's hungry."

Those gallant policemen would not have appreciated being asked to look for a Coco in the rooms of some gentleman in Vichy, some Parisian taking the cure and staying in one of the best hotels, or to search the house of some country squire known for his taste in schoolgirls.

Attitudes have changed since the turn of the century. In those days poor people did not get particularly upset if a wealthy young (or even not so young) man began to pay attention to a poor but pretty girl — whose background would have doomed her to the life of a peasant's wife or a laborer's bride. Such contacts between money and charm were viewed as an opportunity for upward mobility. It could happen that the prince married the shepherdess, though it was rare, to be sure. But often enough he at least set her up in a home of her own and gave her jewels. When the shepherdess "knew her way around," she came out of it with substantial gains. The proof was Adrienne.

Coco had other aspirations. She said: "When I begin to ana-lyze myself, I find at once that my need for independence came into being when I was very young. I heard a great deal of talk about money among my aunts' maids, who used to say, 'When we have money, we'll leave.' "

With what is now known of the truth about her youth, it is easy to make the necessary transpositions.

Coco felt humiliated in the convent in Moulins. As a charity pupil, she was in a position of inferiority, and it rankled. In order to break out of the stereotype of poverty she invented a father who was seeking his fortune in the Americas. The image of the avenging father — avenging because rich — was quite naturally replaced in her unconscious by that of a rich man. The process seems elementary.

She never talked to me about her adolescent years. It has been supposed that she spent them in Moulins, with Adrienne and An-toinette, Coco's younger sister, and that all three, who were known as the Three Graces, worked as dressmakers and also en-tertained the most dashing officers of the cavalry regiment in their house, under the chaperonage of Maud M.

According to another legend, Coco at that time was singing in a music hall — the Blue Angel of Moulins, as it were. "You know perfectly well you were the Madelon of Moulins," her "godson" Serge Lifar once spat at her in my presence. She merely shrugged, her lips tight and her face full of contempt.

She did have a very pleasant voice when she was twenty, and she did enjoy singing in public. Perhaps she would rather have become Maria Callas than Coco Chanel. But that is a long way from singing in a soldiers' saloon and then passing the plate: "For the artist, layeezngents."

Yet every bit of gossip about Coco yields a gram of truth. And suppose it were true? Suppose Coco did sing for the soldiers, or the officers, in Moulins or Vichy? Nothing could soil her because she already sensed her destiny above destiny. She had still to fulfill it, and, for this, to go up to Paris. And then go back to

Paris — this time not on a prayer but with someone solid on whom she could rely, who would help her to make a real start.

In that chic light-cavalry regiment in Moulins the most eligible young men of Paris came one after another year after year: wealth, family, youth, all in dashing uniforms, white gloves, bearing great names and money, charming, bounderish. The right to be a bounder has been more or less lost. "A real bounder" — that was said with a certain admiration.

What did all these young bucks want? What did they ask of Adrienne, or Coco? (Antoinette, the youngster, was not there: she was taking care of a hatter's children in Clermont-Ferrand.) The Parisians, of course — and the rest — wanted everything. They went after it with flowers and casual charm, with the certainty that they were overwhelming the pretty creatures to whom they condescended. Without referring to this period, though the observations are none the less interesting on that account, Coco said to me:

"I have my defenses; I've always been able to defend myself. I don't like people who don't like me. I can spot them at once. When I am not liked, I know it right away, and I leave. I can't live among people who dislike me. I don't ask that people love me — that's a big word. And I don't love everyone, either. There are very few people I love — really love, which means being devoted to someone body and soul. That kind of loving is rare."

That kind of love was not what she felt for Balsan. He had by now left the army and already plunged himself completely into his career as a gentleman rider.

And before Balsan? Anyone is free to imagine his own story of those years. The Three Graces would have provided Zola with a problem novel about money tainting innocence. Balzac would have been involved in Maud M. and Adrienne's lover. Victor Hugo would have seen Cosette in Antoinette. Stendhal would have understood Coco. Was she not of the same mold as Fabrice del Dongo, and did she not have a face whose purity would have sent the saints to hell? One can only dream.

A FACE THAT LOOKED
LIKE NO ONE ELSE'S

She said: "No one kept telling me I was pretty.
I had no idea I was. I didn't care about it.
I think I was born twenty years too soon."
She said too: "No one has a neck as long as mine."

Collection of Boris Kochno

COCOTTES IN FLOUNCES AND FURBELOWS RULED OVER PARIS

First, holding her pearls in her hands, is Emilienne d'Alençon, the official mistress of Etienne Balsan, the chevalier whom Coco followed to Paris to become "No. 2." Balsan liked only old women, Coco sniffed. At right, above: Otéro of the magic eyes. At right, below: Liane de Pougy before a costume ball. When Coco appeared, the *cocottes* vanished.

HER FIRST DRESS: SEM PROCLAIMS THE END OF A PUPPET SHOW

These splendid drawings by the great Sem are taken from his album *Real Style and False*. While those on the left-hand page require no commentary, it is important to point out that the dress on the right-hand page was Coco's first, made at the request of Premet, himself a dressmaker, for a very-much-talked-about courtesan, Forzane.

Private collection

BEFORE FAME,
HER ONE LOVE

These pictures were taken in 1917, which was the tragic year of the Great War. Coco is shown getting a tan at Biarritz and playing golf with her friend Marthe Davelli. They were known as the grasshopper and the ant, Coco being the ant. The gentleman in the boater is Pierre Decourcelle, the author of the serialized novels that enthralled Coco. The dark-haired man picnicking on the beach at Biarritz with her is the man she loved, Boy Capel, an Englishman. He made his fortune by procuring coal for France during the war.

Collection of J. Loste

MISIA LEADS THE PARADE OF THE SEVEN HUNDRED

The Seven Hundred were the privileged caste that in the view of Paul Morand constituted Paris society when Coco made her appearance in it, under the chaperonage of Misia Sert, the wife of the painter José María Sert. Very beautiful, intelligent, amusing, Misia knew everyone. At left, she is shown in her home on the Esplanade des Invalides. Without the Serts, Coco said, "I would have died in a kind of idiocy." At right, above: Coco with Jean Cocteau; below: in a Watteau costume at the Comte d'Orgel's ball — named for Raymond Radiguet's second novel, which had that title — at the Beaumonts', with Serge Lifar and Countess Montgomery, now the wife of General Bethouart. Comte Etienne de Beaumont was the model for Radiguet's title character.

Shown between Christian Bérard and Boris Kochno, Coco was already wearing blue jeans many years ago.

SURROUNDED BY THE PRIDE OF PARIS FOR A HALF CENTURY

"Everyone who was anyone" in literature, painting, music, film, who was the target of the camera and the spotlight, jostled his way in to pay tribute to the empress of taste and fashion, bowing to her most awesome judgments.

A talk with Louis Jouvet, actor and director, after a success by Jean Giraudoux.

In conversation with Salvador Dali, then an unknown.

Chatting with Georges Auric, who was beginning his career as a composer.

And with Jacques Chazot.

Archives Plon

Photo by United Press International

Photo by Roger Schall

A GRAND DUKE, A DUKE, A POET

She had already known Grand Duke Dmitri
(top right) before the Great War. A collab
orator with Prince Felix Yusupoff in the mur
der of Rasputin, he went to France to find
refuge with her. He was still escorting her
when she met the Duke of Westminster (top
left) in Monte Carlo. "At last a man on whom
I can lean," she sighed. She would have liked
to bear him a son. She was then forty-five. At
bottom left she is shown, in an "Anglicized"
version of her Chanel uniform, with the duke.
At lower left on the opposite page, Pierre
Reverdy, the poet, whom she ranked above
Cocteau; at lower right, Paul Iribe, the artist
who died playing tennis at her villa, La Pausa.

Collection of René Dazy

FIFTY YEARS OF
THE CHANEL STYLE

Archives Vogue

1931

1922

1931

Photo by Hor

1925

1935

1938

1949

1955

1964

1971

Photo by Roger Schal

THE HONORS OF THE STAIRCASE

An honor much coveted was the right to see the collections from the top steps of the mirrored staircase. At extreme right in the front row, Marie-Louise Bousquet.

What a setting Moulins was in 1900! The silence, the closed shutters, the High Mass, the military concerts, the old ladies all in black, the lawyer in his frock coat, the bishop who was never seen, the annual reception at the prefecture, the Tuesdays given by the colonel's wife . . .

What a horror, what a hell, Coco would have said if she had ever mentioned it. Did she ever, when she was alone with her truth, think back to her adolescent years in Moulins? Did a face come suddenly back into her memory? A face earlier than Balsan's? A strange woman, Coco Chanel. Did she remember Balsan simply because he had brought her to Paris?

Had she guessed immediately that he was not like the others? That this man would say to her "Come with me"?

"My Uncle Etienne," according to his nephew, the explorer François Balsan, was "thoroughly antisnob." And on the day when Coco saw this Parisian enter her life, the colors of this handsome gentleman jockey were already known at the tracks: the turquoise shirt and the black cap. He was twenty-five, and a fountain of natural energy. And still a source of scandal to his family, which learned only later how much it owed to his triumphs after all.

The Balsans had been in the textile industry for centuries. Until the Boer War they had supplied the blue cloth for British police uniforms. But the business did not interest Etienne, who was an undisciplined, prankish boy not at all given to studies. By way of developing his character his parents sent him to a British "public school." He took along his dog and, when he arrived in England, bought two horses. He was seen at every fox-hunting meet but rarely in his classes. He was a tremendous favorite socially — much too tremendous, in the view of his father, who summoned him home and very firmly requested that he enlist in the African light cavalry. Fathers were still obeyed then.

One winter day when the young soldier of the republic was on guard duty outside his garrison, he was anything but hospitable to a civilian whom he subsequently called a "pasty-faced abortion." This was the governor. During the guardhouse confinement that followed, Balsan learned from the conscript country boy who brought the food that the weather was so cold that the horses' pasterns were splitting. "Tell your corporal," Balsan said, "who will repeat it to the sergeant, who will tell the lieutenant, who will pass it on to the captain, who will inform the colonel, that Cavalryman Balsan, who is in the guardhouse, knows how to take care of horses." He was given his chance. Escorted by an armed guard, he went into the town of Constantine to get a pharmacist to make up a miraculous remedy, the secret of which is still in the Balsan family: a quart of Goulard's extract, a quart of oil, and a quart of water. The ailing horses' pasterns were bathed with this solution. Three days later the squadron was back in the saddle, and Balsan had a corporal's stripe.

Horses were in his blood. Women interested him just as much, but he spent less on them than on his horses. In the saddle he spared neither his mounts nor his competitors, even if they were professional jockeys. He rode with one eye closed — in reserve, he explained, in the event that the other was blinded by a spatter of mud. Frequently it was difficult for him to make the weight, and this enraged him. When he raced at Chateauroux all the workers in the family's factory bet on him.

There was one beast that only he could master. Having forgot his whip one day, he borrowed a silver-handled cane from one of his brothers and broke it. François Balsan described the scene in the family's privately written and printed history:

Suddenly (after having lain back at the end of the pack) Etienne seemed to have been stung by a wasp. He became a demon! His vigorous legs went into action, his arms almost flew from their sockets, and in a perfect rhythm the cane struck the horse's flank with each flexion of its hindquarters, shining in the sun. The sound of the cane against the flesh could be heard in the stands. In great strides the chestnut mare began to pass her rivals. It was a magnificent if overfast spectacle by a mediocre horse under the influence of a master of the whip. She had only a tiny reserve of strength left: Etienne called on her for it neither too soon nor too late. "Etienne wins!" the spectators shouted, and the stands vibrated to their stamping feet. My uncle came in pale, panting, ill-tempered, deaf to the cheers; it was a wonder that he did not attack the admirers who were blocking his way.

Etienne asked François, who was still a boy, to tell the family chauffeur that his uncle would have to be driven to the station to catch the Paris train.

"But what about tomorrow's race?"

"Tomorrow my other horse will certainly win. My apprentice will ride him."

Systematically antisnob. This was extraordinary in 1900. This Etienne Balsan had a heart. Oh, the others had too — the dashing, bounderish, handsome, rich young officers whom Coco met in Moulins (where Maud M. had a discreet little place), but in their case the heart had been conditioned: I mean it clung to its condition and pretty generally beat according to caste rules. When they formed a friendship or fell in love outside their class, they did so with condescension, if not with a feeling of betrayal. There was nothing of this in Etienne Balsan.

Coco, of course, grasped the situation from the first: Balsan, the systematic antisnob, was Amphitryon, the messenger of fate. Did she make him beg hard or long before she accepted him as a lover? It is quite conceivable that, guided by her intuition, she trusted him from first sight.

5

The First Victory: Poverty Routed

Coco left Moulins without regrets. The fact that a dashing man was taking her to Paris gave her confidence in her own uncommon beauty. She no longer was afraid of her past, and she won her first victory, over poverty and desertion. Warm, amusing and unlike the ordinary run, Balsan, the first of the lovers whose names were to be important to her, moved her into his château at Royallieu. She was not to be alone there: Balsan was not married, but he had a mistress in residence, Emilienne d'Alençon, who was a famous cocotte. *Would Coco be kept in second place by the lord of the manor?*

Even before his tour of duty in Algeria with the African light cavalry, Etienne Balsan had been acting the gentleman rider; and on his release from military service he threw himself completely into horses. His training ground was at La Croix–St.-Ouen, near Compiègne, and he bought the château of Royallieu in the vicinity. Château? Hardly: Balsan's predecessor in ownership, an energetic farmer, had raised chickens there in huge numbers. Today, if local people are asked where the château is, they are perplexed. "Is there a château around here?"

Many hundreds of years earlier it had been fortified, and was known as La Neuville, no doubt an outpost for the defense of Paris; it had served also as a hunting lodge for the Capet kings. It became La Maison du Roy after Philippe le Bel stayed in it, and then Royallieu. A queen called Adélaïde turned it into an abbey, which quite soon became a priory. Later still it was a stud farm, and its huge stables remained standing though silent.

What remained of the royal castle in the large, rather ordinary house in which Coco was to spend several years? A few stones, no doubt, by now part of the moss-covered walls. The entrance to the estate is still attractive, with a door of rough wood studded with great nails.

Coco had a gift for conciseness. This is how she described Etienne Balsan to me: "Etienne Balsan liked old women. He adored Emilienne d'Alençon. Beauty and youth didn't concern him. He adored *cocottes* and he lived with that one to the scandal of his family. He was very independent. He had a racing stable."

Actually, Emilienne d'Alençon was only a few years older than Coco. She was at the height of her beauty. But what is striking in Coco's account of her is not its dishonesty (which is self-explanatory, automatic) but the total absence of any sign of protest. Not for one minute did the little girl from Moulins dream of challenging the rights of the "other woman," whom Balsan had brought back from Paris and installed in his home in Royallieu as his official mistress and the lady of the house. She was *homely*, Coco sniffed. But Coco accepted the situation. Why? Because, like a good little girl, she was thinking only of the happiness of the man she loved?

It must be admitted that she was in a very strange position. But it was in no sense unexpected. When she left Moulins she

knew what was awaiting her. Otherwise, when she found someone else in residence she would have gone back home, there can
be no doubt. So she was ready for . . . for what? Sharing?

But what about the "other woman"? Would Emilienne d'Alençon have tolerated a competitor in *her* house? She had interests
to defend! How were matters worked out? What a young
womanhood for Coco! Like the heroines of her serials, she went
from one untenable situation to another, and apparently with
great ease. She adjusted herself to everything.

The current Balsans suppose that Coco "amused" Uncle
Etienne with her wit and with something acerb in her manner
that made him laugh. For him she was a "playmate-mistress,"
while for her, the "charming provincial," he was an "interesting,
attractive lover." Handed down from one generation to the next,
these appraisals enable us to glimpse something of the difficult
conditions under which Coco was introduced into "society."

She knew from the start that she would not be the mistress of
Royallieu. What pledge had she given? That she would keep out
of the way? There has been gossip to the effect that in her early
days at Royallieu Coco ate some of her meals in the servants'
quarters. If this were true, it would in no way damage Mademoiselle Chanel — quite the contrary. At worst one might reprove
her for having concealed so disconcerting a truth.

The Balsans have categorically denied this version. There
were times when Etienne entertained friends of his own class
(people still talked like that), some of whom, especially
Edouard Barante, were accompanied by their wives. At such
times, it seems, and for all kinds of obvious reasons, Coco simply
disappeared. But this does nothing to clear up the mystery of the
relations among the three principals. Etienne Balsan must have
had remarkable strength to manage that team of two creatures,
each as difficult as the other.

He was a generous, friendly man, overflowing with vivacity
and energy; very much at ease in his emotional anarchy, in love
with freedom above everything; and no doubt that was how he

kept his two women in line: "If you don't like it . . . !" He never put a threat into words — that was not necessary; he showed it on his face, he let it play in his smiles, his gaiety, his dynamism.

To his nephews, the young Balsans, he was a god: they were fascinated by him. They would judge any action by saying *Uncle Etienne would do this* or *wouldn't do that.* The Balsans of the older generation, obviously, were more reserved. It is hard not to put oneself in their place for a moment, to try to imagine what they answered when they were asked for news of Etienne, with all the insinuations that they thought they heard. It was no everyday occurrence in that exalted world for a brilliant young man to live as Etienne Balsan did, with Emilienne d'Alençon, his official kept woman, on his right arm, and a kid that didn't look fifteen years old on his left. And how old was Etienne? One was certainly a man at twenty-five, but what was to be expected of a man like that if at twenty-five he was the scandal of Parisian society! Sometimes Coco said: "Everyone was talking about me and I had no idea. If I'd known, I'd have hidden under a table."

She almost never went to Paris at this time. During the early years she stayed in Compiègne, spending most of her time at La Croix–St.-Ouen with the trainers and jockeys; the magnificent Emilienne never as much as dirtied her shoes there. But there Coco could have Etienne to herself. She loved horses because he did. As we shall see, she was always deeply interested in whatever concerned *the man* — the one who was with her for the time. It might be thought that she overdid her boyish characteristics, not her girlish ones.

"I looked like nothing," she said. "Nothing was right on me but my little school suit, which made everyone laugh. Dresses didn't fit me, and I didn't give a damn."

Her remarkable beauty brought her long stares and compliments that were sometimes strange. She said: "I was told I looked noble. I was told I looked like a Kalmuk. Kalmuk? I looked it up in a dictionary: a Russian tribe. A Russian tribe? They don't think you're pretty, I thought. I resigned myself."

I resigned myself. Really? She said: "When a very pretty woman was pointed out to me, I said: '*I* don't think she's pretty. Why do you? What is it about her?' "

To whom did she say that? A groom? A jockey? About some guest at the château? She said:

"I was very hard on all those ladies, especially the society women, whom I considered dirty. But I thought the *cocottes* were ravishing with their hats that were too big and their heavy makeup. They were so appetizing! They resembled my novels. The kept women and the world they lived in were my stories. Whereas the nice people, as far as I was concerned, were unreal. No, they were my aunts! (They had hard lives.)"

She said: "When I came to Paris, I had to learn everything. I'd never before ridden in a vehicle with pneumatic tires — I'd ridden in cars with solid tires. They were so ugly! And the poor coachman who had to drive them, sitting out front and so high up. I was afraid he'd fall. It was dusty, and one wore *gimmicks* — I hated them, they were ugly. All the same, it opened my mind. I said to myself, If life goes on this way something else will be invented that will be better and you'll profit by it."

She had everything to learn — for example, a taste for oysters, which revolted her. As a little girl she had spent a vacation near Arcachon with her sister Antoinette. They had been sent to strengthen their lungs with the good air of the pine forests. Coco said: "We didn't stay at a hotel but with some plain people. He was an oyster picker at an oyster farm. I used to go with him in his old boat every morning. He would fix an oyster for me: open it, clean it, cut off the end and hand it to me. Bah! I would spit it out!"

She could not spit out the oysters that were served to her in Paris. When she went there with Etienne Balsan she stayed at the Ritz. In order to accustom herself to oysters, she had them sent to her room. She said:

"I invited the chambermaid to share them with me. She didn't want any. 'Listen,' I told her: 'make an effort. You're young, you're pretty, one day perhaps you'll have to eat oysters — you'll find . . .' "

I can still see her as we sat with the tape recorder, her mouth open around her unfinished sentence. It was so clear that she was about to tell the chambermaid, *Because you're pretty you'll be taken to Maxim's or somewhere else to eat oysters. Like me! You'll find a rich lover, like me. So teach yourself to face the oyster problem, as I'm doing. One must know what one wants out of life, my girl.*

That was surely what she had said; the words were jostling one another now on her lips; but when in her inner fortress forbidden truths raised themselves out of their dungeons an alarm system went into action at the last moment: she recaptured them and thrust them back into their holes. She finished: "You'll find a nice husband who'll want to please you by buying you oysters, which are expensive."

She said: "I had the good luck to fall into the most elegant set when I came to Paris. I didn't know it, though. At first, to tell the truth, I thought they were all dreadful. In any case I didn't see anything remarkable about them. The only men I'd known had been my father and a few farmers, local men, the priest, the lawyer, the mayor. So I was very *receptive* when I came to Paris, but scared. I thought all the men in Paris were like the ones I knew. I had no idea there were rich young men whom all the women coveted as husbands for their daughters or lovers for themselves." She said: "I felt lost. What could I do?"

How, first of all, ought she to behave with Etienne Balsan and his friends, all of them horsemen, Anglophiles, smart, wealthy, polo players, charming cynics who talked about people who meant nothing to Coco, volleying mysterious catch phrases with the attitude, apparently, that everyone must understand them, laughing over even more mysterious witticisms. Coco laughed too. She was funny.

"I felt I was very different from the others," she said.

And that was the reason for her charm, which was arresting and in no way affected: she rode very well, she was always on hand when her presence was desired or when she was needed. Nevertheless, if fifty or sixty years later Mademoiselle Chanel could say of Etienne Balsan: "Youth and beauty didn't interest him," she must in those days have had to choke back an ocean of pride.

She said: "Above all I didn't want to be taken for a little yokel. I lied in order to be taken seriously."

Unlike Colette's Gigi, she did not have two aunts in the very best-kept world to show her the road; she had to learn everything on her own. One might suppose that Emilienne d'Alençon helped her as much as she could. "The only serious person I met in those days," Coco told me, "was Emilienne d'Alençon."

In a delightful passage written for the semicentennial of Maxim's, Jean Cocteau presented this sketch of the "older woman":

> She was a handsome girl. Blonde, uncondescending, her eyes always laughing, she did not behave like her colleagues (the other kept women). After the great tragic actresses of Maxim's, now there was a comedian, a dimpled Jeanne Granier of Pleasure, who could hold her own with the jockeys and the gigolos. She would pause among the tables, shake hands, ask and answer questions. But if that Emilienne should appear among us now, our faces would bewilder her. She would be vaguely lost, wondering whether she had not gone to the wrong restaurant. She would look up, with those ingenuous eyes, and recognize the brass escutcheons, the mahogany scrollwork, and she would not understand.

But she understood the Prince de Sagan very well when he said to her, "There are certain physical indulgences that I never permit myself with women," and she retorted: "Ah, Prince, you are laying up a very sorry old age for yourself."

"She was an old woman," Coco repeated. "That was all Etienne Balsan liked. He didn't understand me at all. Nevertheless, when I left him . . ."

When, in her early days in Paris and in the Balsan group in Compiègne, Coco disguised herself as a Decourcelle heroine, she had another defense, besides the lie, against the snobs and anyone else who *scared* her: the weapon of every fearful person, aggressiveness.

"I heard a lot about a beauty of the time, Pauline de St.-Sauveur," she told me. "I invited her to tea. She wanted to meet me. One thing I'd learned: one must invite people to tea. Later I was asked what I thought of her.

" 'Horrible!'

" 'What do you mean, horrible?' With a laugh.

"I said: 'She seems mean, hard. Not clean. There's face powder in her hair. Why does she have so much hair? Her profile's so hard!'

"She was thirty. She was the perfect example of the woman I still find horrible — painted, tarted up, hard as stone. Oh, they taught me plenty, those people!"

That observation is worth remembering: *those people taught me plenty!* It was a declaration of war. And *those people* had a great laugh: "Did you hear what Coco said about Pauline?"

"No, what?"

"She said she was awful!"

"It can't be true!"

"She said Pauline was dirty!"

"No!"

They were breathless with laughter. "Can you imagine the gall of that kid?" Translation: *take her out of her chicken run and nothing surprises her, everything's ugly and dirty to her.*

Coco must have wondered privately: Why do they laugh at the awful things I spit out like that just to reassure myself?

She said to me: "I was a little girl scared of everything. A little country girl who knew nothing, absolutely nothing about anything."

She learned that aggressiveness paid. She opened her eyes and ears. She had not yet become a monologuist. She was finding that *tout-Paris* made a great deal of noise over nothing, that its self-confidence was a pose, that it took very little to amaze it or destroy its defenses.

She said, "Cocteau told me after the Liberation: 'It isn't hard to succeed in Paris. What's hard is surviving. But *I* — I've been shitting on them for twenty years.'"

"Them"? Cocteau meant the same people Coco meant when she sighed, "Oh, *they* showed me."

"She is terrible," Jean Cocteau said of Coco; "she is a judge. She looks at you and bends her head. She smiles. And she sentences you to death."

In Compiègne and Paris, when she was twenty, Coco had little time in which to evaluate the men and women on whom her life depended. And besides, Balsan could leave her or send her away. Nothing held them to each other. If her father, the first man in her life, had deserted her, why wouldn't Balsan? She did not trust men. That was instinctive. It was now in her blood. If anyone spoke to her as her father had done, or told her stories as he had told her stories — well, she made no scenes, nor did she close her ears. Distrust. "She looks at you, she judges you." Cocteau was right, and wrong. She did not judge from the summit of her superiority; she asked herself, from the depths of her desertion, What hurt can that man inflict on me?

Or *that woman*? If she needed only a glance to measure and judge a man, she did not even bother to look at a woman. She executed women without trial. She said to me:

"All those ladies [the *cocottes* and the others] were badly dressed, in their body armor, with their bosoms out, their behinds jutting out too, bound in at the waist until they were almost cut in two. They were dressed to the teeth. Actresses and *cocottes* set the fashions, and the poor society ladies followed, with birds in their hair, false hair everywhere, and dresses that dragged on the ground and gathered mud."

And how did Coco dress? "Like a schoolgirl. I couldn't dress any other way. At eighteen I looked fifteen."

Did she dress that way by design? Of those kept women who were so fanatically in fashion, Coco said in a surge of nostalgia: "I didn't think the *cocottes* were all that bad. I thought they were very pretty with their hats broader than their shoulders, and their big, heavily made-up eyes. They were sumptuous. I admired them far more than the society women. The *cocottes* were clean and well turned out. The others were filthy.

"I remember Marthe Letellier, who was beautiful and very elegant, walking in a white woollen dress with fur at the hem to do a better job of sweeping the dust off the paths at Longchamp. I looked at her with a good deal of amazement. I admired her. I didn't know how to walk on high heels. I wore flat heels, which were abominated then. I'd have fallen on my face with high heels." And she added: "I still can't walk on high heels."

Listening to these recollections about Marthe Letellier or Pauline de St.-Sauveur, one understands that Coco had not gone off with Etienne Balsan to spend the rest of her life at the stables of Royallieu or the practice track at the training farm — in other words, to marry a jockey or a trainer. She said: "No one can imagine how bored a young girl like me was! I thought I would die of it! I didn't know what to do with my time."

She laughed, she laughed a great deal, and yet she had no time for laughter. She could not be carefree, like a Balsan. Every day that passed at Royallieu intensified her problems: What is going to become of me? Her whole capital was her beauty and her youth. It may be assumed that she kept up contact with her young Aunt Adrienne. That one was getting ahead! "We'll get married," Baron de Nexon promised Adrienne. And this was no empty talk, because she did become Baronne de Nexon. But what about me? Coco thought. Etienne Balsan was not promising marriage. And in any event Emilienne d'Alençon had precedence over her, and Etienne adored Emilienne! Coco was well aware of that; she still remembered it sixty years later. *If he wouldn't marry Emilienne, why would he marry me?* In Coco's mind and on the basis of Aunt Adrienne, her paradigm, security at that time was to be found in marriage.

"When a man really wants to give a woman presents, he marries her," Coco told me. In the Balsan days it was a concept that was part of her ethic. Only marriage could protect a woman against life.

"Don't annoy me," Etienne Balsan said when she talked about her future. He made fun of her: what a little homemaker! Because he lived on the fringe of middle-class codes, it irritated him when anyone mentioned security to him. Racing, betting, the freedom of his life led him, even more than the other Balsans, to place a relative value on everything that still seemed fixed and determined forever: the gold franc, family, property, credit, honor, all that could be handed down from father to son in families like his own. But the risks that he assumed in order to make life interesting were trifles in contrast to those that anguished Coco. She said frankly: "All I thought of was myself."

The *cocottes* wore huge hats covered with flowers. How can a brain function under all that? Coco wondered.

Her own worked very well. She knew she was being talked about. The society women and kept women whom she found so homely were challenges to her unique beauty, which did not suit the standards of the period. She was all right for a fling, in a pinch, and in Moulins. But Moulins was far away; the army lives on the resources of the country it is occupying, satisfied to have whatever is at hand. Coco was reminded of this when she went to Compiègne. And undoubtedly Emilienne d'Alençon said as much, adding: "Etienne brought her along out of kindness. She wanted to see Paris and try her luck, and naturally he'd like to see what can be done for her."

This must have been what was being said about her in Paris in the beginning, and only this. "Men are so stupid, and you know

Etienne, how generous he is, always ready to do favors; the kid insisted, and he didn't want to say *no* just like that . . ."

But the years slipped past and Coco did not go back to her chicken run. What did she have, then, that little peasant, that Auvergnat that Etienne had found in wooden shoes? The gossip grew more acrid as Coco's elegance became increasingly beyond cavil. She dressed well — and her hats!

Coco said: "All those ladies wanted to know who made my clothes and especially who made my hats. I bought a form in the Galeries Lafayette* and simply draped stuff on it."

Coco's hats, which Gabrielle Dorziat, the best-dressed actress of the time, was soon going to wear, were the first sign of what was to become the Chanel style — the masculine transposed to the feminine without the slightest ambiguity. Men's fedoras with creased crowns, half the brim turned up and half turned down, had a simplicity that obviously was a slap in the face to the constructions of feathers and flowers that were then the rage. She also made a three-cornered velvet hat for Gabrielle Dorziat, who wore it onstage in *Bel Ami*. The press was full of it.

Out of all the sound and fury that surrounded Coco she conceived the notion of "doing something to become independent." Was she still in communication with Adrienne and Antoinette? It is conceivable that the Three Graces of Moulins started to elaborate some concerted plans, and not altogether at cloud level. Really, why should Coco live for years with Etienne Balsan, enjoy the gilded youth of Parisian society and come out of it with nothing?

At a given point another Amphitryon entered her life, the second emissary of her destiny: Boy Capel.

* A large popular department store. Translator.

6

The Second Victory:
Coco Becomes A Milliner

How can one make a lover who is too certain of himself take one seriously? By acquiring a second lover. That was what Coco did when she threw herself at Boy Capel, an English playboy. As a result she escaped the fate that awaited her as a kept woman. "I was able to create my house because two men did battle over my little self," she said, with a certain smile. This was her second victory.

Each autumn Etienne Balsan and his train set up winter quarters in the vicinity of Pau — like Moulins, a horseman's town where there were races, hunts and some polo, a game then very fashionable. It was there that Coco met Boy Capel, an Englishman as dark and dashing as Rudolph Valentino, with very beautiful blue eyes, and she fell in love with him on the spot. This she told Louise de Vilmorin when she was trying to persuade that writer to collaborate with her on a life of Chanel.

"I listened as she spoke," Louise told me, "and took notes,

which I showed her the next day. She tore them up." And Louise raised her eyes to heaven. Her collaboration with Coco could not last. Be that as it may, however, it was from her that I got these details on the lightning that struck in the form of Boy Capel.

Having learned that Boy was going back to Paris, Coco scrawled a brief farewell to Etienne on the top of a table (as it is done in serials: *Forgive me! But I love him*) and, without any luggage, went to the railroad station to wait for Capel. She was extremely apprehensive: how would he react when he saw her?

"He threw his arms around her," Louise de Vilmorin said, and added: "Coco could have left the house later, with a suitcase. She knew the schedule quite well — this was the only train there was."

Boy Capel (according to the same source) carried Coco in his arms to his berth (in those days the French still called it *le sleeping*). "I hope he got another afterward," Louise commented: "even alone, one slept abominably in a *sleeping*."

If fate had not already set its seal on Coco's forehead as the future *Grande Mademoiselle,* this escapade would have come to nothing. It would have got lost among others. Even before Balsan . . . there is still talk that Balsan took Coco away from his captain; others say it was from his adjutant.

I mention these rumors merely to give Boy Capel the importance he deserves. He was one of the rare men in Coco's life, if not the only one, whom she remembered with emotion and over whom (as will appear) she admitted having wept abundantly.

She said: "He had made his own money. And he still found time to write. He was very much concerned with the Beyond. He had lived rather a long time in India. Everything esoteric fascinated him immeasurably. And fascinated me, because I couldn't tolerate his being interested in something that had nothing to do with me."

This in her mouth was a confession of love: *his being interested in something that had nothing to do with me.* She said: "He read, he wrote, he had made his fortune and he found time to give to me. In fact, he found time to cheat on me all day long, which left me absolutely unaffected. It was of no importance. I was so certain that he loved only me. It made no difference to me that he went to bed with various ladies. I thought it was rather dirty, rather disgusting; but I couldn't have cared less."

Said with a pout. She was tearing up — verbally — the few flowers in her garden. She did not want to preserve anything, in her hands or in her heart.

What did Capel give her? First of all confidence, self-confidence. After four years with Balsan (apparently she met Capel in 1907), she was asking herself, What is going to become of me in all this? She enjoyed the good opinion of Jacques Balsan, the aviator and head of the family. "He was ten years older than Etienne, who was ten years older than I," she told me. (Actually Jacques was six years older than Etienne, who was only five years older than Coco. No matter; she looked so young at twenty-five that everyone seemed old to her.)

"Why don't you marry Etienne?" Jacques Balsan is supposed to have asked her.

"I don't love him," she said she had replied. She threw up her hands as she described Jacques Balsan as having done.

"What difference does that make?" she quoted his retort.

"I thought, What a monster!" she said. "It was clear that he was an old man. He started preaching at me: 'You'll come to a bad end, my dear. What's going to happen to you?'

" 'I don't know and I don't care. I want to work.'

" 'But you don't know how to do anything!' "

So Coco opened a hat shop in Compiègne, merely to be doing something. It was a first, timid effort not to be dependent on others, an experiment without a sequel. Who needed her hats in Compiègne? Did she talk to Etienne Balsan about trying again in Paris? He shrugged: what for? Had she not promised, when she followed him to Paris from Moulins, that she would never ask for anything? And now what? What was the matter with her?

And then she went off with Boy Capel. She said: "Like every good Frenchman, like all men in general, Etienne Balsan began to love me again because I'd left him for someone else."

In that family history put together for the exclusive use of the Balsans (some material from which François Balsan has authorized me to use) François Balsan gives the Balsan version of Coco's translation from the arms of the dynamic Etienne to those of the gentle, loving Capel:

While visiting Etienne at Royallieu, Boy was swept off his feet by Coco, the "provisional queen of the domain."

" 'She's terrific, Etienne! I congratulate you on your choice. I hope I can see her again.'

" 'Thanks for the compliments, but don't get excited: she has dinner here every night.' "

Capel's temperature rose steadily during dinner, and the drinks that followed increased his admiration. Profiting by his presence because she sensed an ally in him, Mademoiselle (as François Balsan calls her throughout) began to discuss an idea that had been taking form in her mind:

" 'I'm bored with this shop in Compiègne. The local ladies come in to buy my hats so that they can get a close look at Etienne Balsan's girl friend.'

" 'I'm quite flattered,' " Etienne snapped.

" 'I'm quite annoyed,' " Mademoiselle went on. " 'I have something more interesting to suggest to you. Let's sell the shop in Compiègne and open one in Paris. I have the touch. I'm sure to succeed.'

" 'And that's it?' " Etienne replied. " 'Well, my dear, the answer is *no*.' "

During this rather sharp exchange Boy Capel had been drinking cognac. "His face growing more and more flushed," he went to Coco's rescue: " 'This is a very intelligent suggestion, Etienne.'

" 'For someone else. I'm not a banker.'

" 'Think about it. Have a little heart. *Take care**— if you don't do this little favor for her . . . I . . . I . . .'

" 'Please don't let me stand in your way!' " Etienne, according to the family history, rasped at Boy Capel — his friend, who was dazzled by Coco's beauty. Then, the story says, Etienne called the butler: " 'Michaud, two bottles of Bollinger. Mademoiselle is leaving us. I want to lubricate her departure.' "

"It was all very simple and amicable," François Balsan's account concludes.

But it wasn't really all that simple.

"I could have married Boy Capel," Coco murmured. "I was destined for him. We were made for each other."

Why was there no marriage? Boy Capel valued his freedom. Coco said: "All the women were running after him. I wasn't jealous. I said to him: 'All those women keep looking at you — how strange.' He laughed and said: 'It isn't me they're looking at, you darling idiot, it's you.' "

With Capel she went out. She was no longer in exile among the horses. She was looked at, and this was new. She embarked on the tide of Paris. She was envied because she had tamed the lion of the city's nights. She did not shackle him: *I couldn't have cared less whether he was unfaithful; I found it rather dirty, but it didn't count between us.* How many women talked like that in 1908 or 1910? Morality in those days was very rigid. Paul Bourget could still shock readers with a tale of adultery.

Coco had absorbed something of the anticonformism of Balsan's little group. She was learning what freedoms money conferred when one stopped working for it and allowed it to work for one.

Another point: she was being fought for, Balsan was not letting go. If he had let her disappear with no greater reaction than "Good-bye, have a good trip," she would have felt that she was at

* The English idiom appears in the original. Translator.

Capel's mercy. She would have merely switched escorts. Someone else would have been paying her bills at the Ritz and all the rest. Oh, she must not yet have seemed very demanding, the nice, anxious Coco of those days. With considerable cold-bloodedness, however, she was about to make the most of the situation in which she found herself now that Capel loved her.

"I love you," Capel told her, "but I met you at Etienne's, and he is a friend. You know he'd be unhappy if you really left him."

Even if things did not develop precisely in this fashion, Coco's disclosures re-create the climate that prevailed among the kept women and the men who kept them. A minor breach of contract was overlooked. But the basic commitments must be respected. In plain language, Capel was telling Coco: *Balsan has certain rights over you.*

Coco did not see things that way at all. She objected: "He doesn't love me. He's a little annoyed because I left, but he isn't at all grieved."

And, from Balsan's side: "Are you quite sure you love Capel?" (Occasionally he spoke of Capel as "that adventurer," which was a contemporary synonym for "lousy foreigner.")

"Absolutely sure," she replied.

But, she told me, "I didn't want to say so too soon, either." The little innocent, the tender flower, the guileless girl had no desire to find herself between two stools. An amazing person who risked her skin only for herself. She never put one foot forward until she had been assured that the other could not slip. She felt the stronger between her two men. She said: "I was able to open my shop because two gentlemen were quarreling over my little self."

She went on seeing Balsan, who had never before been so good to her. "Why do you make me so unhappy?" he asked.

"Why are you unhappy?" she countered. "I don't understand."

Which meant, *As long as I lived with you you never told me you loved me. You considered it natural that I should be at your disposal. You didn't even think I was pretty. You preferred*

Emilienne, that old hag! And now you come and tell me I'm making you unhappy. I'm very angry, my dear Etienne, because I'm very fond of you. But remember, you've never done anything for me. What would have become of me if I'd stayed in Compiègne with you? Do you ever give that a thought? You know very well I want to work so I won't be dependent on anyone anymore. Boy understands that. He'll give me a hand. Can you imagine what that means to a woman like me, being dependent on a man like you? I have nothing and I know I can do anything. You have everything and you don't do anything with it.

A man who made his own money. That was what Coco said of Boy Capel at the outset. So there was no need to be born rich: one could become rich. Money, independence.

"Are you sure you love me?" Capel asked her.

"I'll tell you when I'm independent," she said. "I'll know whether I love you when I no longer need you."

To me she explained: "I didn't want him to stop me from doing what I had in my mind. *He* worked. I wanted to work too, so I could be sure of myself. I had learned that one is not the master of one's decisions when one doesn't work."

While Boy Capel was not short of money, he had nevertheless not yet made his fortune. Most of his very considerable wealth was to be acquired during World War I, when, as a result of Clemenceau's friendship, he became one of the suppliers ("procurers" would be more accurate) of coal to France. *Catastrophes bring out people's true selves,* Coco was to observe.

She saw Boy and she saw Etienne: they were always together now in a trio that delighted the gossips. They spent companionable weekends in Compiègne, riding and picnicking. One of the participants in these diversions was the splendid young actress Gabrielle Dorziat, who was to wear Coco's first hats and her first jersey dress. One Sunday the merry group played (if one may use the word) at "country wedding." Coco, dressed as best man, stood beside Dorziat, the maid of honor. The costumes came from the Samaritaine.* Who played the bride — Emilienne d'Alençon? And the bridegroom — Balsan or Capel?

When she went back to Royallieu on a visit, Coco never hesitated to roll up her sleeves, put away her hat and curry her favorite horse. She said: "We lunched and dined together — Etienne, Boy and I. Occasionally Etienne talked about killing himself, and I wept. I wept so! You aren't going to let Etienne kill himself! I said to myself. You'll set them both free. Go throw yourself into the Seine!"

Was there really such drama? It sounds more like a return to Pierre Decourcelle's serials. Whatever the truth, one long revelation by Mademoiselle Chanel must be listened to:

"For a year those gentlemen battled, and all during that time I said to myself, You must do something, otherwise what will become of you in all this? Because who cared about me?

"I was just a kid [she was twenty-six]. I had no money. I lived at the Ritz and everything was paid for for me. It was an incredible situation. Parisian society talked about it. I didn't know Parisian society. I still didn't know anyone. [In fact, she was already going out a great deal; with Capel she came to know much more of Paris life than she had with Balsan.] There I was, and I said to myself, What's going to become of you? [The same question, repeated incessantly.] You must do something.

"I had just spent two years [four or five, at the very least] in Compiègne, riding horses. I couldn't earn a livelihood with that. And, now that I loved someone else, I had to move to Paris. It wasn't possible for me anymore to live on that gentleman's [Balsan's] money.

"It was very complicated. The *cocottes* were paid. I knew that, I'd been taught that. I said to myself, 'Are you going to become like them? A kept woman? But this is appalling!' I didn't want it. There was my family and all the rest. I just couldn't. There was nothing to be done.

"Then they both agreed that I was right. Because the matter

* A large and low-priced popular department store in Paris. Translator.

was discussed by all three of us together. You have no idea how amusing it was, that three-sided discussion that started up fresh every day."

Etienne Balsan left for Argentina, where he was to stay for several months. Was this a kind of cure to purge him of Coco? His friends felt that he was not sorry to terminate his "loving playmates" relationship with Coco. She was of the same mind: for a man of his type such a thing could sometimes become wearisome. "It had to end," Coco admitted. "Etienne Balsan behaved very well."

And there is a story (from a good source, who had it from Mademoiselle Chanel) that Jacques Balsan, the eldest brother, intervened once more. With great tact he explained to Coco that, while Etienne might accept the break, he did not want her to suffer by it. Etienne did not have complete faith in Boy Capel, whom he regarded as a bit too much of a fop, too slick. He said Capel left hair-oil stains on the backs of chairs.

So Jacques Balsan asked Coco what jewel would please her. In both brothers' view, the jewel ought to be one that could easily be sold.

"Jewel?" she murmured. According to her story, she thereupon opened a drawer and took out all the jewelry that Etienne had given her. Pushing aside a gold ring set with a simple topaz, she shoved all the rest over to the head of the house of Balsan. "If that's what your brother wants," she said, "I'll keep this ring. Tell him I'll wear it as long as I live."

Although the tale may be condensed from some serial, she did always wear that ring, even to her grave. I asked her one evening what memories the ring had for her.

"It's a talisman," she replied; "my first ring. A girl friend gave it to me when I was very young."

A girl friend. That particular evening, perhaps, when I questioned her, she did not want to talk about Etienne Balsan.

Before he sailed for Argentina, Etienne Balsan found Coco an apartment in avenue Gabriel, where she could also make her hats. Balsan having supplied the premises, Capel could do no less than provide the means. He opened a bank account for her. "I couldn't sign," she told me; "I wasn't of age yet."

She was almost thirty, in fact; but when she spoke of that period her defenses were never down. She was, roughly, wiping ten years out of her life — the Moulins years and the Compiègne years. She celebrated her "eighteenth" birthday in her own place in avenue Gabriel. She said:

"They [Etienne and Boy] had decided to give me a place where I could make my hats, the way they would have given me a toy, thinking, Let's let her amuse herself, and later we'll see. They didn't understand how important this was to me. They were very rich men, polo players. They didn't understand anything about the little girl who came into their lives to play. A little girl, for that matter, who understood nothing of what was happening to her. It was an unbelievable hodgepodge."

Always this myth of the little girl to whom good things just happened, whereas she had prepared everything, patiently and at length; whereas when she left Moulins she *knew* that she would do what was to start with making hats in avenue Gabriel. She had never stopped thinking about it.

"We've made it!" President Pompidou confided to a friend who visited him at the Elysée Palace on the day of his inauguration. Coco knew the same sense of total happiness the day she first set foot *in her own place* in avenue Gabriel.

"I've done something, all by myself. The House of Chanel isn't a thing made by money. I had no financiers behind me. It didn't cost anyone anything. I had a guaranteed bank credit that I never overdrew. I did it all. I built it all up. I made fortunes. I spent them the same way. I invented the Chanel perfumes. What didn't I do! No one knows everything I've created. I made a revolution. But I was lucky. Everything was just right for it."

In 1938, less than thirty years after Coco first started in fashion, the House of Chanel sold twenty-eight thousand dresses in

Europe, South America and the Middle East, and had four thousand women on its payroll.

Coco said: "How did I manage to do all the things I did and still arrange in spite of everything to have a life filled with love, so much more filled with love than the lives of the women I see? How can they live this way?"

At times she was fantasying, and quite naturally Pierre Decourcelle was available to support her illusions.

7

The Third Victory: Coco Becomes Chanel

She made hats. She invented the jersey dress at a polo match in Deauville. With a sure taste that ruled out any ambiguity, she feminized the English masculine style. Fortified by these initial successes, she brought her family together: the Three Graces of Moulins worked in unison, helped one another, took in an orphaned nephew — and above all, created in Coco's shops a new climate of freedom for women with money.

Her hat business very quickly began to prosper. Soon she "kidnaped" Caroline Reboux's famous chief milliner, Lucienne.* "As soon as I *caught on*," Coco said, "things went well."

She was earning money, she was becoming independent, she was happy, she loved Boy Capel. Why did she not marry him?

Because he knew. He knew everything that she was going to try so fiercely to hide. And, regardless of anything else, before she could contemplate marrying him she had to *rehabilitate* herself by succeeding. One of the many properties of money is its

---

* Caroline Reboux was a leading hat designer in the interwar decades. Translator.

capacity to restore reputation and, almost, virginities. This too she had learned.

The years between 1910 and 1914, her late twenties and early thirties, were certainly the best in her life. This was the period that she would have liked to be the theme of the musical comedy *Coco*. With Boy Capel she had become a personality in the world. She had been one on a more modest scale with Balsan; she was already talked about then, but less than when she was with Capel, whom everyone was watching. His name was always in the papers. Today, the scandal sheets would be running front-page screamers about him: BOY'S HAPPINESS IN DANGER, or BOY'S SECRET — COCO.

Everything that was said about her, even if it did not become an eight-column headline, helped her to sell her first hats. Having seized her opportunity with remarkable foresight, she exploited it with a smiling calculation. From the beginning she had a peasant woman's gift for making her talent pay. She extracted as much money as possible from the frilled and furbelowed ladies who came to try on her hats so that they could get a close look at her. She was no longer dazzled by anyone. As for being impressed . . . Her painful apprenticeship to *le tout-Paris* had left her the lesson, among others, that the right price for the rich was simply *more*. How she must have laughed to herself as she sold her hats. Blocks bought at the Galeries Lafayette for pennies, tricked up with a gimmick, a touch of something on top, and there you are, madame, just for you . . . Meanwhile thinking to herself: idiot, if you're too stupid to make it for yourself, then pay, pay!

She went out a great deal. It was at this time, perhaps even before she opened her hat shop, that she first dined at Maxim's. Her description is amusing:

"I'd been told that the *cocottes* went to Maxim's. [Decent] women didn't go to restaurants. I liked the *cocottes:* they were clean."

This was a leitmotiv with her: kept women are clean. One

could not help thinking of the scene between Gigi and her grandmother, Madame Alvarez, in Colette's novel:

Madame Alvarez: "Did you wash, at least?"
Gigi: "Yes, grandmother, my face."
Madame Alvarez: "Your face, if necessary, you can skip for a day, in an emergency or on a journey, but cleanliness of the lower body is the dignity of woman."

When Coco went to Maxim's for the first time ("in 1913, I was very young") it was indeed popular with *cocottes*. She was escorted by three gentlemen, "one of whom was an Englishman who was determined not to be impressed by anything. A couple sat down at the next table. A woman appeared at once.

" 'Come outside for a moment,' she said to the man.

" 'Let me alone,' he said.

"She broke a glass and began to slash at his face with the base of it. There was blood all over. I fled at once [she imitated hiding under a table]. I went up the stairs, the little spiral stairway. I ran into a room and crawled under a table covered by a cloth. I didn't want to see any more of that quarrel and that blood. How horrible! I was weeping because the three men I was with hadn't done anything. All that mattered to them was that they shouldn't be spattered by the blood.

"The Englishman, who was very much taken with me, asked where I'd gone.

" 'She's gone back home,' the others said.

" 'One has to expect anything from her,' he replied.

"To keep his conscience clear he began looking for me. He went up the stairs and into that room where I was hiding. He lifted the tablecloth [she raised ours and leaned over to call out, like the Englishman]: 'Coco! Come out.'

"I did. But I didn't want to go back to the restaurant. 'You'll go back with me,' the Englishman said. 'One must always try the jump again.' "

On her next venture into Maxim's — this time for lunch — "a

fellow came in with a revolver and ordered everyone to put up his hands. You can understand why after that I didn't go back to Maxim's for thirty years."

Dixit Coco. Obviously the Englishman who made her take the jump again was Boy Capel.

"He really understood me," she said. "He handled me like a child. He said to me: 'Coco, if only you'd stop lying! Can't you talk like everyone else? Where do you dig up the things you imagine?'" In Pierre Decourcelle's stories, she explained sixty years later.

But when she put these questions into Boy Capel's mouth, was she not now posing them to herself? Why lie? Why not tell the truth? At times she was terrified before the abyss in which she was burying ten years of her life. She said:

"Since the war I think about things more than I used to. I had no time before, I was always under pressure. And I needed more sleep than I do now. I was overwhelmed by everything I'd taken on myself. I wanted to forget."

Forget what? Her truth was trying to force its way out from her heart to her lips. If I had been aware of this, perhaps I might have been able to persuade her to free herself, to confess. She went on:

"I've never known just what I wanted to forget. So, to forget whatever it was — probably something that was haunting me — I threw myself into something else."

Right to the end she was to stumble over her own words: "One cannot forget, one never succeeds — things remain in the subconscious, where everything happens." And finally this:

"I wonder whether one doesn't simply try to forget one is alive. One doesn't know. One doesn't put it so clearly. Am I a nervous person? I spend days lying on my sofa. I've always been lazy beyond reason. But inside me there's this need to forget I'm alive, and it drives me to stir myself and do things in order to forget I'm living. Yet living isn't unenjoyable?"

She stopped, as if to underline the question in her tone, though without expecting a reply. She never expected one, except, of course, when she happened to ask what time it was. She said: "I've lived so crowded an existence that I've always been running out of time."

She ran so fast, even before the millinery business, when she was tortured by the anxiety of *what's going to become of me*, that her health was not too good. This in fact was one of the objections raised by Balsan and Capel when she talked of opening a shop.

"I often fainted," she said. Attacks of nerves? Frustration? She added: "One day I fainted three times at the track. I came to in a room, surrounded by jockeys who were looking at me. I heard a gentleman explain to Boy Capel that I was drunk. Things like that happen only to me.

"We'd had lunch at the house of a trainer for Maisons Laffitte. Was I cold? My health is much better now than it was then. I had too much emotion, too much excitement, I lived too intensely. My nerves couldn't stand it. And all at once . . .

"I was standing beside a gentleman who had a horse running. Suddenly I had the feeling he was slipping away from me, fast! What a terrible feeling. I fell to the ground, thinking, this is it, it's all over.

"I'd fainted. The gentleman picked me up and took me to the ladies' room. I came to, hearing the matron saying: 'Please go outside, ladies, it's stifling in here. She'll come to if you let her alone. I have everything she needs.'

"A lady shouted that I ought to be given some hot rum. Someone handed me a glass. I drank it and left, with many thanks to the matron and the other one who'd made me drink the rum. I walked a few steps and fainted all over again.

"That was when I was taken to the jockeys' quarters, in the part where they're taken to lie down when they've been hurt, and it was as I was coming to my senses again that I heard that man insist I was drunk. Which made me furious. Boy Capel objected: 'You are talking nonsense, sir: she's never had a drink in her life.'

"That was true, but the man had recognized the smell of rum on my breath. 'She's drunk and asleep,' he said. 'She's sleeping because she's drunk, that's all.'

"And he was right. I realized I was drunk. I opened my eyes and heard various questions but I couldn't answer, I didn't know what to say, so I made a gesture with my hand to show I didn't want to talk."

Why did she remember these swoons with so many details? For I heard that story more than once, and most remarkably, without any changes. She said: "They talk to me about attacks of nerves! For two years I couldn't cross a street or go into a church. So I stopped going to Mass; until then I'd gone out of courtesy. I couldn't sit through a concert anymore.

"Boy Capel cured me, with exceptional patience, simply by repeating: 'Faint if you want to.' He took me wherever there were people, and said: 'I'm here. Nothing can happen to you. Faint while I'm here.'

"Several times I'd been brought home unconscious. These weren't any hysterical woman's swoons. I fell down, my eyes turned black to there . . . I was taken for dead. That would last a half hour."

And she would end the story with the same sentence, which obviously accounted for its importance: "When I got involved in the House of Chanel, my health came back."

Soon after she began making hats in avenue Gabriel, her younger sister, Antoinette, and her Aunt Adrienne came to work with her. The three of them were not too many to spoil the broth. Coco said: "Luck depends on such trifles. I got there at the right time and I met the people it was necessary to know."

The people it was necessary to know included Etienne Balsan's friends: Maurice and Robert de Nexon, the Marquis de

Chavagnac, Jules de St.-Sauveur and, more than anyone else, a young woman whose beauty was much like Coco's and who sang at the Opéra-Comique, Marthe Davelli. She sang Carmen, Tosca; she created Reynaldo Hahn's Nausicaa. She was a celebrity, and Coco soon became close to her. In the old photographs it is hard to tell them apart: they had the same charm, the same elegance. Which one emulated the other? Those who knew them both admit it was impossible to tell. Old friends think of them now as the grasshopper and the ant — Coco being the ant. But that does not show in their faces. Marthe Davelli married Constant Say of the sugar fortune, who was to lose a great deal of his wealth in a family collapse. She died in the American Hospital in Paris just when Mademoiselle Chanel was making her comeback in 1955. "She came to see me," Madame Say whispered to a friend just before she closed her eyes. "She stayed a quarter of an hour."

But in 1910, when she met Marthe Davelli and their friendship began, death did not yet exist for Coco. Life was beautiful — love, the races, Deauville, polo. With Boy Capel she met Englishmen who came to Paris to escape the hardships of the London climate: the moral climate, of course. She met Russians too, princes and grand dukes who were seeking to throw off the rigors of Moscow. It was still *la Belle Epoque,* and pleasure's name was Paris.

Coco opened a shop in Deauville. In Paris she worked in her apartment. In Deauville her name stood out in black letters on a great white awning over the show window: GABRIELLE CHANEL.

During these early successes, her elder sister, Julia-Berthe, died, leaving a little boy for whom Coco assumed responsibility. It might be said that she adopted him. This was her nephew, André Pallasse. In one of our early conversations, in connection with a baby who had been switched at birth in a hospital in northern France and whose mother did not want him, she said to me, "I'll adopt him! I'll send him to the best boarding school in Switzerland."

That was what she did for young Pallasse when she took him

in, though she sent him not to Switzerland but to England — to Beaumont College, the Catholic Eton. Rather remarkable. She was only just beginning to make money, and already she was modeling herself on *the others,* the Balsans, the Chavagnacs, the Nexons, the St.-Sauveurs, all of whom had either gone to English schools or sent their sons to them.

The wind in those days was blowing from London, which was where one had to get one's clothes and even send one's laundry. All the polo players in Coco's circle spoke English. So did the grand dukes, though they knew French. All Coco heard mentioned was stud books, races, dead heats, starts and — let me not forget — five o'clock tea. That was blazoned in big white letters, in English, on the windows of every pastry shop, even in the country. Did Coco know English even then? I forgot to ask her. It is easy to suppose that she learned it, as she learned to enjoy oysters, with all the concentration that was required. She accepted this Anglomania naturally, as a plant accepts and profits by the rain: it made for glowing foliage and it produced fruit.

She said: "One day I put on a man's *sweater* [using the English word] just like that, because I was cold. It was in Deauville. I tied it with a handkerchief at the waist. I was with some English people. None of them noticed that I was wearing this sweater. None of them told me that it looked good on me, that I looked pretty in it. The English don't tell you anything. I was watching them play polo. I don't know which of them the sweater belonged to — I'd picked it up off a wicker chair. It was around the end of August, and there was talk about the war. I was almost ready to believe the Germans wanted the war to prevent me from making hats."

This, then, is Chanel's version of the birth of the Chanel: a polo sweater caught at the waist with a handkerchief — let us say a scarf. The jersey dress, the first one. One cannot help thinking Coco had some counsel. A dressmaker had gone into business in the house in avenue Gabriel where she made her hats. Coco could not have made more dresses, *real* dresses, without the risk of being taken to court for unfair competition and bad faith. But the jersey? No problem. No one made real dresses out of jersey. Jersey was for men, and anyway in France it was not used. It was worn in English boarding schools. Coco's nephew at Beaumont had navy-blue blazers that he wore at home during vacations. Coco fingered them: Eureka, eureka! All that had to be done was to cut them and sew them. The line and the taste were all innate in her. Her stroke of genius was to transpose the masculine English fashion to the feminine with taste that precluded any ambiguity, as she had already done with hats. She transformed everything she touched — her jackets, her blouses, the ties on the blouses, the cufflinks at the wrists, everything she borrowed from men became ultrafeminine through her magic.

Hers and also that of Marthe Davelli, whom she dressed and with whom she perfected her earliest creations. They seemed to be the twin models of a new elegance. Aunt Adrienne also acted as a model, as did little sister Antoinette. Moulins repeated? No, Moulins had already sunk into the chasm to which Coco had dispatched her lean years.

"I have good news from my nephew," she would say to the jeweled customers who had tried to snub her. "He's studying in England, at Beaumont."

If any young professional high-fashion dressmaker had launched "Chanels" with any ability, she would unquestionably have succeeded. Why did Coco go so much farther than success?

In 1906 Poiret had eliminated the corset, and in 1908 he had cut his models' hair; and he was the first dressmaker to market a perfume, though not under his own name but under that of his daughter, Rosine. Even so, unlike Mademoiselle Chanel, Poiret started no revolution.

But perhaps it is a mistake to say that Mademoiselle Chanel created a revolution in fashion. Was it not rather ways of living that she unsettled?

When Gabrielle Dorziat, the actress, first heard of her, it was in these terms: "There's the most *amusing* little milliner in rue

St.-Honoré." (The avenue Gabriel workshop had already been moved to the mezzanine of 14, rue Cambon, at the corner of rue St.-Honoré.)

Mademoiselle Chanel would not have liked that adjective "amusing." And yet . . . people started going to her because she was *amusing. You know, that one's a real character:* that was what was being said of her. She was unlike anyone else. She made people laugh. Life looked different with her, it became comic, funny, less drab than usual. She brought one out of the commonplace.

She made one of her first jersey dresses for Dorziat — a tailored navy blue, still very long, with a cardigan jacket and a little rabbit collar. The rabbit — as Madame Dorziat still remembers — was supplied by a furrier who was just going into business. His name was Jacques Heim.

In an earlier day — and this was still true in 1910, when Coco was starting out — Chinese women who were intensely beloved, whether empresses or courtesans, never cut their fingernails, the length of which attested to the social significance of their beauty. The *cocottes'* dresses and hats were the equivalent of the Chinese women's nails, which prevented them from working and being part of life among the living. As the curling nails of the most desired Chinese women virtually made them chattels of men rich and powerful enough to pay for their domestic staffs, so the fashions of *la Belle Epoque* threw Emilienne d'Alençon and her colleagues on the mercy of the Balsans and the others who kept women. Their seeming freedom reduced them to servitude.

By stripping them of their finery Coco helped bring about the extinction of a social species that — it must be conceded — was already on the wane. It was the end of a breed: adapted to the ways of the middle class, they were descended from the favorites of the old kings. This was Jean Cocteau's view of them, summarized in Caroline Otéro, *la belle Otéro,* as she was and still is known:

A veritable arsenal of spangles, jewels, corsets, whalebone stays, steel clinchers, flowers and feathers was girded onto this splendid armored car of pleasure. You would see her moving toward you completely alone. But she was not. She was never completely alone, but the very substantial gentleman who escorted her was always a shadow, a hairless shadow with a monocle and evening dress. The shadow in evening dress knew how much her padding and her clackers cost. To undertake to keep her was like managing an apartment house. Her undressing must have approached the scale of moving a household. Otéro! See how she thrusts out her handsome, well-laced bosom. See how she inspects her colleagues with the eyes of a Minerva and rakes them with the spikes of her lashes. See how she shoots forth her black flames. See how she braves the toreadors.

Mademoiselle Chanel did indeed turn the relations between men and women upside down. This would have been recognized long ago if she had not so painfully hidden her truth under a bushel. In avenue Gabriel as in Deauville, women pushed their way close to her in order to breathe the air of freedom. Coco was selling them a new art of living. A struggle had begun.

Suppose that Candide had set up a library in Versailles and filled it with works on the revolution still to come, and that the king had made it fashionable by stopping in every afternoon. That was what was happening with Chanel: she was making her revolution with the women whom she was going to overcome.

I've never cared a damn about money. This never stopped Coco from looking every evening to see what was in the till. Now and then she pinched herself before she fell asleep: *Am I really not dreaming? Is making a fortune really so simple?*

The road from Moulins had not been easy, but nothing was wholly a loss, time was never wasted. The insults that she had swallowed had toughened her stomach. The rich had introduced her to money, and this had helped her to work things out when she was setting her prices. She knew that they would pinch pennies over necessities and bankrupt themselves for frivolities.

What arrangements did she make with Adrienne and Antoinette?

When one stops to think about it that was an interlude of
grace for Coco, Adrienne, Antoinette, and the ravishing Davelli,
who wore happiness on her face. They were so different from all
the other women. They were free! They sold hats and dresses,
and they were free and beautiful. Not old maids — the expression in those days was "prudes" — not prudes at all. But getting
them to say *yes* — well, that was not to be achieved with marriage contracts and lawyers. That depended entirely on them —
on the heart, if you like, or more often on a simple desire for
pleasure, a hope of happiness.

This was something very new. No one understood very clearly
what was happening, and above all no one could guess yet what
was beginning, but it was fascinating.

If Coco had had only hats and dresses to sell, she would have
made a fortune, but what would have survived of Mademoiselle
Chanel? She brought women the great dream of our time: freedom by way of independence, with happiness by way of pleasure.

8

Apprenticeship in the Best Society

The question must be asked how Coco was schooled — how the little orphan who left the orphanage, the docile girl of Royallieu, became that empress of taste whose judgments had the effect of law in all the realms of the Beautiful and the Clever. "Without the Serts," she admitted, "I'd have died in a kind of idiocy."

She said: "The war helped me. Catastrophes show what one really is. In 1919 I woke up famous." She appended, of course: "I'd never guessed it. If I'd known I was famous, I'd have stolen away and wept. I was stupid. I'm supposed to be intelligent. I was sensitive and very dumb."

If anyone had told her that then — that she was stupid and frightened — she would not have agreed. In 1919 she had just raised her flag over rue Cambon, having opened a shop at number 25 in which people bumped into one another. Later she took over 27, 29 and 31. She was *the* personality that was the talk of Paris; and, far from hiding somewhere to weep, she made herself very visible, always gay and dynamic, especially with Grand

Duke Dmitri, the grandson of Czar Alexander II, the nephew
of Czar Alexander III, the first cousin of Czar Nicholas II, the
grandson of King George I of Greece. At the age of eleven he had
commanded a regiment of grenadiers, at fourteen a regiment of
sharpshooters. At twenty-seven, exiled and impoverished but
still haloed in the prestige of the old imperial Russia, he turned
to Mademoiselle Chanel to renew the cycle of the good years. He
had known her before the war, when he used to sally forth with
Boy Capel and the other heroes of the nights of pleasure to forget the cold nights of St. Petersburg. Coco never mentioned him
to me. Some persons, who certainly had no special affection for
her, recalled having heard her treat the brilliant grand duke
curtly: "Let me have a match, Dmitri."

The war had worked out better than she had feared. The Germans had not prevented her from selling hats and jersey dresses.
Marthe Davelli had had a charming house built on the Basque
coast near St.-Jean-de-Luz. During vacations Coco played golf.
When she went into the ocean she kept her stockings on. There
are pictures of her in the bathing suits of the time, her legs
sheathed in silk, and with her, at the height of the war, in 1917,
Boy Capel. He was relaxing between deals in coal. In the background there are some white-trousered gentlemen with dark
jackets, boaters over their ears — right or left according to taste:
Edmond Rostand and Pierre Decourcelle. Coco never talked to
Decourcelle about his stories. She was reading other things. In
order to fill in her areas of cultural deprivation, she was devot-
edly following the course given at night by a new friend, Misia
Sert.

Born Godebska, to a Polish father and a Russian mother, Misia
was what was at that time (in *good* society) called an adven-
turess. She stirred up things and people. Where did she come
from? And what about the money she spent without bothering to
count it: was it chiefly the money of the miserable men she be-
witched? There was something of the Atlantides in her; she was
a fascinating creature. All the good fairies had bent over her

cradle to endow her with beauty, charm, intelligence, wit. Before she could read she was a magnificent pianist. She was five years old when the aging Liszt put her on his lap and asked her to play for him; he worked the pedals. When Fauré heard her, he offered to be her teacher. She drove him to despair when at fifteen she married Thaddée Natanson, the publisher's son, who was putting out the much-talked-about *Revue blanche*. He knew everyone. He brought Debussy to his home, where the composer sat down to the (upright) piano and, acting as his own accompanist, sang all the parts of *Pelléas et Mélisande* for Misia.

She was Renoir's favorite model: he did eight portraits of her, of which one is in the Hermitage in Leningrad and another is in the Barnes Collection outside Philadelphia. In the National Museum of Modern Art in Paris one can see her portraits by Bonnard, Vuillard and Vallotton. When she posed for Renoir he told her about the Commune, while his famous servant, Gabrielle, constantly criticized what he was doing. Occasionally he would stop painting and beg Misia to open the front of her dress: "Lower, I beg you! Why don't you let people see your breasts? That's criminal!" Describing the scene in a book of recollections, Misia said: "After his death I often reproached myself for not having let him see whatever he wanted. Several times I saw that he was on the point of tears. No one was better able than he to appreciate skin texture."

Toulouse-Lautrec called her Hirondelle (Swallow). When he lunched at her house he sketched her on the menu. The menus were thrown out. What a shame! How awful! people moaned later: the same people who, Misia noted ironically, "made fun of Lautrec, twisted their heads in front of a Renoir picture and asked me which way a Bonnard landscape should be hung, people who didn't even know of the existence of Mallarmé."

Mallarmé visited Misia at Valvins on the Seine to read her his poems. He would arrive wearing wooden shoes. One evening she cut him short because she had a headache. He got up and left, and she thought he was offended. An hour later he was back

with some aspirin. As a New Year's gift he sent her some foie
gras with a poem that she lost. But "Why should I have saved
everything everyone gave me?" she demanded. "I'd have been
looked on as an ogre if I'd hoarded things."

She discovered van Gogh and urged all her friends to buy his
paintings at two hundred francs each. They did not want to. The
same friends stopped their ears when she made them listen to
Stravinsky. Grieg played *Peer Gynt* to her: when she heard
Aase's Death she burst into "a flood of tears." Ibsen sent her a
framed, inscribed photograph of himself.

And who but Misia would have dared to silence Caruso?
"Enough! I can't take any more!" she snapped when he was giving her an indigestible diet of Neapolitan songs in her drawing
room. "I have never seen a man so stunned," she noted. In his
Venises, Paul Morand portrayed her splendidly, and I take the
liberty of borrowing from him:

> . . . a collector of geniuses, all of whom were in love with her:
> Vuillard, Bonnard, Renoir, Stravinsky, Picasso . . . a collector of
> hearts and of pink quartz Ming trees; indulging her whims, which
> turned at once into styles accepted by all the imitators, exploited by
> the decorators, described by the journalists, aped by all the empty-
> headed society women. Misia, queen of the modern baroque, who had
> based her whole life on the bizarre, the mother-of-pearl and the shell
> it comes from; Misia the sullen, Misia the crafty, bringing together
> friends who were not speaking to each other "so that they could quar-
> rel better afterward," Proust declared. Inspired in her duplicities, ex-
> quisite in her cruelties, Misia of whom Philippe Berthelot said that
> one must never trust her with what one loves: "Here comes the cat,
> hide your birds," he used to repeat when she rang his doorbell . . .
> Misia of the Paris of the Symbolists, of the Paris of the fauves, of the
> Paris of the Great War, of the Paris of the Versailles Treaty, of the
> Paris of Venice. Misia as soft as a sofa, but, if you were looking for
> rest, a sofa that would release the pitchforks of hell. Misia the unsatis-
> fied, whose piercing eyes were still laughing when her lips had al-
> ready been swollen into a pout.

Perhaps something ought to be said of her dramatic birth. Her
mother, Sophie Godebska, was living in Brussels, pregnant and

awaiting her husband's return from St. Petersburg, where he was decorating a palace for a Princess Trubetzkoy. From an-anonymous-friend-who-was-acting-in-her-best-interests Sophie Godebska learned that her husband was living love's young dream (the standard expression at the time) with a young aunt, who had had sufficient time to bear him a child. Sophie set out at once.

Misia wrote in her autobigraphy:

God knows by what miracle she completed her journey in that gla-cial Russian winter. She arrived at a snow-covered house, made her way up the steps of the veranda and, as she started to ring the bell she leaned against the doorjamb to catch her breath. She recognized the laughing voices that she heard through the door. Her hand did not complete its act. After the superhuman effort that her love had given her the strength to make, an immense lassitude, a profound despair swept through her.

Poor Sophie. She took refuge in a small hotel from which she wrote to her brother. He alerted her husband, who had barely time to see her in her final moments. She had given birth to Misia, who wrote: "The drama of my birth was to have a pro-found effect on my life."

Misia was brought up at first by a rich grandmother, ostenta-tious and greedy, a good musician and a good hostess, whose villa outside Brussels was an open house for everyone in the arts. One of the regular guests was the queen of the Belgians. When Misia ventured into the cellars, she discovered calves, sheep, sides of beef hanging from hooks, "fearful bloody stalactites waiting to be cut to pieces for the benefit of my grandmother and the ogres who surrounded her." She does not add, in her account, that these carcasses disgusted her; but one is nonethe-less reminded of Coco telling how she was revolted by the pigs cut into bleeding halves on a board in the kitchen of her "aunts'" house in the Auvergne.

What was Misia's contribution to the image of Mademoiselle Chanel that Coco was to shape for herself over the years? With

Misia —and Misia's third husband, the Spanish painter José María Sert — Coco spent what might be called her Sorbonne years. They gave her whatever could be taught and at the same time what cannot be taught, awakening in her the talents that were dormant.

Sert was a forerunner of Dali in his attitudes and in his way of speaking. Heavy-set, dark, bearded, always seeming somehow disguised, wrapped in a cape, wearing a sombrero that he insisted he did not remove in the presence of the King of Spain, he of course took it off when Coco appeared. "I can ride horseback into every church in Spain," he asserted.

When he met Misia, he began by asking her: "Did you know, Madame, that a stork can die of hunger in front of a mountain of food?" Though she was rarely at a loss for a retort, she said nothing, and he explained: "One has only to cut off enough of the end of his beak to destroy his perception of distances."

Does this not sound like Dali? Sert like Dali, spoke French with a Catalan accent. Having made his first impression with the stork's help, he went on to describe for Misia the bewilderment of a flock of ducks that he had painted to resemble sea lions when they came upon a family of sea lions that he had equipped with duck feathers.

How could she resist such a man — not handsome but attractive, a giant, with a frightening appetite? At his table, a sharp-tongued gourmet observed, only whole animals were served. When he sent flowers, they were trees, bushes. He gave chocolates in barrowloads. And with all this he had talent, the kind of talent that pays off, that is recognized during life. He always painted huge frescoes. "Yes," the gifted artist Sem commented, "but they shrink."

It would be impossible to imagine a better guide for her journey than Sert. He knew all the painters and he talked about painting without affectation. Coco said: "One felt intelligent when one listened to him."

Misia *taught* Coco Stravinsky, Picasso, music, painting, Paris society, not to mention a certain kind of speech that was already obsolescent but that was based on roots — for example, "mechanic" instead of "chauffeur," "rubber" instead of "raincoat." Sert taught her an art of living that was not natural to her, *that poise that one must never alter,* a way of spending, of squandering without watching what was slipping through one's fingers. *I've earned fortunes and spent them.* She said it, and it was true. But she would never have gone as far as a Sert — that is, beyond not just her means but beyond what would have seemed to her too much.

That first postwar era was a time of marvels, and not merely because of the Boeuf sur le Toit.* The fermentation of the new wine was already straining the old goatskin in which the world was still contained — but not for much longer.

Undoubtedly Coco never gave any thought to her debt to the First World War — the one called the Great. Gide was working on her side, and so was Mauriac, whose incense never wholly blotted out his sulfur. A moral code was disintegrating — that is clear now when the same causes are working the same ravages, but on a much greater number. The crisis that followed 1918 affected only the rich. Today, in a way of speaking, everyone is rich. And everyone claims that right to pleasure that Coco was offering only to the women who could afford her. She would scream and stamp if she could read this — and yet, what is Mary Quant's miniskirt but the emancipating Chanel of the other post-war period?

Through her friend Misia, Coco became interested in the Ballets Russes. "Misia was always talking to me about those ballets," Coco told me. " 'You can't imagine how beautiful they are,' she said; 'once you've seen them your life will be completely different.' She told innumerable stories."

* A famous nightclub of the 1920s and 1930s that epitomized the spirit of innovation, experiment and freedom that marked this highly creative period. The Boeuf sur le Toit was an internationally powerful magnet and symbol. Translator.

Misia was a great friend of Serge de Diaghilev, whom she called Diag. "I love you with your innumerable faults," he wrote to her; "for you I have the feelings I might have for a sister. Unfortunately I have no sister. So all that love has crystalized on you. Remember that we arrived not so long ago at the joint decision that you are the only woman I can love."

Coco was visiting Misia, who lived in the Hotel Meurice (this was in 1922), when Diaghilev burst in with much theatricality. He had just come from London, ruined by the opening of *The Sleeping Beauty*. Coco said:

"He didn't notice me. He wasn't even aware that there was anyone there. I sat quietly and very unobtrusively in my corner.

" 'What's happened to me is a disaster!' he told Misia.

"I realized this was Diaghilev. I looked at him. I observed very attentively. Misia was always telling me about him and about music: she fed me on her memories. I enjoyed her very much. And here I was, unnoticed in my corner, but aware of some great drama taking place for Diaghilev.

" 'What are you going to do?' Misia asked him.

"He had skipped out of London because he couldn't pay his debts, bursting in like a maniac, not knowing what to do. It so happened that Misia went out of the room for a minute to make a private phone call. I leaped up —I, the bashful one, who didn't dare open her mouth to anyone! I got up and I said: 'I live at the Ritz. Come and see me. Don't say anything to Misia. Come as soon as you leave here: I'll be waiting.' "

No matter how accustomed to Coco's understatements one might have been, this would leave anyone breathless: *I, the bashful one, who didn't dare open her mouth to anyone.*

She remembered the emotion that she had felt then. She was more or less aware at the time that she was perpetrating a kind of robbery. What stopped her from telling Diaghilev in Misia's presence the same thing she was going to say to him a little later in the Ritz? Namely: *I have money and I can help you: how much do you need?*

In fact she was putting herself to a test: Are you big enough by now to stand on your own feet? To get along without Misia? She was almost forty years old. She said:

"I went back to the Ritz to wait for Diaghilev. He came. I said to myself, Now that you've had the courage to ask him to come, go through with it, have the courage to talk to him. So I made myself say to him: 'I heard what you were telling Misia. She has no money; she can't give you anything. How much do you need to settle things in London and get back to France?'

"He told me the amount, which I've completely forgotten. I gave him a check immediately. He must have thought it was no good! All I said to him was: 'Misia must never know, never!' "

It was a good friend whom she was deceiving. She could not bear owing anything, however little, to anyone. As soon as she had money she wanted to pay for everything and everyone. As people had paid for her? No: to forget that people had paid for her. Or, in somewhat harsher terms: by paying others' obligations she obliterated her own. She said:

"I'd learned enough by then to know that Misia would be jealous of me because she couldn't do what I could for Diaghilev. I insisted: 'I don't want Misia to know about this. I don't want anyone to know about it.'

"This was how my friendship with Diaghilev began. He must not have been able to present the check without dread; he must have been trembling when he took it to the bank. He never wrote to me. He never compromised himself by as much as a word. I asked Serge [Lifar] what he [Diaghilev] thought of me — I'd got him off the hook a hundred times: 'What were his feelings about me?'

" 'I don't know what you mean,' Serge said.

" 'All right — did he feel friendship for me? Some kind of affection?'

" 'Not at all,' Serge said. 'He was afraid of you.'

"How odd those Russians are! Diaghilev afraid of me! Why? Serge told me: 'Whenever you came to see us, we went into a state of siege. One must not say this or that to you, one must be very careful as soon as you came in.'

"As for me, I felt uneasy in the middle of a group that was intimidated by me. I persisted: 'Why was he afraid of me?'

" 'He'd never met anyone like you, you see,' Serge explained. 'You gave him money and didn't ask for anything in return. He didn't understand: that frightened him. When we went to visit you, he reminded us to be clean, well behaved and well dressed.'

"When you hear something like that, it really shakes you. One thinks one is doing a service . . . So the only feeling I inspired in that Russian was fear!"

An astonishing revelation. Very often, when I was listening to Coco's monologues, I would wonder, When did she start talking? In Misia's apartment in the Hotel Meurice she had not opened her mouth. Diaghilev had confided in Misia as if they had been alone.

I have money; I can help you.

Unquestionably a major landmark. Money had endowed her with the power of speech.

Afraid! Diaghilev was afraid of me! Forty years later she was still flabbergasted by it. She said:

"It required a great deal of money to stage *Noces,* to do *Le Sacre* again — all the Stravinsky things that had filled me with a musical passion. No other kind! But as for him, I think he was in the grip of a different passion, and that made for conflict because I had to tell him there could be no question of anything like that between us. I was very fond of him. He was marvelous. We went out together constantly. It was fun to learn everything from people like him. For ten years I lived among such people."

Misia talked to her about Stravinsky's problems — he was desperately short of money at the time, living in Switzerland. Coco stepped in:

"Something must be done, Misia; he mustn't be left in a mess, or his family allowed to run short."

She told me: "What with the Ballets Russes and all those artists I felt sorry for, some whom I liked very much and others whom I liked less . . . And my gift for meddling in all that, simply to take on fresh troubles, too . . . In the last analysis, what did I have to show for it? Not even those people's friendship! I scared Diaghilev! No, Serge [Lifar] didn't tell me that simply to make conversation; it was part of his youth, he remembered it very well; and besides, that sounds like Diaghilev, who lived in fear — fear of not succeeding, fear of being hit by falling objects, fear that his production wouldn't go on . . . He never gave anyone anything! Not even the tiniest emotion. To his dancers he was merciless. Sometimes Serge [Lifar] hated him. Diaghilev made him work like a dog. He sent him to museums to educate himself, and he talked art to him all the time."

All the same it was fascinating to be with those people. She conceded that.

"What was the name of that decorator who was always around? Bakst! He gave me lots of laughs, that old parrot. He ran after me to let him do my portrait. That one had no complexes! He was very lively, always; he loved to eat, he loved to drink, he loved to do stage sets, and he did them, sets I thought were heavenly. The first time I saw *Shéhérazade* I was in raptures. That's beauty, to me. And so well danced! Ballet today is childish in comparison."

She had met Picasso through Reverdy. She said: "I was a bit baffled by the sets he did for Stravinsky. I didn't really understand. It was all very new to me. I was a little scared and I wondered whether it was really beautiful.

"Later I was seized by a passion for Picasso. He was wicked. He fascinated me the way a hawk would; he filled me with a terrible fear. I would feel it when he came in: something would curl up in me: he'd arrived. I couldn't see him yet but already I knew he was in the room. And then I saw him. He had a way of looking at me . . . I trembled. They were all very rough on one another. They certainly didn't soft-soap one another. They excited me: they were all such great artists. They never mentioned money."

According to Boris Kochno, she gave Diaghilev a check for two hundred thousand francs (gold, again). Others say it was fifty thousand. She never hinted at any amount, and yet the figure was always on the tip of her tongue; she was still impressed by it. Why had she given him the money? And why so much?

Money: she talked about it often, sometimes with a comic touch of which she seemed not wholly aware. She said: "I associated only with rich people. Some of them are quite common, and they bore me to death. But when they're interesting and nice I prefer the rich to the poor, because at least I don't have to worry about their lives."

This was rather close to the remark attributed to Boris Vian — "it's better to be rich and healthy than poor and ill" — though it must surely date back to the invention of money.

Coco said: "To me the only value money has ever had is that of freedom." She added: "Money makes it possible to help people one admires, people who have something to say. I gave the Ballets Russes a great deal of help, and I asked only one thing: that no one know about it."

On this point — *that no one know about it* — Coco's story about Diaghilev completely matched what Boris Kochno had heard from Diaghilev; but as far as the rest was concerned, nothing matched. According to Kochno, Diaghilev had met Coco in Venice, where she was staying with the Serts. Diaghilev had observed that she was pretty, very pretty, but quiet. He had not remembered her name. That is what he told Kochno. Then later, in Paris, at the Hotel Continental or the Grand Hotel, whichever he was living in, a visitor was announced.

It was Coco. According to Diaghilev, she waited for him in the lobby, where she handed him the check for two hundred thousand francs. ". . . But no one is to know!"

Particularly Misia Sert. It is always the details that stand out which lead one to the truth. When she signed the check wherever she gave it to him, and whether it was for fifty thousand or for two hundred thousand francs, Coco was in fact signing a new identity card. She was becoming Chanel: herself! At last! She no longer needed the Serts or anyone else. She drew a patent of nobility on her bank account.

Diaghilev was dying in Venice in the late summer of 1929 when the *Flying Cloud,* the sailing yacht belonging to the Duke of Westminster, stood out to sea from the port. Mademoiselle Chanel was on board.

Diaghilev had sent a message to Misia Sert: "Come at once." She rushed to him. Boris Kochno and Serge Lifar were nursing their master. The heat was stifling, but Diaghilev was shivering with cold. They had wrapped him in his dinner jacket in an effort to warm him. He recognized Misia, though he was already speaking of himself in the past tense: "I loved *Tristan* and the *Pathétique* so much. Promise me, Misia, you'll always wear white — I liked you best in white."

She went out to buy him a sweater, but she could not get him into it: he was too weak to raise his arms and it was impossible now to budge him. At three o'clock in the morning Misia sent for a priest. When the priest learned that the dying man was a Russian, he got angry and refused to shrive him. Misia made such a scene that he agreed to give Diaghilev a "short absolution." Diaghilev died at dawn, just as the rising sun touched his forehead. The glorious daybreak made the sea radiant. As the nurse closed the dead man's eyes, Misia wrote,

a characteristically Russian phenomenon, the kind that one encounters in the characters of Dostoievsky, took place in that little hotel room where the greatest magician of his art had gone to die. Serge's death must have been the spark that detonated the reserve of hate amassed within the two young men who had lived with him. In the silence characteristic of the finest dramas, a kind of roar burst out: Kochno threw himself on Lifar, who was on his knees at the other side of the bed. They rolled on the floor, tearing at each other and biting each other like animals.

A place had to be found in a cemetery, "the last service that I could do for the friend who had lived in my heart for twenty years," Misia wrote. She had a check in her bag, and she sent it to the Baroness d'Erlanger with a note asking her to make the necessary arrangements for the funeral service and the burial. And then she found that she had no more money. Diaghilev left a total estate of six thousand francs, which Misia turned over to Lifar and Kochno — "to the boys," as she put it.

In her book she wrote:

Fortunately I was wearing my diamond necklace. I decided to borrow on it. But on my way to the jeweler, I ran into a very dear friend who, at the urging of a strong premonition, had hurriedly come back to Venice. In fact, she had left the city only the night before on the yacht of the Duke of Westminster, when Diaghilev was already very ill. The boat had barely got into the open sea when she began to fear the worst, and she asked the duke to turn back. This was no minor matter, because this was a planned cruise with a detailed itinerary, which had to be completely changed; and the yacht was a large vessel with a big crew. In any case I was happy to see her. She immediately took me with her and went to the burial with me. Catherine d'Erlanger had arranged the sad ceremony beautifully.

The very dear friend was Coco. Misia does not mention her name in the book. What a coincidence! Once more Coco was at hand with Misia to save Diaghilev from the ultimate disaster of his ruin. She stepped in less timidly than the first time. "The boys," Lifar and Kochno, to demonstrate the depth of their Dostoievskian despair, announced that they would follow the coffin on their knees from the mainland pier to the grave; Coco said to them quietly: "Up!" They obeyed.

Corrections and clarifications from Boris Kochno: the Venetian priest did not have to be pressured in any way to minister to Diaghilev. But Kochno and Lifar — who were afraid that in the midst of being dispatched their master might come out of his coma, fly into a rage or suffer even greater agony at the fear of being at the point of death — were nagging at the priest: "Hurry!" Diaghilev was dying of diabetes.

"On weekdays," Kochno said, "he stuck to his diet, but no one could have prevented him from stuffing himself with sweets on Sundays."

"Was Diaghilev really afraid of Coco?" I asked Kochno.

"Afraid? No, he liked her too much."

"But Coco was convinced of it."

Then Kochno explained: "Diaghilev was a Russian. He believed in gratuitous acts — to him they seemed natural."

A silence. I spoke again: "Coco was an Auvergnat, in spite of everything, no?"

"In spite of everything," Kochno agreed.*

* The Auvergnat in French folklore is the person who never does anything for nothing. Translator.

9

The Seven Hundred Who Count

Cocteau, Radiguet, Stravinsky, Picasso, Bakst, everyone who mattered — those whom Paul Morand called the "seven hundred" — rubbed elbows in relays at Coco's. She had never been more beautiful: her forties were a decade of triumph. She was so lovely, so miraculously young that she was able to cheat on her age by ten years. No one suspected it and no one paid attention to it.

What of love? What of Boy Capel? She said: "My emotional life was thrown into confusion. The man I loved was dead. Nothing interested me anymore except the occult, because I refused to believe that everything had been cut off between us forever."

This book does not have the chronology of a military history. The story that I am about to tell took place before the episode of the Russian ballets. But when did it become important to Coco?

The man I loved was dead. Boy Capel was killed in a car accident on the Côte d'Azur in January 1919. (By coincidence, Etienne Balsan also died in a car accident, but later, at Rio de la Plata, in 1951; he was seventy-three.)

By 1919 Coco was seen everywhere with the Grand Duke

Dmitri. Boy Capel had married; not only did Coco dress his wife, who brought her English friends to Chanel, but Coco was the godmother of one of his children. Naturally, this did not temper her sorrow at his death. Coco said:

"The Serts saved me from despair. Perhaps it would have been better if they had left me to it. I did nothing but weep. They dragged me to Italy, against my wishes. I ran away. Misia found me in tears in a church. One day a miracle happened."

A fine miracle, Coco said, describing it with a certain smugness. She took her time. "We were in Venice. Misia said to me: 'We ought to go to St. Anthony of Padua. That will do you good. You can touch his tomb and ask him for peace, and he'll give it to you.' The Serts — splendid people of a kind that doesn't exist anymore — were right out of the Renaissance. They didn't have a cent and yet they lived in a magnificent style."

When Coco traveled with them, she paid. She always wanted to pay; this too was one of her ways of subjugating. The word may seem strong. She liked, however, to have people dependent on her — a frequent eccentricity among strong characters. For Sert the magnificent, the finest of traveling companions, nothing was too good. At every stop, the best rooms were kept available to him, he was offered the rarest wines, he was enticed into hours at table with the most exquisite dishes. Coco said:

"With the Serts one had no idea how life was going to go. One went to bed at dawn and then set off again . . . Those people never washed themselves. [See, Misia was not really her friend. Like the rest, all the others who had impressed or tried to impress Coco: *dirty!*] In that little clan of ours I was the only one who washed at night. I wanted to start off clean in the morning.

"But they [the Serts] were very entertaining people. They weren't married yet, so there was no formal social life. After their marriage they became very social. Both of them were divine to me. Sert had taken a real liking to me. He taught me a great deal. We went to museums. Without the Serts I'd have died in a kind of idiocy."

In Padua Coco took Misia's advice when she was led into the church and shown St. Anthony's tomb: "Go on, kneel down." Coco said:

"I had no belief at all in this kind of thing. I knelt in front of the tomb to please Misia. I don't share her kind of fanaticism. I have superstition rather than faith. But there beside me I saw a man who was so unhappy! He laid his hand on the tomb. I watched him. I was smaller than he. I saw his face, which showed such desperation, such unhappiness, a life so abominable that I felt ashamed. And I had dared to weep! I almost got up and said to the man: 'Sir, I beg you, please trust me; tell me why you're unhappy, perhaps that will make you feel better.'"

Always these impulses that she did not obey. Why? Remembering her emotion, she said:

"And I dared to complain! I'd never seen so much misery in a face. I at least knew that the man I'd just lost was beside me, on the *other side*, and wouldn't leave me for a minute. And I said to myself, As long as he's there, with you, as long as he's waiting for you, you have no right to weep, it doesn't matter that you're alone *on this side* still for a while. You're still with him — we aren't on the same plane, but he hasn't left you, he wants you to be happy. Above all, he doesn't want you to be miserable."

She was smiling. When she described this trip to Padua with the Serts it was that evening, after the opening of the collection, when I found her sleeping on her couch. She said: "My nicest journeys take place on this couch." Then she came back to Padua:

"That was what I realized when I saw that despairing man kneeling beside me at the statue of St. Anthony of Padua. Here, I said to myself, You know you're not alone and you'll never be, and you dare to feel sorry for yourself in the face of this man, who has nothing left and has come here to touch this tomb because it's his last hope!"

You know you're not alone and you'll never be. I listened to this woman talk on tirelessly, I knew she was alone, and I did not really hear her. Didn't she have *everything*? Didn't she have fame and money? Hadn't she had a fabulous life? What was she still looking for? She said:

"I came out of that Paduan church transformed. I was no longer the same. I — who didn't react anymore to anything, who had turned into a shadow — I ate a fine lunch.

" 'Why, you're eating! You're laughing!' Misia commented.

"I said to her: 'Yes, I'm eating and laughing. The miracle has happened. I'll never weep again — it's all over.'

"Sert took us to Rome and the Coliseum, where he began describing the marvelous parties we could give there. We prowled about until three in the morning. I was discovering Rome, that divine city. I loved everything. I loved life. The next day I sent a long telegram to Paris, ordering everything to be taken out of my apartment. I didn't want to set foot in it again. When I went back to Paris, I moved into the Ritz again."

The Ritz, she said, was her real home. She moved in only a very few things to personalize her room. On her night table, however, she kept a little replica, the kind of souvenir that is sold to tourists, of the tomb of St. Anthony of Padua — a gift from Gianni, her Italian chauffeur — I ought to say her mechanic.

When Misia died at the age of eighty-five, Coco got up in the middle of the night and had herself driven at once to Misia's home. She washed the body, made up the face, dressed the dead woman in white — everything was white; Coco would allow only white flowers. In all this whiteness (the snows of the Auvergne?) there was a touch of red: Misia's lips; of pink: her cheeks, and the very pale pink of a broad satin sash on her bosom. Marvelously rejuvenated by death, she had never been more beautiful, never even in the pictures of the great painters who loved her.

Discussing the period after the Great War, Paul Morand offered the opinion that there were then seven hundred people who mattered in Paris. As under the Directory, or at Versailles, or under Louis XIV. And today? Who matters in Paris today? Coco said:

"It's difficult to talk about an era. It's all gone out of phase. That was another life. When I talk about it I feel I'm making myself ridiculous. I say to myself, My God, how can you still remember all that? But then I say to myself, How can you still go on living? Nothing gives me pleasure anymore, do you understand? I don't enjoy putting one period beside another, another period that isn't even that far behind us! But everything's *something else*. It's frightening."

The seven hundred persons whom Paul Morand said constituted Paris did not all parade through rue Cambon, but it is legitimate to suppose that almost all of them wanted to go there and that for most of them the wish was realized. Misia brought to Coco's everyone on whom the Paris spotlights shone — writers from Giraudoux to Drieu La Rochelle, musicians from Satie to Georges Auric, film directors, tennis champions, and boxers too, arriving on the heels of Cocteau; and I am not listing the Russians of the imperial clan, the cream of the emigration. A Russian collection dressed Paris society in beautiful adaptations of the muzhik's blouse, with boots and bonnets of assorted furs. Coco sat her throne in a whirlwind of which she said little.

She no longer saw the survivors of those gay revels — people like Paul Morand and others — who had known her before she was clad from head to foot in Chanel. She avoided, for example, meeting Elise Jouhandeau, who, when she was a dancer under the name of Cariathis, had given Coco some friendly counsels and even a few lessons in deportment when she was taking her first steps in the Parisian stratosphere. Sometimes, during a ceremony or even a funeral, she would turn her back on someone who was approaching her with outstretched hand, and she would ask: "Who is that old fool?" Perhaps a former lover, whom she pretended not to recognize. To her last day she never stopped wiping out the past, whether it dated from yesterday or from the orphanage.

Always eager to know the celebrities of the moment, she was delighted to have them at her table; but, as soon as they had closed the door behind them, Coco tore them to shreds: *What vulgarity, and to think that one represents France abroad . . . Why, this one ought to go straight back home and give herself a good wash . . . As for him, he calls himself a writer, and did you ever see anyone but him spread mashed potato on his bread? Where do such people come from? What a time we live in!*

She professed to mourn for her own heyday, and yet she *forgot* the survivors who, with her, had made it illustrious. What did they matter beside Mademoiselle Chanel? Only the unknowns found favor with her, such as Reverdy. Her claws sprang out almost in spite of herself when she heard the name of Cocteau. The most intelligent, the most gifted fellow she'd ever known, she said, but as a poet he was a fake. He had never done anything, he had stolen everything from others, especially from Reverdy. She was angry with me when I defended him. Her reaction to Cocteau was the bull's to the muleta: she attacked. She said: "Only Reverdy and [Blaise] Cendrars will survive."

Nevertheless Cocteau was invited to every party in rue Cambon, where he introduced Raymond Radiguet. One evening in January 1969 Coco talked about Radiguet's death:

" 'I'm afraid he's dying,' Jean whimpered [she imitated him, with fake sobs]. I handed him a thermometer: 'Here, Jean, go see him and take his temperature, and the right way — put the thermometer where it belongs — and then put it in this little case and bring it back to me. But don't do anything else.' "

She called me to witness: "Certainly I couldn't take care of Radiguet before I knew whether he was ill. I barely knew him. He came to lunch occasionally. And he drank! Some Americans who were there said to me: 'How can a boy so young drink so much?' "

Cocteau brought back the thermometer. Radiguet's temperature was over 104.

"I telephoned a doctor. 'It's eleven o'clock at night,' he said to me. 'I've had a hard day. I'll send my assistant.' But I insisted. 'All right, I'll do it for you,' the doctor said, 'but I'll take my assistant with me, and he'll call you.' Which meant, clearly, that the assistant would go to Radiguet's by himself. I said to the doctor: 'Tell him not to call me too late, please. I need my rest too.' "

Why all these details? Did she manufacture them as she went along, to suit her monologue? She created, or rather re-created, her world. She said:

"After all, I didn't know this Radiguet very well, but I wanted him taken care of, I didn't want him left to die in a dirty hotel because he had no money. Cocteau was weeping. He said: 'I'm ill.' He went to bed. The doctor saw at once that Radiguet had typhoid. One can smell it. It gives off an odor. He was taken to a hospital. The doctor said to me: 'Mademoiselle, you are assuming a responsibility.'

"But it would have taken a day to find his parents. The father was a newspaper man. The mother died shortly afterward. She wanted to die: she got into Radiguet's bed and she caught typhoid, and she died. As for poor Radiguet, I was told that when he was finally put into his bed in the hospital, he sighed: 'At last.' At last someone was taking an interest in him. I took care of his burial.* I don't really like to concern myself with such things, but since he had no money . . . I had flowers sent. There were very few people. Cocteau went home to bed with the flowers, which he put under his pajamas and on his skin, and he was still weeping."

She looked at me in irritation: "Really, you're the only writer I know who has a good opinion of Cocteau."

If Cocteau had come into the room at that moment, she would

---

* He was twenty years old. Translator.

have thrown her arms around him. She admired him, no matter what she said. She spoke to me at length about his film *Le Testament d'Orphée*. Cocteau had invited her to a private screening. She described it:

"Of course I arrived late. There was no usher, no one. Fortunately the film hadn't started. I heard Jean's voice: he was explaining his film. Some poor young woman standing near the door said to me: 'Go that way, there are seats in the back.'

"I'd never gone into a film theater alone. I don't see well enough. Someone has to take me by the hand. As soon as I go into a cinema I go blind. For a half hour I can't see anything. I disturb everyone.

"So I thought, Damn, if that woman thinks I can find those seats . . . I stayed near the door. I took off my coat so that I could put it on the floor and sit on it: it wouldn't have been the first time I'd seen a film that way. Doudou (Cocteau's adopted son), who was watching for me, ran to me: 'I've saved a seat for you down there — come on.'

" 'No, no, Doudou, this is marvelous — I'm quite happy.'

"But he put me in the second row. I thought I was alone. But every now and then a hand dropped onto my thigh and stroked it. What gall! I didn't dare look. I said to myself, just watch the film and don't try to see who has the gall to caress your thigh that way in the dark. He'll look pretty silly when the lights go on.

"What a shock when they did! It was Jean! He'd come and sat next to me and from time to time he was touching my leg. I said to him: 'Listen, that's not to be borne! I was watching you on the screen and you were sitting next to me. I find that frightening. Your film is marvelous.'

"I was right about the film. When one thinks of all the slop they throw in our faces and then criticize us for not liking!"

Could I and could she believe what she was telling me — that she had not known it was Cocteau next to her? Forgetting the compliments that she had just paid to the film, she remarked: "I fell asleep twice." What did she want? What was she looking for?

We wandered far from the concerns of the time between the wars. Anyone else would have expanded upon such glorious memories. Not Coco: as she had told me, her life began tomorrow. In order to enshroud forever the very distant past that she disowned, that she forgot, she was constantly strewing dead leaves on everything that was *yesterday*. Talking of her most dazzling years, she said:

"One day Paris decided that I had charm [*du chien*]. What a horrible word. What does it mean? So that was what the French had discovered: I wasn't pretty but I had charm [*j'avais du chien*]. It's degrading! Does that mean I looked like a dog? It meant, I suppose, that I had a certain chic. Another horrible word that doesn't mean anything. That ruins the French, to use words like that to describe fashion or women. 'She has dog!' 'she has chic!' There are words that upset me. Even the sound of them annoys me. Finally I realized that these are things one says of those little tramps that wiggle their bottoms in the street. I have nothing to do with that at all!"

The question comes up again: what did she want?

She reigned. She made black mandatory. No woman would have dared before to go out dressed completely in black by day — still less by night — unless she was in mourning. Coco said:

"For four or five years I made only black. My dresses sold like mad, with little touches — a little white collar, or cuffs. Everyone wore them — actresses, society women, housemaids."

"It gave women great delight to play at looking poor without having to be any the less elegant on that account," Lucien François, the fashion expert, was to write. He added, in fact, that Raymond Poincaré, "the austere savior of the franc, was Chanel's involuntary accomplice."

Nothing annoyed Mademoiselle Chanel more than the charge

that her style looked poor. Some went as far as to call it "soup-kitchen style." In the United States it became known as the poor-girl fashion. She was furious:

"Nothing is more idiotic than confusing simplicity and poverty. I wonder how a suit cut out of the finest cloth, very meticulously finished, luxuriously lined, can look poor, especially when it's worn with the accessories I've made fashionable — the chains, the necklaces, the stones, the brooches, all the things that have enriched women so much and so cheaply, since they're imitation. This is all just the opposite of the poor girl. Thanks to me they can walk around like millionaires."

The idea for black was born when she attended the first charity ball for the Petits Lits Blancs, which was organized by Léon Bailby, the editor in chief of *l'Intransigeant* and the great press lord of the period after the Great War. She said:

"I went to that ball at the request of Flamant, a friend of Bailby — a very kind, very gentle, very patient man. He was quite fond of me. 'I would like it so much if you'd come,' he said. We had a box. Colors were horrible in those days. After a look around the room I said to Flamant with a laugh: 'I don't believe it — the colors are too awful, they make women ugly. I think they ought to be dressed in black.'

"That was what I did, and it set off all kinds of tales. Elsa Maxwell wrote in a New York newspaper that since I couldn't wear mourning for Boy Capel because I hadn't been married to him I was making the whole world wear it. What bad taste."

Elsa Maxwell's story was illustrated with a sketch showing a woman in a black veil bowed over a grave. Coco went into detail: "Black veil over a dress in *mousseline de soie*. The lady was supposed to be me. I got thousands of letters from American men who offered their consoling services. Women wrote too: 'Your eyes were not made for tears.'"

I might observe, by the way, that when it came to volume of mail she had a tendency to exaggerate, as if to convince herself that she was really from the South. "Do you get many letters about your broadcasts?" she asked me once, when she had just appeared on television. "The letters I got after my appearance would overflow this room." She meant her dining room.

She did not start the bobbed-hair trend, as her legend would have it. Poiret, as I have mentioned, cut his models' hair in 1908. But she accelerated the fashion by giving it her blessing. This, however, was the result of an accident. In 1917 she was still living in avenue Gabriel, where she made her hats. She was supposed to go to the opera (it must be admitted that she had no vocation for nursing). Her gas-burning hot-water heater blew up, and some of her hair was scorched and charred. At first she thought of breaking her engagement, and then she took a long pair of scissors and cut off some of her long hair. All that was necessary now was to wash it, which she very often did herself anyway.

This, then, was how a style was born. First there was Poiret's boldness: who would dare to follow? Women working in arms factories were cutting their hair out of necessity. And then came Chanel . . . It was noticed at once at the opera that she was wearing her hair short, even though she was also wearing a hat. (The hat to her was the ultimate privilege of the privileged woman, the mark of distinction, the patent of membership in the cast of the true *happy few* — she used the English phrase — the rare possessors of wealth and eminence: *her* aristocracy. For them, the very well provided for, she believed, the hat would always be mandatory.)

So Coco had cut her hair. It brought forth a song: "She had her hair cut." I was eight years old when I heard it in my vacation camp in Montfort-l'Amaury, where my brothers and I were in residence as guests of the state. The bigger boys used to sing it softly at night in their tents.

"She had her hair cut." That made the big boys chuckle. Why? In one verse I overheard something about "running to my mistress." The only mistresses I knew anything about so far were schoolmistresses. Mine, the one by whom I was influenced then, had beautiful braids wound around her white head like a crown. I mentioned this to Coco. Occasionally, during the last years of her life, she listened and even paid attention, asking questions in search of details.

"Did she cut her long hair, out east there in Alsace?" Coco asked. She was dreaming. She said: "Sometimes I ask myself, Have you really done anything? I just don't know. I think I've upset a lot of people. I was harassed, I wanted peace, a peaceful life."

And marriage? We would talk about it later. There was a succession of men. She said: "They ran after me. I had to lead two dozen different existences. I had no time to live."

This was frequently repeated: *I had no time to live.* She harbored in herself an unsatisfied romantic. Did her Venetian adventure occur before or after the Duke of Westminster?

The Arrivabenes were giving a party in honor of Coco and the Serts in their palazzo on the Grand Canal. It was an exquisite September night, and Coco was beautiful in white, with magnificent jewelry and a diamond star in her hair. She was alone, or she felt alone (*What am I doing here? What am I looking for in this life I'm leading? What can I expect from it?*).

She slipped away and set out on foot to go back to the Hotel Danieli, on the Molo degli Schiavoni. It was two o'clock in the morning, and absolutely silent. She wrapped herself in her ermine cape. It was easy to get lost in the streets and alleys of Venice, winding in and out among the canals. She crossed a bridge, then another; she turned right, then left. She was exhausted.

Coco came out into a little square whitened by the moonlight. A young man was sleeping on a bench — a remarkably beautiful fellow, she recalled. She sat down on the same bench to rest and to admire the young man, whose amazement when he awakened can be imagined. Was he seeing a vision?

"I'm lost," Coco explained. "I'm trying to get back to the Danieli."

"Come with me."

In front of the hotel, as she was about to go in, the young man, who had barely spoken during their walk, took hold of her ermine cape, drew her to him and asked: "Do I go to your room or do you come to mine?"

She admitted that then she was rather frightened. She said: "I got hold of myself and went into the hotel. When I was awakened a few hours later by the arrival of breakfast, and I began to remember the walk, I felt so relieved: what luck that I hadn't given in! How embarrassed I'd be now."

10

The Fourth Victory:
The Duke of Westminster

However radiant Coco was still, however perpetually nubile, age was nevertheless about to do her a nasty turn. She was in love with the Duke of Westminster. For the Moulins orphan this was the peak of her life. The richest man in the world, she sighed when she mentioned him. He loved Coco and wanted to marry her. Each had found his match in the other. If, as she wanted so much, Coco had been able to bear him a son, her destiny would undoubtedly have been different. But she was already forty-five when she met him.

Grand Duke Dmitri was still Coco's escort when she met the Duke of Westminster one evening in 1929 at the Hôtel de Paris in Monte Carlo. "Well!" breathed Lady Abdy when they got up to dance. Lady Abdy, whose delightful given name was Ia, was a very blond and very Russian sculptured beauty who had fled to Paris after the revolution. She designed handbags and dressing gowns for her fellow exiles to sell to shops. Misia had introduced her to Coco, saying: "You'll see! She does remarkable things."

As it happened, that season was not so good as earlier ones had been for the House of Chanel. Patou was scoring a triumph as a result of a stroke of genius: he had put the feminine waist back where it belonged. This was major news in the world of fashion, and its repercussions were felt at the ends of the earth. The waist was back where it came from! Only Paris could have thought of that.

"Come and show me what you're making," Coco said to Lady Abdy.

Everything she brought was at once put on sale in the accessories department, and Ia herself was hired. Recalling those glorious times, Lady Abdy sighed: "She would have done anything for her house. She started right out by addressing you as *tu*, which gave her an edge over you. Sometimes she had strange ways of working."

Etienne de Beaumont was in charge of jewelry for the House of Chanel. It was he and Misia, Lady Abdy believes, who established Coco's social foundations. A relatively short time after his wife's death Beaumont asked Mademoiselle Chanel to marry him. "I'll do for you what I did for my wife," he promised. "I'll never contradict you."

But according to Coco: "My real life began with Westminster. I'd finally found a shoulder I could lean on, a tree against which I could prop myself." She called him Bonnie.

Related to the royal family of England, the Duke of Westminster was the richest man in Great Britain. Among other things, he owned hundreds of dwellings in the section of London that bears his name, as well as others in the West End. (I learned this when I was in England on a scholarship from the Chamber of Commerce of Paris, at the same period as Coco but not for so long a time. I lived in a little two-story house that belonged to the duke: I lived under the roof, paying twenty-five shillings a week, of which five went to the duke. The first time I went for a walk in Hyde Park I was trapped in the horde of Hunger Marchers and, like them, I was chased by the mounted police. As I was racing frantically to safety, an old fellow grabbed my arm and thrust his ear trumpet at me: "Who started it, young man, the police or the strikers?" I was discovering England.)

Of those days with Westminister Coco said: "I had nothing more to fear. Nothing more could happen to me — little things, yes, but nothing important."

Is it difficult to imagine what was going on in Coco's heart and mind? The orphanage. Moulins. Royallieu and the mistress keepers. She closed her eyes and refused to remember all that. It was not true. It had never been true. "I'm not an orphan!" she had screamed in the orphanage, "I have a father. He's making his fortune in America. Soon he'll come back and fetch me, and we'll live in a big house."

She had Eton Place, the duke's palace, with its hundreds of gardeners who cultivated roses, carnations and orchids all year round. But, she said, "he preferred to pick the first daisies from the fields for me."

She was impressed by the duke's fortune, and she spoke of it rhapsodically: "He was so rich that he completely forgot about it. No thought of money ever influenced any of his reactions, his acts, his thoughts. He was never calculating."

By the grace of his fabulous wealth, as listening to Coco made clear, the duke managed to achieve the innocence ascribed by the gospels to the poor. Lady Abdy found him "rather a guttersnipe, but Coco liked that. With Westminster Coco behaved like a little girl, timid and docile. She followed him everywhere. Her life was a fairy tale. Their love was not sensual."

Coco said: "If I hadn't met Westminster I'd have gone crazy. I had too much emotion, too much excitement. I lived out my novels, but so badly! With too much intensity, always torn between this and that, between this man and that, with that business [the House of Chanel] on my back though I still didn't understand very much about it . . . I left for England in a daze."

She led an open-air life in England. She said:

"I rode a great deal. In winter there were hunts, three a week — boar hunts and fox hunts. I preferred hunting boars; foxes bored me. It was very healthy. One played tennis. I've never done anything by halves. I learned to fish for salmon. For a year I watched, and I found it very dull. What, spend whole days casting flies to catch a fish? That was not for me! And then I tried it, and I fished from daybreak to eleven at night. I adored it. Obviously I was lucky: I fished only the best rivers. I even went to Norway, but up there I wasn't allowed to fish because the salmon were too tough. They'd bite off your finger easily."

A Scot once accosted her at the Ritz. " 'Are you related to a Mademoiselle Chanel who used to fish for salmon in Scotland?' She acted out the questions and answers, imitating the Scot's mannerisms.

"Have you been to Lochmore, monsieur?"

"Yes, madame, and in the record book there I saw that a Mademoiselle Chanel had done some remarkable things."

"That was indeed I, monsieur."

"You're making fun of me! Are you joking?"

"Not at all, monsieur. You were at Lochmore, weren't you? Visiting the Duke of Westminster, or, rather, his heirs?"

"But was it really you who fished like that, Mademoiselle Chanel?"

"Don't believe me if you don't wish to, monsieur, it makes no difference to me, but it certainly was I."

"You really caught all those salmon?"

"I did nothing else, monsieur, all day long. And you must have seen that I fished only the best places. Never the lake! I hated fishing the lake, it was a bore."

Remembering, she said: "I became very healthy in England. I did a lot of sports. No one expected you to be a champion in everything. But one had to be a champion in something."

It is well known that the Duke of Westminster refused to trust the mails for the letters he wrote to Mademoiselle Chanel when she was in Paris. Three gentlemen messengers maintained their communications lines. To give me some idea of the duke's wealth, Coco told me — not without ingenuousness — that even in midsummer a fire was lighted in every fireplace in his houses, because it was a Westminster's duty to burn coal in order to keep the English miners working. No doubt I had mentioned the Hunger Marchers to her; and she believed in the obligations of wealth. Nothing seemed more natural to her than the privileges of wealth and birth. Apart from some exceptions (remarkable ones, like herself, but so rare!), the poor were intended not to become rich but to be content with their condition, be honest, and work hard. Furthermore, did they not have the hope of a better world in the Beyond? As long as she continued to go to Mass, she said it was to set the example. Like a duchess.

It has happened more than once in history that a prince has loved a peasant, or even a prostitute from some den of iniquity. Between the duke and Coco, however, there was no question of the elevation (through love) of an *inferior* woman, but rather of an alliance between the first free woman of the New Day with one of the last great exemplars of high birth and divine right. Was Mademoiselle Chanel aware of this? The Duke of Westminster wanted to marry her. The marriage did not take place. Why not?

She said: "He was not free. His divorce took three years. No one could make me marry a man with whom I'd lived for three years.*

"Besides," she continued, "I wasn't free either. I didn't want to give up the House of Chanel. *They* didn't understand that, any of them."

There are stories that she refused the duke's proposal with the comment that while there were plenty of Duchesses of Westminster, there was only one Mademoiselle Chanel. "The duke would really have laughed if I'd said anything so imbecilic," she told

---

* The duke's first wife was the former Constance Cornwallis-West, who bore him a son (he died at fourteen) in 1901 and two daughters, Ursula, born in 1902, and Mary, born in 1910. It was Mary for whom the party described below was given. M.H.

me. Actually the story came out of a dinner party where there was talk about Coco and her duke. "Why should she marry him?" Sir Charles Mendl, counselor to the British embassy, is supposed to have said. "She's the only Coco Chanel in the world and there are already three Duchesses of Westminster."

All this is virtually essential to the legend of Mademoiselle Chanel, like the famous dinner that she gave in her home (in London she had a house next door to the duke's) before the reception held by the Duke and Duchess of Westminster to introduce their younger daughter to society: a ball at which several members of the royal family were expected. Coco had been invited by the duchess herself — the woman who in spite of her divorce was still called the Duchess of Westminster because she was the mother of the duke's children. It was predicted that her appearance would cause a sensation. Immediately after the dinner in her house Coco urged the duke — who was one of her guests — to join the duchess in welcoming their guests. Everyone else at her dinner left at the same time.

Coco undressed and went to bed, having sent for the newspapers. The next day she sent the duchess a mass of flowers with her apologies.

Was Coco telling the truth when she said she would not have married a man with whom she had lived for three years?

She hoped to bear a son to the duke, to replace the boy who had died at the age of fourteen after a commonplace but belated operation. It can even be said that she tried to bear him a son, for, after consultations with doctors, she adopted a regimen of exercises that she had been told would facilitate childbearing, principally leg movements; for example, she kept her legs in the air for long periods. The revelation may be surprising; but I found it confirmed by an outburst of Coco's against motherhood and confinement. She was speaking of a mutual friend, a young man whose recent marriage was not going well.

"His wife insisted he be present when she gave birth," Coco

said. "Ever since he saw her in that disgraceful state, he's had no desire to touch her."

Her face was distorted. There was panic in her eyes. She recalled a cat giving birth: "It seemed she'd finished, but no, there were still more [kittens] mewing inside her to get out." Her voice vibrated with disgust. "And dogs swallow all that! Even a colt; it's horrid, it's messy."

She was frightening. Actually, as I realized too late, what she was giving voice to was despair. She had had everything, but she had not had *that!* Not what she hoped when, on the deck of the *Flying Cloud*, Westminster's yacht, or on the lawn of la Pausa, her country house at Roquebrune above Monte Carlo, she did her exercises intended to facilitate childbearing. She was forty-five when she danced with the Duke of Westminster at Monte Carlo for the first time. (If Coco had had a child by Boy Capel, Gabrielle Dorziat thought, they would have married.)

To be or not to be the Duchess of Westminster, after all . . . It was true that she was the only Coco Chanel. And true that when a friend told her of the duke's death, she gave no apparent sign of feeling. But to be the mother of a Duke of Westminster! To become a woman like all the rest (a mother) in order to be all the greater an exception . . . It is understandable that she might have had such a dream and that her disappointment lay heavy in the depths of her heart.

She said: "I've known luxury such as no one will ever know again." This was her way of expressing her love for Westminster. She went to Gibraltar with him. At that time they were traveling aboard the specially renovated historic destroyer *Cutty Sark*. She said:

"We were shown everything that was inside the rock. I felt very unhappy, and absolutely out of place: a Frenchwoman seeing all that. We rode in a boat over bodies of fresh water. Then we sailed on canals of pure petroleum. Of course one had to remove anything that might cause a spark."

On the *Flying Cloud* she had freshwater baths. Sea water was bad for her skin, she said.

There were times when she showed jealousy. During one cruise on the *Flying Cloud* she insisted, successfully, that a very pretty woman, at that time a well-known painter, be put ashore at the first port of call, which was Villefranche. Rather embarrassed, the duke went on to Nice, where he found a breathtaking emerald. He gave it to Coco after dinner. The perfect full moon made an iridescent carpet across the whole deck; the two lovers were leaning on the rail. Coco gazed on the emerald in the hollow of her palm, and then let it fall into the sea — Cleopatra dissolving Caesar's pearls in vinegar. (Notice to underwater fishermen: the yacht was standing off Villefranche.)

Essentially, Coco preferred long stays at la Pausa to cruises. Once again she was establishing a style, by making summer vacations in the South of France fashionable; previously no one had gone there except a few penniless painters, and they protected themselves against its climate. Coco was a sensation when she returned to Paris all bronzed — to say nothing of her white pajamas. She had launched them in Venice, with matching turbans and black tops.

At the Casino in Juan-les-Pins one evening the doorman refused to admit her. She was on her way to meet the duke, who was a great gambler and very generous. (He was very absent-minded too, money meant so little to him. He would leave it on the table, and the bet would double and redouble; someone would call him away, and he would stuff the bills and chips into his pockets and give away the surplus, if it may be called that. Needless to say, he was very popular in all the casinos.) At Juan-les-Pins Coco was rescued from the doorman's ban by Baudoin himself, the founder and general manager, who said to her: "Mademoiselle Chanel, you are living proof that one must be not merely dressed but well dressed." A witticism and a compliment that she recalled with pleasure.

There was great freedom at la Pausa. Coming back from a swim, one found a buffet set up on the terrace, with cold things on one side — ham, roast beef, fish — and hot dishes on the other, kept ready by antique silver warmers from England — stew, cassoulets, risotto, country and regional dishes. One sat on the grass, protected by tarpaulins of coarse linen. There was no protocol, no ceremony, Coco said. Regular guests, besides the Duke of Westminster and his friends, included Salvador Dali, Jean Cocteau, the composer Georges Auric, the actor Marcel Herrand, the Duchesse d'Ayen, the Beaumonts, Prince Kutusov and Serge Lifar, whom Coco called her godson because Diaghilev had got him out of Russia with the money that she had given him.

In the hotel rooms in which she had lived since she had given up her first apartment in avenue Gabriel and the house of splendors at 29 Faubourg St.-Honoré, Mademoiselle Chanel clung to the anonymity that they afforded her: the brass bed, the Louis XVI furniture in its gray lacquer, the Mapple wardrobes, with just a few personal things on her night table — an ikon, a Byzantine cross, and that replica of the tomb of St. Anthony of Padua that one of her "mechanics" had given her.

But her bedroom in la Pausa was much more personal: a vast Spanish bed in gilt iron, on the uprights of which she hung amulets (for fertility?) and artificial and fresh flowers all commingled: a bed for a gypsy queen. Most of the furniture too was Spanish. The windows looked out on a very simple garden with cypress and olive trees; under the olive trees there were iris that seemed to have grown at random, and the most natural-looking lavender. One giant olive tree, one of the oldest, stood like a sentry before the entrance to the house: the driveway circled it. "It watches over me," Coco said; "it protects my threshold against intruders."

It was at la Pausa that she finally broke with Westminster. The guests slept badly that night, kept awake by sharp exchanges.

Churchill had stepped in, had reminded the duke of his obligations. As proof of his surrender, the duke was to marry the
daughter of a chief of protocol at Buckingham Palace.

What was Westminster to Coco if not, first and foremost, the
dazzling symbol, visible to the ends of the earth, of the success of
the House of Chanel?

Of this Chanel of the thirties, not at the peak of her fame but
at the height of her splendors, Maurice Sachs has given a marvelous portrait in *The Decade of Illusion*, written in 1932 and
dedicated to Jean Cocteau:

> Chanel created a feminine character such as Paris had never before
> known. Her influence went beyond the reach of her work. Her name
> was etched on minds in the same way as the names of men eminent
> in politics or letters. She represented, in sum, a new being, all-power-
> ful in spite of the legendary weakness of women and, it seemed, essen-
> tial to the city's life. . . .
>
> She was a general: one of those young generals of the Empire in
> whom the spirit of conquest ruled. Yes, that was it: the swiftness of
> her vision, the logic of her orders, her care for details and, most espe-
> cially, the loyalty that she manifested toward her army of workers. . . .
>
> She was not conventionally beautiful, but she was irresistible. Her
> words were not magic, but her mind and her heart were unforgettable.
> And, though her work may not be of the kind that is preserved by
> future ages, I should like to think that those who will write the his-
> tory of the first decades of this century will keep Chanel's great under-
> taking in their memories.

11

The Unexpected Friend: Pierre Reverdy

What part did love — real love — have in Coco Chanel's life? At the end of her lifetime, she recalled only a few men. This does not mean that she had forgotten the others; but she no longer spoke of them because they added nothing to the legend of herself which she was constructing in her solitude. One of those of whom she did often speak was Reverdy, a great poet who is still unappreciated.

"Love begins with love, and it would be impossible to go from the strongest friendship to anything but a weak love." Having picked up La Bruyère's *Pensées* by chance and opened it at random, Reverdy, the poet, copied this sentence for Coco and added his own commentary:

But he did not say that one could go from a great love to an imperishable friendship. I have written that there is no real love without friendship, as there is no great friendship without love (as between men, the word "love" being used in a special sense). But one has to have real gall to write like this when one has read that fellow. Order La Bruyère's *Caractères* (or, if you have it in your library, find it),

Rochefoucauld's *Maximes* and Chamfort's. Read some of them every so often in the evening.

Again, it was Misia through whom Coco had met Reverdy. She showed him some of the aphorisms that she was writing. "I congratulate you on those three *pensées* that you sent me," he wrote to her in one of his many letters, none of which is dated. "They are very good — the last is perfect and absolutely in the top rank of what one strives for in this form."

This Reverdy was a curious man. "His faith kept him untouched by the flatteries of the world," Misia wrote, rejoicing that she had been able to help him fulfill a desire that was especially dear to him: to withdraw to the Abbey of Solesmes, where he wrote with discipline and zeal.

What did Coco find in Reverdy's prose? When she was breaking with Westminster, the duke told a friend: "She's losing her mind, she's in love with a priest."

Reverdy did live among the monks, and almost like them. Like Cocteau, Maurice Sachs and several others, he had become a convert under the influence of Jacques Maritain and his wife. But Coco Chanel was not the only person on whom Reverdy made an impression. His friends among writers included Guillaume Apollinaire, Blaise Cendrars and Max Jacob. He had known André Salmon at the Bateau Lavoir, where he went to meet Picasso, Braque and Juan Gris. They all became prominent and very rich (except Gris, who died too young to enjoy his success). Reverdy lived on a small salary from a publisher.

"If you wrote your poems on separate sheets and signed each one as your painter friends sign their pictures," Coco observed, "regardless of what snobbery has to do with it [and she would have seen to whatever was necessary for that!], you would be as rich as they are."

But at thirty Reverdy was still working as a proofreader for *l'Intran.* One night, as he came out of the composing room into a drizzle, he fell in the street and banged his knee painfully against the curb. The colleague who was with him heard him sigh bitterly: "Allow me, O Lord, to continue to be an unknown poet."

That his peers recognized his genius was certainly a consolation and an encouragement, but it did not make his sufferings from poverty any lighter, and this occasionally influenced his judgments. He was a harsh critic. In his monastic exile he kept current with the news from Paris and knew everything that was happening there; in conversation he had a storyteller's dash much like that of Christian Bérard, who wallowed in gossip. A newspaper man turned book publisher brought out some of Reverdy's poems with illustrations by Picasso: nothing but bones, in reds of varying intensity. Today the book is sought after by collectors and commands a high price. If Reverdy knows it, wherever he is, the irony will make him smile.

He had very handsome teeth. He was *common:* that was what Lady Abdy remembered about Reverdy. She was also very positive that Coco was tremendously fond of him. They could have married, she thought: they would have been happy. If Reverdy had been free, would he have married Mademoiselle Chanel? It is not certain. It would have meant taking an incalculable risk.

It is not uninteresting to compare Reverdy's correspondence with Misia (what she published of it in her book) with the letters that he wrote to Coco. He wrote to Misia:

I love you so much. I think of you with such tenderness. You are one of those whom I love to the point of pain. Often my arms, my lips, my heart long for you. You are a fragment of my life. A lovely part. Here, in this silence that some would call mortal (only the birds are heard to speak, only the monks to sing), I listen to God and I love my friends with a divine love. God has used you to make possible for me this life of tenderness and love that was the only life possible for me henceforth. The choice was to die, to wither away, or to live in the unique light. It would be a dreadful thing, Misia, to leave the world with a cold heart — it is something delightful and gay to leave it in an excess of love.

For Coco he changed his tone. I have seen a number of letters that Reverdy wrote to Coco during World War II.

With Misia the sky was blue, the birds spoke, the monks sang. It was a happy, relaxed man who was writing. Reading his letters to Coco one cannot help thinking of Diaghilev, who, according to Lifar, was afraid of her. "I will come to see you soon," Reverdy wrote in response to a rather imperious telegram from Coco, "but I will not stay long." He spoke of the peace of Solesmes. "I need this solitude," he said. "It is time for me to change my life if I do not want to end in complete self-contempt. Running after pleasure is like running after the wind. One loses one's breath and all that is left is a gnawing bitterness."

Everything that Reverdy wrote to Coco was serious, tainted by the need for self-justification. In the two months that he had spent in Solesmes, he explained, he had not stopped working and he had produced the equivalent of a new book. He was thinking, seeking: he wanted to regain his faith in order to become a real member of the monastery, he declared. "For too long," he wrote, "I have given free rein to that poetry in me that asked only to chase after pleasure."

These are almost letters to an anxious mother who must be reassured, even at the cost of dramatizing things somewhat: let her make no mistake, regardless of certain appearances, time is not being wasted — one is writing and making progress.

It might be supposed that Reverdy and Coco found each other mutually intimidating, if there were not evident in her that "common" side that struck Lady Abdy in Reverdy. One must, obviously, clarify the word. In Coco, as in her poet, being "common" meant shrewdness, extremely quick wit, rapid repartee, the refusal to be taken in by the respectable and the pretentious; with, in addition, something of the comic, a slightly low charm, some sentiment as required; all of which puts a word to a great many uses. Both Coco and Reverdy were always very close to the popular, if not to the people; for it would be preposterous to contend that Mademoiselle Chanel had kept the slightest trace of a child of the people. Nevertheless, she recognized something of her own childhood in Reverdy's, for she appropriated it without the least scruple. Did she perhaps tell some scrap of her truth to Reverdy or any of the other men in her life? Never; and this power to keep silent was clearly her weakness as a woman. One can love a woman without a past; to live with her is more difficult.

Reverdy wrote his letters all across the page, occasionally in a script of normal size with some fifteen words to the line, particularly when he was sending Mademoiselle Chanel things he had written for her — rather professorial commentaries on La Bruyère, or reflections on the art of writing. On his book *Le Gant de crin* (*The Massage Glove*) he offered this commentary:

"The secret, and the danger, of this kind of expression is that it demands conciseness, substance and depth, preciseness and lightness. One is constantly torn among the difficulty of maintaining preciseness, the accuracy of what one wants to say, and the good taste that constantly imposes sacrifices, etc."

An ill-disposed mind might bracket this letter with a correspondence-course lesson. In actuality a different comparison thrusts itself forward: one must go back to what Coco said of Boy Capel in connection with occultism: "I wouldn't tolerate his being interested in something that didn't interest me." In Reverdy's case the same reflex made a bluestocking of her. Besides, she had undoubtedly found a way of strengthening her ties with him and making his life easier by paying him for the job of polishing the aphorisms that she was writing.

When Reverdy was not playing professor, when he allowed his heart to speak, his handwriting grew larger and there would be no more than five or six words to a line that stretched across the whole page. And then suddenly, when every page was full and there was no margin (though the message was much shorter than it seemed when one first opened the envelope with its three or four sheets), there would be something further to be added, in a microscopic line almost indecipherably squeezed in on the very edge of the page. A curious man. Not very big, stocky, Catalan in type, a lock of hair over the forehead.

"One must remain alone, a layman and without faith." When he thus defined his vocation as a poet withdrawn from the world, Reverdy touched Mademoiselle Chanel's heart. She was alone. Lay? That did not mean much to her. Without faith? She had no more than Reverdy, if, as Reverdy did, one associates faith with religious conviction.

One Sunday when she and I were talking, she had heard Mass. She clarified:

"On the radio. I don't go to Mass anymore. But hearing it did me good. For the first time I listened without rebellion to a priest talking. Catholicism is the hardest religion . . . We haven't believed in the devil for a long time now. People wore themselves out talking that kind of nonsense. This priest I heard on the radio didn't mention it at all. He said one must tolerate and understand all religions. That was the first time I'd ever heard that from a priest's mouth, and it was well done, he used parables. Radio is educational."

She called herself a Theosophist. That was fashionable at the turn of the century, it was in the air then. The Gurdjieff* of the period was Annie Besant, by then an old lady. Her followers believed in metempsychosis. Death was no more: one changed dimensions. Coco said: "I believe in the fourth, fifth, sixth dimension. That comes from the need for reassurance, for a belief that one never loses everything and that something happens on the other side. I believe in the unreal, I believe in everything that's full of mystery; but I don't believe in spiritualism or hypnotism."

She turned to the talks that she had had with Abbé Mugnier, the best society's confessor, who was credited (he too) with a few sensational conversions. Coco said:

"One day I said to Abbé Mugnier: '*Monsieur l'abbé*, I'll tell you right now why I no longer know whether I'm still a Catholic. In any event, I'm not a practicing one.'

* Georgi Gurdjieff, a Russian mystic who enjoyed a certain vogue during the 1920s and set up an "institute" in Fontainebleau to cure bodies and souls through a variant of anthroposophy, itself a derivative from Theosophy. Translator.

" 'Some people are made to be practicing, and you aren't one of them,' he said. He launched into a disquisition.

" 'No, *Monsieur l'abbé*,' I said, 'I'm not equipped to talk about these things, and besides I don't get any pleasure out of it; it doesn't interest me.' I hope he forgave me: I told him the Mass bored me extremely and I didn't go anymore, not even to set an example."

Abbé Mugnier reassured her: yes, he told her, hell does exist, but there is no one there.

In the last book of mine that I was able to give her, *Et Moïse créa Dieu* (*And Moses Created God*), Coco found this statement: "God is the strength that makes it possible for man to accomplish God's work." During the conversation about my book, we also talked about a Polish novel that was having a success.

"Why Moses?" she asked. "Do you think those old stories — the Bible — still interest people?"

It irritated her that my book was not in the little bookshop in the Ritz while the Polish novel was prominently displayed there. She found it dirty and degrading. "Where do people dig up the terrible things they dare to write and other people print?" Then she came back to *Moses:* "Do you think the Jews will like it? They won't buy it."

Often, especially when there was talk about the fashion shops that were springing up then like mushrooms after a storm, she would give vent to a febrile, passionate anti-Semitism that was never corroborated by an act, a deed, or demeanor. I tried vainly to convince her that Moses, who to me was the greatest of the great, was becoming also the most modern, because it was necessary to remake what he had achieved — to create or, if you prefer, to reshape God to the exigencies of today, so that in order to protect them he might serve as the common denominator for all the races of man.

But Coco preferred my previous book, a novel called *Belle de Paris* (*A Beautiful Woman of Paris*), perhaps because sometimes the heroine spoke for her. Moreover, she did not really understand why I had gone from *Belle de Paris* to *Moses*. "To catch my breath," I explained.

"You don't know how to make money," she observed.

After Reverdy there was an artist, Paul Iribe, who induced Coco to put out a rather disastrous newspaper. Iribe never felt the slightest monastic vocation: he led a very full life. His father, an architect, had explained to the Communards of 1871 how they would have to go about knocking down the column in the place Vendôme. In order to warn Coco against Iribe's "follies," her friends said to her: "Don't forget that his father brought down the Vendôme column."

Iribe died during a tennis game at la Pausa. Coco, who had loved him, never talked of him. He had never catered to her pride.

Marriage . . . probably she thought about it. But *they* disappeared, almost always. A woman who was the richest and the most beautiful, and yet ran searching for love: that was the theme of my novel that Coco liked, *Belle de Paris*. She kept it beside her bed for quite some time.

Only Westminster gave her what every other man, whatever his position, offers his wife: happiness with security. With Westminster there was an average-couple balance — no need to wonder who was giving and who was taking. She neither kept nor was kept; there was no calculation, no mental reservations, ever. The natural simplicity of love, for Coco, was to be found only with the richest man in the world.

As for the rest . . . Cocteau spoke one day about "pederastic women": women who have men, as men *have* women. It is a breed that is increasing.

12

The Silence of the German Occupation

No one has ever really understood why Coco closed the House of Chanel in September 1939, when war was declared. "I thought no one would go on making dresses," she said unconvincingly. She spent those dark years as she spent the rest of her life, alone, thinking only of herself — that is, of her house. A German visited her in rue Cambon and they spoke English. She never mentioned his name in my presence.

In 1939 the House of Chanel occupied five houses in rue Cambon. "I was going to hang on," Coco said. "Fortunately I sold. What kind of money would that take today? Now, thank God, everything's on a small scale."

She broke off all her activities when war was declared. This was poor judgment. There were insinuations that she was withdrawing from the field because Schiaparelli had eclipsed her. But she said:

"I stopped working because of the war. Everyone in my place had someone who was in uniform — a husband, a brother, a father. The House of Chanel was empty two hours after war was declared."

She employed only women, however.

She cut off the incomes which she had been pouring out to her brothers, Alphonse and Lucien. In one of the rare letters written in her own hand which we possess, she wrote in pencil this explanation for Alphonse: "I am very sorry to have to give you this sad news [the cutting off of his monthly check], but my house having been closed down, I am myself almost in the state of misery."

Some newspaper accounts of her death implied that she had always resented the 1936 labor agreements, the social-welfare laws, paid vacations, etc. She had placed a vacation home in Mimizan at the disposal of her workers.

She said: "How could I suppose there would still be people who would buy dresses? I was so stupid, such a *dummy* about life that it seemed impossible to me. I said to myself, You'll just put everything in order and find something else to keep you busy. I can do anything — except get up at five in the morning! Well, I made a mistake. Some people sold dresses all through the war. That will be a lesson to me. Whatever may happen hereafter, I'll go on making my clothes. The only thing I still believe in is my work."

Pallasse, her nephew, was mobilized. He was a pessimist and anticipated disaster. "In England he was an officer [it will be remembered that she had sent him to school at Beaumont]. He wanted to serve in France as an enlisted man, and so he went all through that phony war, which, he said, was phony only to those who weren't there. He was stationed in one of the farthest outposts. When the Germans came . . ."

She mimed a battle scene as she imagined it: the Germans sitting two by two in their armored vehicles. She gathered her skirt under her, held her knees close and sat up straight. "They were everywhere," she said. After a pause: "And then, my nephew told me, they saluted us." She saluted her nephew, the brave soldier, her hand forming a visor over her eyes. Her nephew spent four years in a prison camp. Before the collapse he had asked Coco to stay with his wife near Vichy (I think) if things went badly. ". . . But I didn't leave Paris on the Germans' account. I would never have left. What could they do to me? I was behaving myself. My business was closed."

The tide of the exodus washed her up in the vicinity of Pau, at the Château de Lambeyc, which she had bought from Etienne Balsan for her nephew. This gave her the opportunity for a reunion with Balsan, who was now married, in a nearby country house. But Coco was bored in Pau. She went frequently to the hairdresser's, where she found an old friend, Marie-Louise Bousquet, who was very much the Parisian, very lively and very funny. She had had an academic salon between the wars; after the Liberation she became one of the fixed poles of French-American snobbery. At that time she represented *Harper's Bazaar* in Paris.

"Let's go back to Paris together," Coco suggested to her. They made the trip with a third woman, a doctor. "The car smelled of oil," Coco said. She remembered the smallest details of the journey. "A friend had given me forty-five liters of gasoline* because he thought I might need it."

The first stop was Vichy, where the ladies dined at the Hôtel du Parc. "Everyone was laughing and drinking champagne," Coco said. "Those ladies were wearing hats as big as this [she gestured]. 'Well,' I said, 'it's the height of the season here.'"

Someone overheard her. "A gentleman turned to me: 'What do you mean, madame?' I said: 'I mean everyone's very gay here and it's quite pleasant.' The man's wife calmed him down."

Where were they to spend the night? Someone got Coco a militia man's bed: "The poor devil had to go on duty that night so that I could sleep." But she managed to prevail on the owner of a large hotel by asking him to give her "anything at all." He had her put in the attic, where she "died of the heat. I got up every

* About ten gallons. Translator.

hour to go to the toilet just for fresh air. It was stifling there under the roof." Marie-Louise Bousquet slept on a chaise longue set up in a linen room.

"A gentleman offered me his room," Coco said, "provided I would share the bed with him. Thank you very much, but no monsieur." She must have known him reasonably well, however, because she dined with him.

In Vichy a letter from Paris was waiting for her: to her surprise, the manager of the Ritz was advising her that the Germans had not seized her apartment.

"They didn't even look in the luggage I'd left — big trunks that had been put in the hall, with my name on them in large letters. A German general saw them and asked: 'Is this the Mademoiselle Chanel who makes the dresses and perfumes? She can stay, we don't need her apartment.'" She added: "The Germans weren't all gangsters."

If one took seriously the few disclosures that Mademoiselle Chanel allowed herself to make about those black years of the occupation, one's teeth would be set on edge. But the truth was that the war simply did not interest her. Her overpowering egocentricity protected her better than the Maginot Line had protected her country. No one could impinge upon what one might call her splendid isolation. She said: "There will always be wars because so many medicines are being invented that soon people won't die anymore."

In Vichy, through the good offices of a prefect of police, she managed to have the gasoline tank of her car filled, and she resumed the journey to Paris, still with her friend and the woman doctor. Soon their road was blocked. "They wouldn't let anyone through," she said, "except Belgians going back to their country in ancient wagons pulled by oxen. It was an exodus back to prehistoric times. And the exodus took place only because the weather was good. If it had been bad, the people would all have stayed home."

What was to be done? Coco told the "mechanic" to turn around, not in order to go back to Vichy but to find a side road. "But they were jammed too," she said. "And there was nothing to eat wherever one looked. Finally we reached Bourbon-l'Archambault, which is a watering place. The people there were very uneasy. Everything had been booked for the season, but no one had come."

At the first hotel she saw, she asked whether there were rooms available, and she got three, each with a bath — a miracle. Before she went up for her bath, she noticed a child sitting on a wall: he was about to fall. And in fact he did, head first. She ran to him: "No one touch the child until we know whether he's broken anything!" The little boy was crying, and so was his mother, a poor woman. Coco took a hundred-franc bill from her purse:

"I don't like to say it, but as soon as that kid saw the bill he stopped crying. He took it and gave it to his mother. 'We'll be able to eat tonight,' he said to me. The mother had another child, and she was pregnant. She showed me her purse: she had exactly five francs. She was living on whatever people chose to give her. But people get tired of giving. It was all so sad."

As if to excuse herself for a certain emotion that had infiltrated her story, she added: "You know, one was in a very strange state at that time, one felt all kinds of things."

But of the Germans she said only, "I had nothing to blame myself for. What could they do to me?" And the defeat of France was not her affair.

She remembered the bath that she had finally been able to have in Bourbon-l'Archambault: "*Afterward,* the water was so black! And my stockings were all in holes."

Nor had she forgotten the menu of that night's dinner: a hot salad with soft-boiled eggs on it. The owner of the restaurant went to her table: "Are you really Mademoiselle Chanel?"

"I was by now doing so many things, my dear," Coco ex-

plained to me: "making clothes, jewelry, perfumes. I was beginning to be a famous person. This woman said to me: 'My parents
would be so happy to meet you!' They were textile workers. We
went to see them. 'Would you like some anisette, Mademoiselle
Chanel?' they asked. They looked at me, they touched my hand,
the old lady got out a newspaper with my picture in it and murmured: 'Why, yes, it's really you, Mademoiselle Chanel.'"

What about the Germans? "They gave one gasoline. There
were signs: 'French gasoline.' One simply asked for it."

Back in Paris at last, as she approached the Ritz an assistant
manager made a gesture: *"Don't go any further.* She saw sentries. She replied to the man's gesture with one of her own: *"If I
can't go any farther, then you come to me!*

"You must go to the *Kommandantur,"* the hotel man explained.

"What do you mean? All dirty like this? I must change. Is my
maid upstairs?"

"No, she hasn't come back."

"Then you go to the *Kommandantur!* Say that Mademoiselle
Chanel has arrived. I'll go when I'm clean. I've always been
taught that it's better to be clean when one is asking for something."

This was 1940! Coco's recollections dumfounded me. She
brought them out very spontaneously. She said:

"During the war we could sell only about twenty bottles of
perfume a day in the House of Chanel. People lined up long before opening time, chiefly German soldiers. I laughed when I
saw them; I thought, You poor fools, most of you will go away
empty-handed. And I said to myself, when the Americans come,
it will be the same thing."

War or peace, she lived to herself, entrenched in her Fortress
Chanel, letting down the drawbridge when she was in the mood
to allow entrance to whom she wished. During the occupation it
was Baron von D., whom her friends nicknamed Spatz (Spar-

row). He was a handsome man who in his youth had had ambitions. After World War I he had taken part in the suppression of the Spartakist movement, which had sought to extend the Russian Revolution to Germany. He was known in Paris before 1940; he was one of those charmers in the "parallel" diplomatic missions that Ribbentrop* had sent to Paris and London to lay the groundwork for him. In those days Spatz had made a smashing conquest of a beautiful, rich Parisian who was not quite "Aryan": she and her husband left France when the nation fell. Spatz took over their apartment in order to "protect" it. Very much the gentleman, he knew wines, cigars, good clothes — nothing was too good for him. Women took turns keeping him in his accustomed style.

Spatz was assigned to supervision of the textile industry, which was interesting work at the start, but after the opening of the Russian front everything changed. What mattered above everything else to Spatz was to stay in Paris, to hold out — and, therefore, not to attract attention. He concealed his cars. He did not appear in public with Coco, not even for the briefest of dinners at Maxim's. They kept to rue Cambon. When some friend took it on himself to warn Coco about "this friendship with a German," she objected: "He isn't a German! His mother is English."

It was true. Spatz's mother was an Englishwoman of the highest nobility. To Coco he was more than a lover, he was a companion. Did he assure her of certain amenities? I never heard her mention the difficulties of the occupation, except once: in connection with a ring. Complaining of the condition of her hands, she gave me to understand that she had suffered from chilblains, like almost everyone else; so she could not have been very warm or well fed.

After the Liberation, questions were asked of her. By whom?

* Joachim von Ribbentrop, the Foreign Minister of Germany, who was hanged at Nuremberg. Translator.

"Those Parisians of the Liberation with their shirtsleeves rolled up. Four days earlier, when they were with the Germans, they didn't have their sleeves rolled up."

"Do you know this gentleman?" she was asked. This meant Baron Spatz.

"Of course. I've known him for twenty years."

"Where is he?"

"He is a German. So I suppose he's in Germany. When he came to say good-bye to me — he is very well bred — he told me he was going back to Germany."

Did she really reply with such poise to those Parisians-with-their-shirt-sleeves-rolled-up?

"When anyone came to question me about all that, I said: 'Do you have identification? What English colonel do you work with? Who gave you your orders?' When I asked those questions, no one could answer. I could. On the English side it was serious. The English are serious people."

When I pointed out that under the occupation it would have been dangerous to carry English papers, she interrupted: "This was *afterward!* One could ask for them *afterward!* Everyone who did anything serious had papers; no one could refuse to issue them."

But she offered no details of the serious work that she herself had done during the occupation on instructions from an English colonel. She had some problems after the Liberation. Before she left for Switzerland, she withdrew into an extremely modest pension outside Paris. Some say she bought her way out of trouble; others say she had the protection of Churchill, Westminster's friend, who was supposed to have intervened on her behalf.

Had Coco really "worked" for the English during the war? Pierre Artigue, a former journalist who is now president of the Belgian-American Chamber of Commerce in the United States, believes that it is possible, if not probable. Her name might have appeared on the extremely secret list of persons who had remained in France and who were regarded by the English as "reliable." Artigue had occasion to consult this list in Allied head-quarters in Cairo, where he was serving during the war. Hore-Belisha* also told him of Churchill's private list. Obviously, the woman in the Ritz of Paris who might have become Duchess of Westminster would not have lost interest in the English. But this does not necessarily mean that she worked for them. No — it is quite possible to suppose — that was not her affair.

With the perspective of time it becomes easier to understand her. Like many Frenchmen, she had simply gone on living. As for the baron, the charming Spatz, he belonged to the world in which she had blossomed. She was right when she said she had known him for twenty years. He could have been one of the group of polo players of *la Belle Epoque*.

I took virtually verbatim notes on a conversation between her and Serge Lifar one day when the three of us lunched together. They were talking about the occupation.

Lifar said, "Because of my position [he was the ballet master at the Paris Opera] I saw hundreds of Germans. I saw everyone, from Goering to Goebbels, but she [he pointed to Coco] didn't see anyone, ever — not one German. She didn't go out."

"I would have considered it *impolite* to go out." (I translated *ill bred, bad form:* a lady of taste could not show herself in the Paris of the Germans. That, beyond any doubt, was what she wanted one to infer.)

"She was terrifying!" Lifar went on. "Such courage! One day I went to the Gestapo with her. [He ducked his head like a man who hears bullets whistling past.] She said whatever came into her head. I tried to make her be quiet: 'Look, Coco, that's enough; you're going to get yourself arrested. One isn't in a kin-dergarten here.' "

"My conscience was clear," Coco said, "so I was in no danger."

The name of someone prominent in fashion came into the con-versation. "Him!" Lifar exploded. "He collaborated all through

* Leslie Hore-Belisha, Churchill's first Minister of War when he became Prime Minister in 1940. Translator.

the war — he and So-and-So! They were the Germans' creatures. And they popped up as members of the Resistance at the Liberation! Christ, I saw them at the Ritz with the Germans for four years! Oh, it doesn't matter to me, but just the same they shouldn't have done what they did to the marshal.* Resistants! Those two! Neither one had Coco's courage."

"I told X [one of the two, the one who no doubt had claimed a part in the purges after 1944]: 'My dear, the only resistant is me.' "

"You closed your business!" Lifar cried. "The others went on working; they did whatever the Germans wanted."

"The Germans paid," Coco observed. She added: "People said to me: 'They're paying with our money.' I replied: 'The Armistice compelled us to pay them that money. So it's their money.' "

She repeated the story that she had heard at the time when Marshal Goering visited Cartier's, the jewelers. She did the dialogue between Goering and the management official who had been instructed to receive him.

"Obviously, *monsieur le maréchal,* we have very little left to show you, but, if you wish, we can have things brought back —"

"Not at all. This is wartime, and in wartime one does not buy expensive jewelry. I came merely to show these young men [the officers with him] what is produced by the genius of French artisans. I'd like them to learn to appreciate your watches."

(Here Coco launched into a lecture on the world's best watches, the details of which I have forgotten. Obviously it was Goering in whom I was interested.)

"Do you really wish to buy nothing, *monsieur le maréchal?*"

"Perhaps some little token to give Madame Goering pleasure . . . That is, if you have something that isn't too expensive."

Let no eyebrows go up. The dialogue as Coco reconstructed it is too splendid. And besides . . . I do not know why I feel as if I

---

* Henri-Philippe Pétain, who headed the Vichy regime after the fall of France. He was tried and convicted for treason and died in prison after de Gaulle commuted his death sentence. Translator.

were hearing, in some ingenuous form, the echo of a monstrous truth. *Something that isn't too expensive!* I was in an *Oflag** at that time, I was dying of hunger, I was crushed by the Germans' victory — the triumph of evil, total horror, the negation of all the divine truths absorbed with my mother's milk. One of the officers of Cartier's, Louis Devaux, was in the camp with me. We were members of a group that met on the sandy *Sportplatz* to draw up the balance sheet of the defeat and to try to evolve guidelines for the reconstruction of France. And back in Paris Goering was examining a bracelet:

"With tiny emeralds, I think," Coco said. "Dirt cheap. It cost very little."

She tapped her bosom above what would have been a man's breast pocket. Goering had no money with him.

"I will send someone for the bracelet tomorrow."

"Not at all, *monsieur le maréchal!* Take it with you. You can pay for it whenever it's convenient."

"Certainly not!"

"Yes, of course."

And Coco went on: "He took the bracelet, but the money was there five minutes later."

"Of course," Lifar said. He called me to witness with this staggering question: "Why shouldn't Goering have paid? He could have bought half of Europe."

Around Christmas of the year of my release from captivity I had to go to Cartier's to deliver a message from Louis Devaux. I remember the empty show windows. In no case could there have been any question of my buying even the cheapest thing. What would I have done if I had seen Goering walk in? But let no one think that Mademoiselle Chanel would have spoken to him, or smiled. She did not see *them,* she declared, and I am sure that she was telling the truth. "That did something to *them,*" she told me, "when a woman who still had something left ignored *them* completely."

* A German prison camp for captured officers. Translator.

A woman who still had something left. That was truly touching. She was sixty years old when Spatz "hid" in her house in rue Cambon. No doubt it is rather an exaggeration to say that he was hiding, and yet . . . He was so afraid of being noticed, watched, sent away from Paris, where, because of Coco, he was leading the easy, comfortable life that suited him. A shirker (the usual word), an aging Don Juan, very well bred, very assiduous.

Is it so difficult to imagine the life of this strange couple during the occupation years? Coco going out of the Ritz and walking between the two sentries, who perhaps recognized her. Coco in rue Cambon. "I didn't see *them*," she repeated. *They* stood in line in front of the House of Chanel in the hope being able to buy a bottle of perfume for a *Liebchen*. And Coco with that blood-red mouth, with her saber tongue: "Idiots!" Though she did not see *them*, she knew they were there.

Spatz would be waiting for her upstairs, in her private drawing room. He would be wearing civilian clothes, and he would have a glass in his hand — champagne or whiskey. He would light a cigar. He would kiss Coco's hand. "How are you this morning?"

They spoke English to each other. "He isn't a German. His mother is English!" She discussed the news. What did she call Hitler? The word *yéyé* did not exist yet. Perhaps she called him the madman? Or the savage? Or the utter imbecile? Or perhaps *zazou*? That word was used then, in France, as *yéyé* is today, and by very nearly the same (young) people.

Spatz soothed her to the best of his ability. He knew only too well that she was not wrong when she said the *zazou* was leading Germany to catastrophe. And not only Germany — a world was going to disappear, an era was ending in the horror of mediocrity. To Spatz, as to Coco, the war was primarily that — mediocrity. Vulgarity. Nobodies at Maxim's. Spatz never set foot in the place, and not only because he was determined to be forgotten. How could one take Coco to Maxim's and ask her to sit next to *the others?* There were no cars, and the cigars were bad. And so poor Spatz pined away.

And Coco? She was sixty.

"Nature gives you the face you have when you are twenty. Life shapes the face you have at thirty. But it is up to you to earn the face you have at fifty."

She remembered having said that before the war, in the glory of her fifties, when she was the uncontested queen of Paris. She had in fact put matters more directly: at thirty a woman must choose between her face and her bottom, she had said one day, perhaps thinking back to the counsels of Emilienne d'Alençon (*the only sensible woman I met when I was twenty*).

"I've said so many stupid things," she murmured when she was reminded of the remark about the face. But she did nòt renege. "What I really said was this: a woman of fifty is responsible for her face. No one is young after fifty. But women defend themselves better than men, they are better preserved. A man can't have his hair dyed."

Of whom was she thinking? Of Spatz, her last companion?

"A man pays less attention to his dentist than a woman who can afford it does. I know a good dozen women between forty-five and fifty-five whom I consider more attractive than three-quarters of the young women who don't take proper care of themselves. They smell good and they're properly washed. Obviously they spend whole days with hairdresser and company."

How did she spend her time? How did she prepare herself for Spatz? To be sixty, in that Sahara of the occupation . . .

"What a lovely day," Spatz would say. Of what and whom did she think as they chatted in English together? Of Westminster, the richest man in the world, who neglected the orchids in his greenhouses to bend and pick the first violet "for you, darling"? The richest man in the world had placed his wealth and his name at her feet, and now . . . a German baron whom she was resigned to disguising as an Englishman.

In the depths of her soul the truth of Baron Spatz was lost among all the others — the truth of the orphanage, the truth of Moulins, the truth of Royallieu, already interred beneath the dead leaves of time. More leaves were falling on the baron, even as he leaned toward her: "Could I have some cognac?"

During the occupation she used the subway. "It didn't smell as bad as people said. The Germans, who were afraid of epidemics, had it disinfected." This was to be translated: *Thank God they took those precautions, or where would we have been?*

Why did she turn provocative when she talked about the Germans and the occupation? In her subconscious she recognized she bore a certain guilt. But let no one take it on himself to judge her! She was something of a chauvinist, and she was aware of her importance for France: of the importance of Chanel for France, I should say. In her moments of depression, when she thought of putting the key under the doormat, she would whimper: "The Americans will realize what closing the House of Chanel would mean."

During the franc crisis of 1968 she returned in shock from a visit to Switzerland. Her French francs had been refused! She was outraged: "There were people who left in May with suitcases full of currency. Someone should have said to them: 'Halt! This is your country that's at stake.' But no, they were allowed to go, and now when you arrive you're told the franc is at zero. So what can one do? Nothing but defend the country's prestige once more!"

13

The Fifth Victory: Coco, Businesswoman

*After the war, and before reopening her business, Coco Chanel
embarked on one of the hardest battles of her career. This time
the little orphan from Vichy declared war on finance. There was
an attempt to deprive her of the profits from one of her perfumes.
With the guile and stubbornness of a peasant woman and ably
backed by her lawyer, she was to wrest from the great financiers
terms of payment that would make her the best-compensated
business head in the world.*

One day in 1935 a young lawyer specializing in international
law, which was then a novelty, was anxiously awaiting his first
client. The client turned out to be a woman.

"I sat her down in this chair," he told me. "It looks old, but I
refuse to get rid of it."

The lawyer was René de Chambrun. The client was Coco
Chanel.

"I know you have just come back from the United States," she
said. De Chambrun had spent four years in an important New
York law firm. "Did you meet Pierre Wertheimer in New York?"

"No."

She looked at him suspiciously. Could it be that he did not know Pierre Wertheimer?

"He's cheating me," she said. "I need your help. You are young and you are stubborn — I know, I've been told. What's more, I need someone who can give me a great deal of time."

"I had hardly anything else," the lawyer said to me, describing the interview. His father, a five-star general and a director of the National City Bank of New York,* had just given him the vast, luxurious office in which he was advising Coco. "You'll give us bad advice," his father had grumbled at him, "and in return we'll absolve you of the rent."

Mademoiselle Chanel was consulting a lawyer because of her perfumes. She had been selling them since the First World War. By 1935 she had three labels: Bois des Isles, Chanel No. 5, and Cuir de Russie, which could be bought only in her shops in rue Cambon and Deauville (and, somewhat later, in the shops that she opened in Biarritz and Cannes).

In 1924 she had had a visit from the Wertheimer brothers, Paul and Pierre, whom she knew very well. They were intelligent, rich and aggressive. Pierre was a member of that category of society that might be called "the great mistress keepers." Undoubtedly his feelings for Coco went beyond mere admiration. Be that as it may, he and his brother, after many blandishments, suggested that they and Coco incorporate as Parfums Chanel for the promotion of the sale of her perfumes in France and throughout the world. "Because they're the best in the world!" the brothers reiterated. "And, dear Coco, you will be president of the company."

She agreed, and turned over to Parfums Chanel the rights to all the brands she had thus far marketed under the name of Chanel, as well as the chemical formulas and the manufacturing processes. She received two hundred shares worth five hundred francs each, exempt from all obligations and representing ten per

* Now the First National City Bank. Translator.

cent of the capital. She would also have ten per cent of all branches set up abroad.

One can guess that Coco began fairly soon to sense that she was being cheated, since ten years after her agreement with the Wertheimers she sent young Chambrun into battle against them. Actually, hostilities had begun some years earlier. Mademoiselle Chanel would not tolerate being used as the milk cow: ten per cent for her and the rest for the others! How could she ever have signed such an agreement? She had certainly come to regret it. In his files René de Chambrun found an amusing document — a notice of a meeting, addressed by Parfums Chanel to its president, Mademoiselle Chanel. The agenda concerned a summons. By whom had the corporation been haled into court? By its president! The notice dated from 1934 (when de Chambrun was still in the United States). The cup was by then overflowing.

The Wertheimer brothers were having the Chanel perfumes made by their own company, Bourjois. They granted sales rights to foreign subsidiaries which they created and in which Mademoiselle Chanel always had the same ten per cent. In a word, the more the business grew, the more Coco regretted ever having made the deal.

In 1939 she insisted on being released. But it took a long time to start suit, and the war intensified the conflict between her and her associates.

Before leaving France for the United States the Wertheimers sold their shares to an airplane manufacturer. It would be more accurate to say that they entrusted them to him. This "managing director" marketed the perfumes during the dark years of occupation. Some were sold in Germany. The Wertheimers, meanwhile, were selling Chanel No. 5 even in the United States Army PX's. They produced it to the best of their ability in a little plant in Hoboken, across the Hudson from New York City, and naturally their product did not follow Mademoiselle Chanel's original formulas calling for natural essences from Grasse. This activity, which was contrary to the 1924 agreement, went on after the war. And what did Coco Chanel get out of it? Ridiculous royalties on the order of five thousand dollars a year, on average, during the war. The Wertheimer brothers, who were the big majority stockholders in Parfums Chanel, had taken advantage of that fact to sell the old corporation for twenty-five hundred dollars to a new one set up in the United States: Chanel, Incorporated, New York. Coco's share was cut back to virtually nothing.

Worse still, in their advertising as in their commercial promotion, the Wertheimer brothers began linking Chanel perfumes more and more with Bourjois. Under tie-in contracts of which Coco knew nothing, merchants who wanted to sell Chanel had to buy Bourjois as well. Outside France, Chanel and Bourjois addressed joint New Year's greetings to the world in the same advertisements.

"I want my revenge," Coco finally told René de Chambrun. "It's got to be all or nothing."

In 1946, and exclusively in her shop, she offered a new perfume for sale under the name of "Mademoiselle Chanel." According to the bylaws of the original corporation, Parfums Chanel, she had the theoretical right to do so. Parfums Chanel, however, obtained an order of attachment against these new perfumes on the ground of trade-mark infringement. This was enough to crush Coco. She could do nothing but bite her nails. In the wake of the occupation, in 1946, not only was she not in the public eye, but it was still to her best interest to remain out of it. Her lawyers attempted to convince her of this, though they did not insist too much. I say lawyers in the plural because Chambrun on his own volition called in Chresteil, the president of the French bar association, to assist him.

"An amicable settlement will bring you much more than litigation will," both lawyers reiterated to their client. But she was out for blood. All or nothing! she retorted. In addition to a rather favorable public climate (they had just returned from exile in New York), the Wertheimer brothers enjoyed the advantage of a solid legal footing: the rights acquired by third parties in a corporation. Although they had departed from Coco's 1924 formulas, they had nonetheless made substantial financial contributions, they had worked on behalf of Parfums Chanel, they had built it into a big business on a world scale. Who could negate the importance of the Wertheimers' contribution to the joint undertaking? In addition, they were to contend that their associate, Mademoiselle Chanel, was *obsolete*, too old, no longer a public figure at all. In 1924 she had had talent, youth, creativeness, energy, but in 1946, when she was over sixty . . .

The suit (for the restitution of capital invested) was by no means won in advance, as Chambrun well knew. It was no pleasure for him to have to inform his client of her adversaries' line of argument.

"So I'm too old!" she raged. "They think I'm too old, those ———s!" She minced no epithets.

The case went to trial, but the decision was postponed for two months. Wasting no time, Coco launched a master stroke that would have delighted Balzac. She handed Chambrun a number of tiny phials that she took from her purse.

"Don't bother opening them," she said. "Take them home and ask Josée to smell them." Josée was Chambrun's wife. Under her breath Coco was still muttering: "So I'm too old. They'll find out."

She had made up new perfumes. "With a little still, at home. I have the right to do what I like there, don't I?"

"Absolutely," Chambrun said.

"And what I make at home I can give to Josée?"

"No law can prevent you," Chambrun agreed.

She had not got over the seizure of her new perfumes. Josée de Chambrun thought the samples were exquisite. Her husband, however, thought it best to submit them to an expert. One of his friends, who was in the top level at Coty, sent him a "nose," a Russian who having sniffed at Coco's little phials could not contain his cries of enthusiasm.

Coco dragged Chambrun to Switzerland, where a subcontracting perfumer (if I can call him that) who was working for her very quickly made up enough from her raw materials to fill a hundred bottles with Mademoiselle Chanel No. 5, Mademoiselle Chanel Bois des Isles and Mademoiselle Chanel 31 rue Cambon. The bottles were different, and they had different labels.

"Do I have the right to give these like this to my friends?" she asked. She was exultant. "So I'm old, am I?"

The friends for whom the new bottles were intended were the owners of certain large New York department stores that were very solidly entrenched in the perfume trade and in fashion. They had barely received Coco's "presents" when Chambrun saw the Wertheimer brothers arrive from America with their lawyers. The burghers of Calais in shirt sleeves, the ropes around their necks.

"What does she really want?"

It was a remarkable reversal of the situation. Having been virtually stripped naked, Mademoiselle Chanel was about to obtain — with Chambrun's help — far more than she had asked in her summons and complaint, to which her associates had responded without much show of feeling. No decision was ever handed down in the case, because everything was settled out of court. Mademoiselle Chanel received:

a. the right to make and sell Mademoiselle Chanel perfumes everywhere in the world (a right that she employed thereafter as a powerful threat);
b. substantial damages with interest, calculated on the basis of the sale of her shares in Parfums Chanel in the United States for $180,000, plus £20,000 in Great Britain, *plus* 5,000,000 1947 French francs;
c. a royalty of two per cent on all gross sales of Chanel perfumes throughout the world;
d. a kind of monopoly conceded to her in Switzerland, her fief, her kingdom.

What a masterful woman! During the negotiations between

Chambrun and the Wertheimer brothers, she kept to rue Cambon. Her lawyer would go into another room to telephone her, and then return and tell the others: "She's in Switzerland and won't be back until tomorrow."

It must be emphasized that all this took place in 1947, immediately after the war, when, let me repeat, Mademoiselle Chanel was still not *persona gratissima* in Paris, not really "cleared through Customs," as the contemporary idiom had it for those whose behavior during the occupation had given rise to doubts. If the Wertheimer brothers had wanted to do so, they could have whipped up embarrassing publicity with their suit against Coco Chanel. Was she aware of this?

The Wertheimers were good losers. Not only did they never consider challenging the new agreements; but whenever Coco returned to the fray to acquire further advantages, Pierre Wertheimer went far beyond her demands, with complete cordiality and exceptional devotion. Until her death he was the most understanding of financiers for Coco, a friend whose loyalty truly withstood every test.

Coco knew very well what she had won in these amazing negotiations over the perfumes. After the agreement had been signed, she took the Chambruns home with her to rue Cambon for a champagne dinner. "My dear Bunny," she told her lawyer, "I have already made a great deal of money in my life, but, as you know, I've also spent a lot. Now, thanks to you, I shall never have to work again."

Stretching out in her chair, she rested her feet on a well-designed little table equipped with drawers and a lamp, a very low table that she could pull up to her couch when she wanted to work, because she stored quantities of indispensable objects in the drawers. "I'm not going to need this anymore," she said, "because I'm not going to do anything anymore." She pushed it toward Josée de Chambrun. "Let me make you a present of it."

The next day she had it delivered to Madame de Chambrun. As if indeed she imagined she would never go back into harness.

But she could not have stayed idle. Recalling the years at Roy-allieu, she used to say: "No one knew how boring it was for a young girl like me." After the war the same boredom gripped her, cut off her breathing. Wait? Why wait? In 1953, when she made her decision, she was seventy years old. "One must never reveal a woman's age," Louise de Vilmorin always said. For Mademoiselle Chanel's comeback, however, the fact of being seventy was important. Indeed, it was vital.

14

The Sixth Victory: The Comeback

What was there left for Coco Chanel to conquer, unless it was life itself, by reversing the flow of a river, by forcing fashion to go back to its Chanel sources? Nothing is more difficult, and this is true in every area, than to start one's career afresh, to bring off a comeback. Coco Chanel won such a victory over time when she reopened her dress house in 1954. She was seventy-one. No one made any allowances for her. She offered no one any bribes. It was a battle that took several years.

Was it Marie-Hélène de Rothschild, the wife of Baron Guy, who was behind Coco Chanel's comeback in 1954? The Baroness thinks so.

The year before, Coco had spent several weeks in New York visiting Marie-Hélène's mother, Maggie van Zuylen, one of her closest friends. One day Marie-Hélène brought home her debutante gown. She thought it was very pretty. Coco thought it was atrocious. In a matter of hours she improvised a dazzling gown out of the red taffeta of a curtain.

"Everyone asked me who'd made it," Marie-Hélène told Coco

after the dance. To me Marie-Hélène said: "That's what made her decide to go back."

In fact, Coco Chanel had for some time been contemplating reconquering the kingdom she had abandoned in 1939. The success of the perfumes sharpened her appetite for a return to glory. She had never stopped thinking of this return since her first trip to the United States, after the Liberation, in 1947.

As the ship docked in New York Coco was locking her suitcases herself. There was much hustle and bustle on the deck. Al Brown, the well-known boxer, was on board. ("He hadn't been allowed to travel first class," Coco recalled. "Things have progressed since.") Coco thought it was Brown who was the cause of the excitement; she noticed dozens of reporters jostling one another as they attempted to board the ship.

"A cabin boy came to ask me to go to the salon," she said. "But I had no time to waste. Besides, I had no appointment with anyone. Finally the captain himself came for me. The reporters were there for me! The captain had put all the reporters into the flower shop. 'I can't hold them back,' he said to me; 'they're savages. They'll smash everything if I don't bring you back.' "

Had she been asked to dine at the captain's table during the voyage? I dared not ask her. Shortly after the Liberation there were still too many stories about Coco — both absurd and false, since they accused her of having lived with a German who was in the Gestapo.

At the train in Paris and at the pier in Cherbourg there had not been one reporter who wanted to interview Coco. In New York there was a crowd. She learned again that she was a major planet. It was a remarkable moment for her. Under suspicion in her own country, she was welcomed in triumph to America.

The captain was tugging at her arm. "Come with me, come."

"But, Captain, I have to finish with my luggage."

"I'll send someone to take care of it for you, mademoiselle."

All her powers had been restored. She had the domestic staff of the French Line at her disposition. Once more she was Coco Chanel *la Grande Mademoiselle*. What a victory.

Above, in the flower shop, the "savages" began by asking her what she thought of Dior's "new look." She said: "I had taken along two suits from my last prewar collection. I was wearing one of them. I said: 'You've had a look at me.'

"They laughed. They understood! 'If you want to know what I think of the "new look," just look at me.' They asked whether I wouldn't make dresses again. I said: 'I have no idea. I closed the house of Chanel because of the war. I've come to New York because of my perfumes, nothing else.'

" 'Where should one use perfume?' a young woman asked.

" 'Wherever one wants to be kissed,' I said.

"Those American reporters are children. I saw this answer printed everywhere. It was a bore; but I think it earned me the friendship of the American reporters: I'd told them something that made everyone laugh."

It must be pointed out that by the time she attempted her comeback in 1954 the press as a whole was poised for attack. She had made no attempt to manage her return without disturbance. She behaved like a boxer who had once held the championship in every class and now was putting on his gloves again with considerable boasting: "If there were any real boxers left, I wouldn't come out of retirement, but unfortunately the manly art has been degraded by fakers whom I find myself obliged to discipline as they deserve."

In essence that was what Mademoiselle Chanel repeated whenever she was asked about her plans, and naturally such remarks did not calm the emotions aroused by her comeback. She was upsetting. She was irritating. What did she want? It was assumed that she was incapable of competition, discredited by her age and also (though no one dared to say it too loudly) by the rumors that had been spread about her behavior during the occupation.

She was getting ready to launch "atomic ready-to-wear," some said; others said that she would bring out "something unprecedented." And there was one very menacing rumor: there was not a model whom she wanted to hire.

Again one must emphasize her age: seventy. "Never mind building, but *planting* at that age . . ." What could she plant at the age of seventy? Nothing more nor less than the Chanel myth.

Suppose that she had not reopened in rue Cambon, that she had not returned to her place at the summit of high fashion, that she had been prevented from recapturing it . . . that *the others* had succeeded in blocking her way. Who would remember her? Like other dressmakers, such as Poiret, she would be known by the specialists. She would leave silhouettes in the catalogues. But not "the Chanel," which is at once a suit and a style, and which circumstances may turn into a way of life.

Was she aware what was at stake for her in this comeback? In the beginning, perhaps, she was merely yielding to an impulse to throw off her boredom. When rest wears you out at seventy, what else is left except work? Love? Pleasures? Pleasure? I can still hear her bewailing a rumor about her that had to do with her supposed feelings about one of her models: "Imagine — me, now! An old lesbian! It's unbelievable how people dream up these things."

It was shattering, and I can only repeat her complaint as she expressed it, in all its nakedness. One touches depths that allow no trifling with words. She said too: "Love? For whom? An old man? How horrible. A young man? How shameful. If such a terrible thing happened to me, I'd flee, I'd hide."

Why, indeed, should she have disguised her past if, letting herself drift into the comforts of an old lady's retirement, she had renounced her future? Her comeback was the recompense for all the sacrifices that she had accepted, all the renunciations that Coco had made in favor of Chanel.

When Mademoiselle Chanel reopened her house in 1954, something marvelous was coming to an end: the Liberation, a period that was probably unique in the life of a rich capitalist country. For almost ten years money had had no importance. Tainted by the occupation, money was in hiding, as a hurt bear keeps to the depths of its cave and licks its wounds. After the Liberation of Paris, newspapers and fashion houses were established on hope and prayer. Plays were put on without backers or producers. A reporter with an expense account could mistake himself for a Rothschild. It was a time of miracles — existentialism born in the basement of the Tabou,* scribblers scrambling up the bases of statues to bellow oratorios of words without meaning to audiences of spellbound loafers, and plainclothes policemen trying to understand. Everyone met in St.-Germain-des-Prés. In the Flore, the Montana, the Bar Vert and the Tabou the *Life* correspondents could find everyone of any interest or unusualness who had emerged from the night of occupation. It was there that I made my first acquaintance with the dress industry, through a friendship with Pierre Balmain, who used to dress up as a cowboy and dance to the rhythms of Boris Vian,† and with Jacques Fath, who was showing Paris to young Americans. The old salons were still dozing in the aroma of mothballs. When the Faths had me to dinner in their château in Corbeville, their Vietnamese chauffeur doubled as butler. In the house itself there was nothing in the drawers and not a bottle in the cellar. The hens on their model farm laid only when stimulated by Geneviève Fath's storming rages.

None of these mirages of liberty was left in 1954 when Mademoiselle Chanel went back to rue Cambon. She did not launch her venture *on nothing*, to paraphrase the French generals who were at that time bogged down in Indochina.

She could take nothing for granted. But "in spite of the depression that is raging in high fashion," the *New York Herald Tribune* said of Mademoiselle Chanel, "she should be able to

---

* A café frequented by the intellectuals who fostered the existentialist movement. Translator.
† A novelist, poet and jazz enthusiast who died young. Translator.

take her old position. According to her, there are still three thousand women in the world who want to be dressed by Chanel."

The *Tribune* had stated the position badly: it was precisely
this crisis in high fashion that gave Mademoiselle Chanel her
chance. After the other war, the one called the Great, she had
pushed Poiret off his pedestal by dressing those same several
thousand women mentioned by the Paris edition of the American
newspaper. In order to overcome Dior, the same privileged persons' new favorite, she was going to "Chanellize" the world. Was
she aware of this? Did she have any intuition of what was going
on? In a word, of the industrialization of fashion?

There was already a dress industry in the United States, with
its headquarters in New York's Seventh Avenue. The dress industry was analogous to the old Ford car. Like Detroit in 1920, Seventh Avenue in 1954 was mass-producing usable things, which
did clothe (as old Ford's cars did run). But what of elegance?
The equivalent of coachwork? This was what Mademoiselle
Chanel was going to perfect. She was going to issue letters of
nobility to the mass production of the suit. That, though she did
not know it, was why she was settling back into her old routine
in rue Cambon.

When one reflects on it . . . Sometimes a bicyclist reckons
that with so many million turns of his pedals he has traveled the
equivalent of a thousand circumnavigations of the earth. Or a
flier finds that if he puts end to end the miles he has flown, they
would amount to a complete journey around the cosmos with
stops at Venus and Saturn. Or, again, a swimmer, who under
training from a California coach has done the crawl as far as the
Cape of Good Hope and beyond. How many steps Mademoiselle
Chanel must have taken between her "house" and her home!

I should like to have been in her shoes that day when she went
from her home in the Ritz to the House of Chanel for her comeback. It was 5 February 1954, six months before her seventy-first
birthday. She had chosen the fifth because of her perfume. What
was she going to show? "She finds the present fashion too com-

plicated," *le Figaro* said; "she has her eye on the simple, the ultrasimple; she moves with her time."

She was in her drawing room with its lions, its crystals, its wild boar dropped from the skies, in her setting of lacquer and gold, among the flowers that came to her by the armload. And with shadows and phantoms.

"We were all rather moved," *l'Aurore* said. "It was a whole past, virtually an epoch that we had been invited to watch coming back to life after fourteen years of silence. One felt somehow as if one were entering the palace of the Sleeping Beauty."

Mademoiselle Chanel, backstage, was listening to every sound from outside. "Who's there?"

"Everyone," she was told. What will the names of "everyone," as listed in the next day's newspapers, mean today? Mapie de Toulouse-Lautrec, Maurice van Moppès, Boris Kochno, Comtesse Pastré, Sophie (soon to be if not already) Litvak,* Carmel Snow, editor in chief of *Harper's Bazaar* and fashion dictator for the United States. The wife of the President of France did not attend (though Madame Pompidou, years later, did go to Coco's posthumous collection).

A religious hush spread as the first model appeared on the stage, wearing "a black coat-suit, the skirt of which was neither tight nor loose, with a little white blouse," as *l'Aurore* described it. "It was followed by other suits in rather dull wools, in a wan black, matched joylessly with melancholy prints. The models had the figure of 1930 — no breasts, no waist, no hips. The dresses gathered at the waist, with their full sleeves and their round low necks, offered nothing but a fugitive reminder of a time that it is difficult to specify — perhaps 1929–1930. What everyone had come for was the atmosphere of the old collections that used to set Paris agog. But none of that is left — nothing but

---

* Comtesse Mapie (Marie-Pierre) de Toulouse-Lautrec, a member of the same family as the painter, was a society woman who became a journalist, writing about food for *Elle*, a women's magazine. Maurice van Moppès, a painter, has since died. Comtesse Pastré was a society figure. Sophie, who modeled for Fath, married the American film director Anatole Litvak. Translator.

models parading through a room that cannot make up its mind to applaud. A rather sad retrospective, like all retrospectives."

Marcel Boussac* was already financially involved in *l'Aurore*, and he was backing Dior. Does this suggest that the *Aurore* reporter had his mind made up in advance? Not in the least: he was voicing an almost universal reaction.

AT COCO CHANEL'S IN PODUNK IN 1930, *Combat's* headline read. Its very Parisian fashion columnist was Lucien François, whose authoritativeness was conceded by everyone. He was not pleasant to see; and one saw him everywhere. He was dreaded, rather like an oracle. His account, a regular anthology piece, must be quoted:

> The cream of Paris, blended with the finest flowers of the buyers, rubbed elbows on the mirrored staircase that leads from the Chanel shop in rue Cambon to the huge salon through which the world's most privileged ladies paraded in 1925. Nothing there had changed — not the well-known calamander screen nor the interplay of the mirrors. As Ruggieri the Florentine traced the future for Marie de Médici in mirror arrangements, would we see the future of elegance etched in these, that for fifteen years had been blind? Such was the question in the minds of Madame Lopez-Williams, Comtesse Pastré and Mapie de Toulouse-Lautrec, all old customers of Chanel who had been invited to her sensational comeback. Sensational, unquestionably . . . The fact that this tireless, haughty, despotic little woman, who had left her mark on an era and then cast off her glories for a decade and a half, was going back into harness at the age of seventy was already sensational enough. But disenchanted lips have been heard to utter cruel rumors bound to arouse a perverse curiosity. Even as usually well-informed sources whispered that she was reopening her house in order to further the publicity for her perfumes, Chanel was busily denying this, saying that it was only her revulsion at the bad taste of today's Paris dressmakers that had impelled her to emerge from her pleasant retirement. And the eagle eyes of this Cassandra, made new by plastic surgery, were sparkling . . .
>
> We would see!
>
> We did see — some quite badly, though they had every reason to

---

* Boussac was a textile magnate — in cotton — and the owner of a large racing stable, who also dabbled in newspapers. Translator.

see otherwise. Others saw very well, though it would have been better had they not seen so clearly. The first were the observers sent by the world's greatest newspapers and scattered at random in the crowd. The others were the buyers from abroad, who had bought the collection as a whole sight unseen, purely because of the promise implicit in the label it bore . . .

The reporters went back to their offices in a deep sadness, and the buyers returned to their stores in severe anxiety. With the very first dress it was clear that the Chanel style belonged to a time that was gone. Fashion has progressed in fifteen years. New fabrics and unforeseen inventions called for new techniques that have changed the habits of the eye. At the same time, Chanel was entrenching herself in the legend idealized by her memory, idealized so effectively that it had been forgotten that even in 1938 her vogue had been dealt its deathblow.

What is there to say of those swatches of lace inserted in other swatches of mousseline? What is there to say of those deflated shirtwaist dresses spattered with contrasting bias panels that no one would wear any more even in Podunk? . . . Not even 1938 clothes! They were ghosts of 1930 things.

Mademoiselle Chanel is not worried by the fact that life is difficult for those who dress the living. But how can it help being even more cruel to those who dress only the dead?

Paris society turned out yesterday to devour the liontamer. She remained invisible. In her games of the future we saw not the future but a disappointing reflection of the past, into which a pretentious little black figure was disappearing with giant steps.

It is impossible, as one transcribes this prose, not to raise questions in one's mind about journalism and its practitioners. This Lucien François was widely read. He was the nephew of the writer t'Serstevens.* Everyone toadied to him. Dress designers gave him the best seats at their showings. His opinions were feared. In a book that he published in 1961 he paid tribute to Mademoiselle Chanel: no one contributed as much as she to the renown of Paris, he admitted. He added that she had shown her

* Albert t'Serstevens, a poet born in 1886, was also the author of a number of forgotten novels and of a treatise on the peoples of the Greek Archipelago. Translator.

talent by baring her talons. His opinion had not gone up, however. Here are samples: "Demanding very steep prices for her little cardigans and her daringly austere jersey sheaths, she subjugated the whole world to the snobbery of the poor look . . . At that time (1925) she was an enchanting person, dark and imperious, with her half-savage charm, her stubborn child's forehead and eyebrows belied by her doelike eyes, so much so that she had the look of who knows what sexless urchin. . . ."

Recalling the comeback that he had so brilliantly described seven years earlier, he now characterized it as a historic event and her as a "seventy-year-old child prodigy." He sent a copy of the book to Coco with a flowery inscription. She said she threw it out without opening it; but it may be supposed that she looked through the part that dealt with her.

Simone Baron drew up a balance sheet in *Paris-Presse:* the collection consisted of one hundred thirty creations, she said, ranging from the very simple little jersey suit to the white lace gown with dual colors, white and red, red and black, all worn by beautiful models. In a feature story in the same newspaper another reporter recalled that Bernard Grasset, the book publisher, had nicknamed Coco *la Grande Mademoiselle.* "She is still a character," the woman reporter wrote.

L'Aurore plucked the daisy. "You will like the schoolgirl coats *a little,* the wreaths of artificial flowers on the mousseline dresses *a lot,* the evening suits in gold-trimmed brocade *madly,* and the 1925 pleated collars *not at all.*"

The English reporters evidenced scarcely better judgment. CHANEL DRESS SHOW A FIASCO, the *Daily Express* headlined; its story said that as people came out of the House of Chanel after the show they dared not look at one another, bewildered as they were by the spectacle that they had just seen and wondering sorrowfully: "Is it possible? Did we really see what we saw? Why was that poor Chanel so determined to display that stuff?"

To the London *Daily Mail* it was a FLOP.

After the showing Coco was at home to no one. Nor had her

exhausted-gypsy profile been seen in the staircase mirrors during the collection. "Mademoiselle is tired," her staff said, turning back the curious who tried to throng into her apartment to see in her face the work of humiliation and defeat.

It is at such times that one fully recognizes the ferocity of Paris. Was Coco Chanel loved during her first reign, between the two wars? When she came back she had virtually everyone against her. There were sniggers: "What did the old woman expect, then?" There were some circles in the dress industry that called her that regularly: "the old woman." "Doesn't she have money enough for a comfortable retirement?" "Why does she come back to bother us?" "She has nothing left to say!" "What does she know about the young?"

She heard all that, she divined that she was being laughed at, regarded as "out of it." She said:

"My dear, I was overcome when I heard them talk about the young. This is the worst possible thing, this is decadence. When one begins to talk about youth, one has lost it. Being young is a question of health, of the time, of the moment. When I'm not bored, when I'm with someone who understands me, why should I worry whether I look young? To hell with that! I'm not at all young anymore, but why that should keep me from feeling happy with someone who doesn't bore me?"

Then came that gem that I quoted earlier: "Youth is something very new. Who talked about it twenty years ago?"

When did she first recognize that she was no longer young? In 1939, she said. Actually, she was speaking of the war:

"It hadn't occurred to me yet that I could grow old. I'd always been among bright, pleasant people, friends. And all at once I found myself alone, separated from everyone I liked. Everyone I liked was on the other side of the ocean. And around me there were people of an abominable cynicism who talked of nothing but that — youth. I had no choice but to accept the reality: I was no longer young."

Once again, in one of her monologues, she was juxtaposing

two occasions in her life: this time, very clearly, the closing and the reopening of the House of Chanel. The cynics-with-their-mouths-full-of-youth were the enemies of her comeback, who laughed at her defeat, while, behind locked doors, she was suffering the first test of loneliness.

Actually, she was not completely alone in her gloomy drawing room. A few close friends — Hervé and Gérard Mille and Maggie van Zuylen — were there to congratulate her on the victories yet to come. She did not want to listen to them that day. Destiny was handing her her little black orphanage apron again. The ironic laughter of Paris awakened the echoes of Etienne Balsan's resounding laugh. And, too, in this very room a shadow still hid behind the calamander screens — the shadow of Spatz. The occupation was not so far in the past. She was coming face to face with everything that she would have to *sweep away* in order to resume her place at the top, to make the world forget her age, her money, her past successes, her hibernation during the dark occupation years.

Completely in control outwardly, in spite of her setback, she explained at first to her friends: "My name doesn't mean anything to the young." As for the *old* customers, they were afraid it would date them to go back to rue Cambon. Both explanations would have been sufficient to defeat anyone other than Mademoiselle Chanel. Could she admit a failure that would allow *the others* to take over the battlefield?

Between the start of the war and Coco's return, homosexuality had acquired a kind of official status — if indeed it had not become institutionalized. It was no longer concealed; it was flaunted, particularly in fashion. To Coco this was one more reason for her to join the battle.

"Everyone to his own work," she said. "I spend afternoons in dressing rooms with almost-naked women. Can a man do a job like that? Fiddling with dresses, working for women? I'm naïve enough to think it's impossible. Those who do it aren't men."

Nevertheless, the male designers who were in the spotlight seemed not at all prepared to yield their eminence to Mademoiselle Chanel.

It may be supposed that before the war she had felt no particular affection for those designers sufficiently talented to compete with the House of Chanel; but nonetheless she had accepted them as a reality. She considered it normal then, to combat recognized, admitted adversaries. But now, when she was making her comeback! She felt surrounded by usurpers. It was rather as if one had asked Raimu,* at the height of his glory, to appear in a screen test with aspiring actors.

She said: "Someone came to see me, a gentleman, to ask my advice. He was no longer sure whether he still loved his wife and children or whether he ought to start life over with a young man. People like that I throw out of the house. They talk to you about their complexes. I'm allergic to complexes. All these new words. No one had complexes *before*. They were called vices. I'd rather have people with vices than people with complexes. There've always been people like that, who have to have remarkable complications in order to do the simplest things. Now they're talked about all the time. And that's called sickness now! How can one cure people who don't know whether they love men or women?"

Complexes and homosexuality made her angry because they were connected with the problems of her comeback. Yet the substance of her complaints against the modern fashion trade was restricted to its technical side. Men do not know how a woman moves, she believed. One of her models, showing a man's designs, had told the dresser: "I can't raise my arms."

"The dress isn't made for that," she was told.

"A dress made right should allow one to walk, to dance, even to ride horseback!" Coco protested vehemently. She told a story: "The other day I put on a lady's jacket made by a man. One sleeve hung down to here. I had no more shoulders, I had no

* A gifted French film actor. Translator.

more anything — I'd dissolved, they had to look for me, it was impossible to see me. From the back I looked like a starving beggar. Everyone died laughing."

Success was to come to her from the United States, as it did for Roger Vadim and Brigitte Bardot — for this was also the time of *And God Created Woman*. The comparison would appall her. But it makes it possible to mark a postwar milestone: already it was not enough to dazzle Paris, the blessing of New York was required. The fashion trade would not concede this. "Those men take themselves very seriously," Coco said sarcastically. "They think they're irreplaceable."

In six months America was Chanel-ized. The buyers for whom everyone had felt sorry because they had had blind faith in the Chanel label were smoking bigger cigars than Darryl Zanuck's. "Finally you've come back," Charlie Chaplin said to his friend Coco. "Now I can copy your style again for my actresses' clothes, as I did in *City Lights*, because it doesn't go out of date." First *Vogue* and *Harper's Bazaar*, then *Life*, with a four-page spread, hailed the new reign of *la Grande Mademoiselle*:

"The woman who hides behind the best-known perfume in the world, No. 5, may have made her comeback a little too soon, but already she is influencing everything. At seventy-one she is bringing in more than a style — a revolution."

This appraisal was published after the third Chanel collection. In one year she had won by a knockout in the third round.

But not without anxiety. Not without having felt the cold breath of defeat (as will appear from an unpublished document that will be discussed presently). None of which prevented her from explaining:

"I am logical and I do logical things. People must be dressed. They're offered absurdities, grotesque diversions in which one can neither walk nor run. The American women rejected them before the French did because the Americans are more practical. That's why America went for Chanel right away. Life in America isn't amusing, but it's practical. People live outside the cities; they go to the country every evening. They leave their cars on the outskirts of the cities. Everyone walks, everyone runs — it's a different life. American women like change. They're clean — they wash properly. This is what makes New York, a repulsively dirty city, look prosperous. Real luxury to me means having well-made clothes and being able to wear a suit for five years because it still looks good. I adore old suits, things that have been used. In America things are thrown away. Nothing is solid. Nothing is washed or sent to the cleaner. I sent a dress out to be cleaned over there, and all that was left of it was a button. That's America: the opposite of luxury. *Cheap.* [She used the English word.] I find it horrible."

It was this America, however, this cheap America that put over the Chanel style — first of all because the style lent itself to the machines for the mass cutting of suits and also because this mass-produced suit could be raised to the level of nobility by the Chanel legend born of the perfumes, especially of No. 5.

There is the story of the interview with Marilyn Monroe, in her day the glory of Hollywood:

"What do you wear in the morning?"

"A sweater and skirt."

"And in the afternoon?"

"Another sweater, another skirt."

"What about the evening?"

"The same, but in silk."

"And at night?"

"Five drops of Chanel No. 5."

(The story is well known. What is not so well known is that it drove the manufacturers of pajamas and nightgowns to despair. They prevailed on the actress, by way of reparation, to make the imprint of her lips on a white tissue, which they copied on thousands of miles of fabric converted into night wear for both men and women.)

No one had a better grasp of the commercial value of her legend than Mademoiselle Chanel herself. Miss Monroe could not have mentioned any other perfume without being accused of a deal with its maker; but she could mention Chanel No. 5 as she would have revealed a secret for attracting men, or the potency of a love potion. One could never be a poor girl if one were clean, wore a Chanel suit and used No. 5. Coco was deeply convinced that with her combination of style and perfume she had contributed something very new, and not merely to a couple of thousand fortunate women.

Chanel-ization went more slowly in France. By choice or otherwise, Coco remained aloof from the Parisian merry-go-round. Everyone went to Corbeville for square dancing at the Faths', and the gossip writers concentrated on the two Christians, Dior and Bérard. It must be pointed out that the Parisian fashion writers, hatched out of the egg of the Liberation, still knew nothing but what they were part of — the skin, or, more precisely, the outer scab, so that they were ignorant of the real taste of the fruit or the suppurations of the sore.

"What a time," Coco sighed. Then she corrected herself: "I have no right to criticize it, because it isn't mine. Mine is over. I judge this period with eyes that are not the eyes of the people who live in it. I should say heart rather than eyes. Frequently I feel so alien to everything around me. What do people live for now? I don't understand them; I'm behind, I'm a leftover. My mind no longer keeps up with the times."

And where did this realization lead her? To this brilliant conclusion: "I'm very well aware that everyone is out of date." Her long, arduous French comeback gave her pleasure but did not satisfy her:

"I brought off something when I recaptured my place at the top. Now the working people know me. When I go to the flea market everyone says *bonjour* to me. People come up and kiss me. I let them — it doesn't cost anything and it gives pleasure, as Picasso says."

Had she heard the shot whistle past her head after her first collection? While she had never doubted she would succeed, she had nevertheless thought in terms of a different comeback, one on a more commercial level. On 30 September 1953 she had asked René de Chambrun to deliver a letter in New York to her friend Carmel Snow, the editor in chief of *Harper's Bazaar:*

My dear Carmel,

During the summer I came to the conclusion that it would be amusing to return to my work, which is my whole life. Surely I've told you that one day or another I'd start to work on creating a new style, adapted to a new way of living, and that I was waiting for the right moment. I have the feeling that that moment has come.

The highly paradoxical atmosphere of Paris today, when more and more women go to see the collections without having the means to buy the clothes, leads me to do something totally different.

One of my main objectives is naturally mass sales through some manufacturer in the United States, on a basis of compensation through royalties. Nor have I any doubt that what I do will have a tremendous appeal throughout the whole world.

My first collection will be ready on 1 November. I think it would not be wise to go farther until I have received an offer from the top wholesale manufacturer* you can recommend. The best thing for him would probably be to come to Paris. Nothing, naturally, would please me more than to have you here at the same time. For the present I have no plans to present the collection myself in America, but that might be done later.

As ever,†
GABRIELLE CHANEL

This plan, which was carried fairly far, fed the rumor that for her comeback Mademoiselle Chanel would launch "atomic ready-to-wear." She was to do so by means of copies. To her the project had the advantage of worrying Pierre Wertheimer. As profitable as the new agreement with him was, it still did not

---

* "Top wholesale manufacturer" was in English in the original letter. Translator.

† "As ever" also in English in the original letter. Translator.

give Coco complete satisfaction. With an American manufacturer she could have introduced her Mademoiselle Chanel perfumes at the same time as her mass-produced suits. She had the
right to do so.

It is easy to guess how she exploited this new situation to her
own advantage. Wertheimer had agreed to finance her comeback
in rue Cambon. At the start Coco criticized him for not providing sufficient money; but when he heard rumors of the merchan-
dising device she had in mind, he at once became very generous.
Coco prevailed on him to have the perfume corporation pay all
her expenses, including her servants and her taxes. No one in the
world had ever obtained such terms. Furthermore, she arranged
for renegotiation of the privileges granted to her under the 1947
agreement, gaining a substantial compensation for giving up the
manufacture of the series of Mademoiselle Chanel perfumes.
Later, in the same fashion and against hard dollars, she surren-
dered her Swiss fief, where her perfumes — those of the original
series — were sold for her exclusive benefit.

Did these financial victories gained at the expense of Pierre
Wertheimer wipe out the grievances of the past? Wertheimer
wanted a formal reconciliation, a public exchange of kisses at the
races, for example, or Coco's acceptance of an invitation for a
cruise aboard his yacht. At the end of a full life this was one of
his dreams; the other was a Derby victory. And now his horse
Vimy won at Epsom Downs — unexpectedly and so all the more
gloriously. He had an appointment the next day with Coco in rue
Cambon for a kind of privy council at which René de Chambrun
would also be present.

When Wertheimer arrived, the doorman announced "Monsieur Pierre" to Mademoiselle. He went quickly up the stairs, undoubtedly rather faster than he would have liked, but he knew a
stopwatch was being held on him. If he had taken his time, Coco
would have said: "Aren't you well?"

Of course she knew that he had just won at Epsom. In fact, she
had supposed that the celebration of such a famous victory

would have detained him in London. She hastily hid the newspapers with the story of the race.

"You don't look well at all," she greeted Wertheimer.

He went pale. Then he held out his arms. "Aren't you going to kiss me?"

"Why should I?"

"The Derby! Didn't you know? I won the Derby!"

"And you didn't even telephone?" Coco scolded.

She was not easy, *la Grande Mademoiselle,* and, to everyone whom she dominated, she was uncompromising.

She was proud that she had Chanel-ized the woman in the street.

15

Coco's Jewelry: "Fortunes Worth Nothing"

"What haven't I done in my life!" she remarked. "I've even put out a newspaper." For varying reasons, of course, she attached more importance to certain of her creations: to her perfumes, which brought her money and independence; to her jewelry, which made it possible for her, mingling the real and the fake, to toy with her life in a sense, manipulating the play of light on the real and the imaginary — and thus proving that the synthetic can be confused with the genuine.

She said: "I don't care a damn for jewels. They don't bring anything in life. They don't add to the joy of living. As a rule women care a great deal about them, and no one gives them any. I had no interest in them, and I was given so many. I always had to say: 'No, thank you, I have enough jewelry. What do you want me to do with it?'"

She said: "I'm covered with chokers, necklaces, brooches, earrings, stones of every color, so many that no one understands me when I say I don't like jewels. What I don't like is a stone for the stone's own sake, the headlight diamond, the eye-gouger that stands as an identification, an outward sign of wealth for the husband or the lover of the woman wearing it. Nor do I like jewelry for jewelry's sake — the diamond clip, the quote-string-of-pearls-unquote that one takes out of the safe for evening display, that one puts back in the safe after dinner and that probably belongs to a corporation. That's all jewelry-to-be-sold-in-case-of-emergency. Jewelry for the rich. I don't like it."

She said: "If there is jewelry, there must be a lot. If it's real, that's showy and in bad taste. The jewelry I make is fake and very beautiful. Even more beautiful than the real thing."

She said: "Jewelry characterizes a period. I'd like mine to be characterized by Chanel jewelry. It will be! I'm thinking of all those women who because of Chanel jewelry wear fortunes that aren't worth anything. I asked one of my models whether she had any idea what the things around her neck would be worth if they were real, and she said: 'No idea, mademoiselle.'

" 'Six or seven million francs,' I told her. They were emeralds, *larger than life*. When one makes fake jewelry one always makes it bigger. The necklace was worth perhaps twenty thousand francs."

She said: "Do you know what jewelers call gold jewelry with diamonds? War jewelry! Gold, gold, and stones that are mounted and that glitter . . . ! One's afraid to breathe on them, they might blow away."

She said: "A jewel is an ornament. Those that I make are very pretty. Some are so beautiful that I'm dazzled by them myself. They become sumptuous, absolutely Byzantine. Why does everything I make become Byzantine?"

She said: "If I took off all my jewelry, how would that change me?"

She said: "I don't become attached to a jewel any more than to a house. When I give up a house, I've gone for good. But this little ring is my talisman. I was born in August. My talisman is gold and topaz."

She said: "In the street one should wear only fakes. One wears real jewelry at home, for one's own enjoyment, now and then."

To make her jewelry she settled herself in her living room. Sitting on the edge of the couch, she fiddled with a ball of plastic that looked like chewing gum. In front of her, on the very low Chinese table, were boxes and little bowls filled with stones of all sizes and shapes, which she stuck at random into the "chewing gum" that she had flattened on the table. She used both real and paste stones, concerned only with the effect that they would create in a whole. She had some magnificent emeralds and some very beautiful, very rare rubies, but she was just as fond of the pink Thai rubies and the light Ceylonese sapphires, which are not worth very much, and of topazes. "There's nothing prettier than a topaz," she said; "it's golden water."

The Duke of Westminster gave her a creation in emeralds surrounded by diamonds: ring, earrings, bracelet, choker — and, in matching jewel cases, two identical bracelets of Indian emeralds, pigeon's-blood rubies and Kashmiri sapphires. She tried them on: "On me they look ridiculous." She closed the cases: "I'll have to have the whole business taken out of the setting." She did, and the stones were commingled with those that already filled the boxes and the little bowls and with which she played when she was creating her jewelry.

She would very much have liked to pay another visit to the Schatzkammer (treasure chamber) in Munich, where she had admired the jewelry of the Renaissance and Byzantium, particularly the Byzantine crosses encrusted with heavy stones. As she described them she recalled another journey, to Ravenna, with a visit to the mausoleum of Galla Placidia, Empress of the West.

She said: "I made false pearls in order not to have to wear my own. I was told I looked pretty with them. I said to myself, All women ought to be able to wear them to improve their looks. I looked, and I found the people who could manufacture them in bulk. I've always found the people I was looking for."

She said: "I've made fortunes with pearls and fortunes with jewels. I'd have millions if I'd put it all away."

(So she also had a sense of humor.)

16

"The French Don't Like Me"

Honors? Coco refused them. Correction: she refused all distinctions which had been bestowed on others before her. "They want to put me on the same little hill with everyone else," she said. Did she mean that she did not expect from her country or its representatives the official recognition that (in her view) was her due? If she hoped for this victory as well, she never made any effort to win it.

At the time of Mademoiselle Chanel's comeback the high-fashion houses lived in great fear of being copied. In the same (touching) fashion, for the sake of keeping wheezing myths alive, there is a great pretense of fearing spies who steal the secrets of military systems that have no further reasons for being. In all fairness, it must be admitted that at this time a few operators were still able to get outrageous prices for a smuggled Jacques Fath collar, a Balmain cuff or a Dior hemline, thus enabling other operators to market counterfeits even before the designers' own customers could be taken care of. How many copies did this amount to? Pitifully few, of no importance to anyone, when one considers how much is required to supply mass industries whose equipment is not set up overnight. What purpose would be served by stealing a secret that could not be exploited until the whole world knew about it?

And so the fashion spies disappeared. In business one must adjust oneself to the facts. It costs too much to deny them. After all, one cannot maintain a spy force simply to prove that fashion continues to exist, unless one is a minister of defense and exempt from the laws of economics.

Mademoiselle Chanel had long since joined the High Fashion Association, at the request of its president at the time, Madeleine Vionnet. The organization functioned, Chanel ironically explained, "for the protection of seasonal trades. Address me with deference; I belong to the seasonal trades." Nevertheless, she had been pleased at the time by Madame Vionnet's invitation. Coco was not beloved of the fashion world. She said:

"The dressmakers didn't take me seriously, and they were right. I knew nothing about the business. In the beginning, I had my milliners making my dresses; I didn't know that specialized workers existed. But this was just as well, because I learned everything for myself: I had to know because I had to explain things to my milliners. Besides, it isn't all that complicated. Fashion is like architecture; primarily a question of proportions. The most difficult thing to create is a well-proportioned dress for all women, a dress that five different women could wear without anyone's seeing right away that it's the same thing."

She said also: "Fashion is a business, not an art. We don't work from genius; we're tradespeople. We don't hang our dresses in galleries to be seen; we sell them. If mine are copied, so much the better. Ideas are made to be communicated."

There were occasions, however, when she complained bitterly of what she called piracy, especially by women's magazines offering their readers Chanels to be copied to their hearts' content. Doing her shopping one Sunday morning, Coco's associate Lilou Grumbach heard someone shouting: "Come and get your little Chanels, only fifty francs! Don't push, ladies, there's enough for everybody!" The story delighted Mademoiselle Chanel, who commented: "They were going like fresh vegetables — and in fact fresh vegetables were being sold next door."

Lilou brought back one of the little fifty-franc Chanels, in white, coarse linen, with a braided border, a kind of plait effect that gave Mademoiselle Chanel the idea of using raffia. "The street interests me more than the drawing room," she would say on such occasions.

She said: "French fashion existed when it was copied in France, for Frenchwomen. A few people created it, and it was copied in copy houses. One day, with his eye on the Legion of Honor, some gentleman decided to change all that, and so a trade association was founded to protect the interests of (they should forgive the expression!) the miserable French dressmakers. Some did their job well and made money, even if they didn't pile up fortunes."

In the perspective of time, what I find striking in this speech is the reference to the desire for the Legion of Honor in the gentleman who, etc. In those shadows in which Coco concealed herself, the slightest glimmer casts light on the unexpected. Did she crave honors? Yes and no. The cross and the red ribbon did not interest her. Before the war, Paul Reynaud, who was a Cabinet minister and later Premier, offered her the Legion of Honor. Unfortunately it was already being worn by others, particularly Madame Paquin. Still, Coco could not have been made a commander to start, like some ambassador or foreign statesman.

Recalling the beginnings of her fame, she said: "I lived among English people, who don't pay one compliments, who aren't always telling you you're ravishing and a genius. One doesn't talk about those things. It's a kind of spell cast on my life: the English, whom I like, and the Americans, whom I like less, like me. The French don't like me, and there's nothing to be done."

The two disclosures were related. She talked about the "gentleman" who in order to win the Legion of Honor set up a trade association counter to the real interests of Frenchwomen (they could no longer benefit by the fashion created for them); and she wound up with an unappreciated Chanel who had genius but who was not to be talked about because the French (certain French) did not like her. One must recognize the connection that existed in her mind — she could not receive justice in France — and that angered her.

In the midst of another declaration, made on another occasion and dealing with Brigitte Bardot, I caught this sigh: "To think that *that* represents France abroad!"

I also heard her recall, with uncharacteristic intensity, a dinner at the Elysée Palace: "There I was at the table of the President of France! In the President's palace one is not at home. Even if he's one of your friends, he's the President. The servants are there . . ."

She who was always so sure of herself! One could see her being suppliant, too, begging for friendship, for company. But was it conceivable that she hungered and thirsted after honors? Yet were they not the one thing that she could share with the love of her life, the House of Chanel? She wanted to be a monument. Who would attend the unveiling, the consecration? Photographers came to take pictures of the chairs on which she sat. She said: "I've become an object."

Sometimes little dressmakers would write to her: "We can't afford to buy your things, mademoiselle. Would you allow us to come to a showing so that we could see the collection?"

She invited some, when she was in the mood. She also admitted a group of nuns who were teaching dressmaking to girls in a provincial trade school. (Were they orphans?) Coco's models bowed perfunctorily to the nuns; Coco said: "I was thinking of the little girls who would come out of school wearing Chanels." What a mystery, the mystery in which she wrapped herself!

She broke with the High Fashion Association in 1957:

Dear Mr. President:

I have the honor to submit to you, as president of the High Fashion Association of Paris, a resignation that you desire but that, out of a courtesy for which I thank you, you hesitate to request of me.

This will resolve the conflict that has existed between your association and myself.

The "conflict" had arisen out of the liberties that she had taken with a rule stipulating that members of the association must allow photographs of their creations to be made and published only at dates set by the association. The break did not really inconvenience Mademoiselle Chanel very much. In actuality, it established her in her regal solitude. No one could speak of dress designers with more contempt than she. When she condescended to recognize any talent — a crumb! — in one or another couturier, it was always in relation to herself: he had had the intelligence to copy her.

"Perhaps I am cheating myself of a great pleasure by not associating with those people [the male designers]," she said ironically. "After all, I might be able to give them some advice!"

On the table in front of her there was a package, only half opened, from one of those people: his new perfume. She said:

"What is this supposed to be, when a gentleman like that sends me a bottle in a thingamajig all tied up in atrocious ribbons and giving off an ungodly smell that will never disappear? It really clings! If one wears that, one will be spotted a mile off — a stink of old, rotten fruit that gives one a headache. How can I reply to this gentleman? If I send him a bottle of Chanel perfume, it means: 'Here, smell this and see what real perfume is.' I can't do that, though! I'll just forget about it." By way of conclusion: "I couldn't find the right way to handle those people."

She had not looked very hard for it, or very long. Occasionally she felt some affection for Balenciaga. During a dinner she remarked that he had called her three or four times in a few days. "If he phones again," she said, laughing, "it will certainly be to ask me to marry him!"

"How old is he?"

"It isn't worth the effort of figuring it up!"

She did not rank the dress designers of her comeback period on the same level with those of her early days; occasionally she spoke of the latter with some feeling, rather like a man recalling the people he had known in the army. "I started the fashion of making dressmakers fashionable," she said. "Before I came along they weren't noticed at all. No one spoke to Jacques Doucet,* who was a remarkable man and a real lover of the arts — one visit to the Doucet Museum is proof of that. He never enjoyed the slightest social standing."

Was the credit for this advance hers? Many things changed between 1914 and 1919 that seem quite trivial today. She attached to society the importance that a believing Catholic of her time would have ascribed to heaven and hell. To be in or not to be in!

"I never ran after society people," she said. It was true in a sense: she could no longer have endured being *snubbed* as she had been at Royallieu. That was why she never went, so to speak, *to the other people's houses*. "There was a social custom that one did not entertain one's tradespeople."

She repeated this with two stories that, she said, had given her a great deal to think about. By mistake, the great jeweler Cartier, instead of the Belgian ambassador, Baron Cartier de Marchienne, had been invited to a party at Maurice de Rothschild's. When the jeweler and his wife were announced, Rothschild bluntly told them, with that boorishness that all his friends agreed was characteristic of him, that there had been a mistake and he did not entertain his tradespeople. "Of course," he added, "if you would like to see the various rooms with their paintings and furniture . . ." The Cartiers walked out. Obviously, Coco said.

---

* In addition to his eminence in his field, Doucet was known also for his fine collection of eighteenth-century paintings, which he broke up and sold in order to collect van Gogh, Cézanne and Manet. He was a pioneer in the publication of superb art books. Translator.

Another Rothschild, Baron Henri's wife, asked Coco to stop in and see "heaps of old-fashioned jewelry. Come and tell me what to do: what I can do with it." The baroness had contributed to the reputation of the House of Chanel when it was starting out. So Coco went and examined the jewelry spread out on a velvet pad in the baroness' boudoir. A tall man in a frock coat was shown in — Cartier, the jeweler, whom Coco was meeting for the first time. He was treated like a servant — "an obviously superior servant," Coco observed.

What is remarkable is the fact that she did battle to the end of her life to defend a "superior equality" that no one any longer denied her, or, one might say, that no one denies her even now. She never managed to get out of her black orphanage apron. A girl of her talent, of her genius? She was of a hyper-middle-class era, a rigid time in which genius was still not enough, especially for a woman. Money, however, became a patent of high birth; but the newer it was, the more there had to be. This explains why Coco never gave up working for it until she died. Even as she was reiterating that she had no need of it, she never left a penny of her change on the counter.

One might say she never was present at any of her customers' fittings, except for some special friends. On the other hand, she always supervised those of such actresses as Ingrid Bergman, Jeanne Moreau, Delphine Seyrig or Romy Schneider; they were the greatest, and she refused to take their money: "I am not going to be paid by women before whom I kneel when a skirt hem has to be taken up."

And then, when she had got home, she would massage her knees: "What weariness! I thought I'd drop. How those people bore me."

She greeted Brigitte Bardot with seeming warmth, but it didn't take. The actress wanted a dress for a party in Belgium for which Coco was to receive a fee. She wanted to appear in a black mousseline de soie like Delphine Seyrig's in *Last Year at Marienbad*.

"They're expecting you there like a sunburst, and you want to arrive in mourning?" Coco asked.

"You can use me for your publicity," Bardot replied.

"I feel sorry for her," Coco sighed when she talked of the actress in the mid-1960's. "She can't go out anymore, she can't even go to a restaurant for lunch. She wears wigs and glasses so she won't be recognized." And, virtually paraphrasing the Scriptures (. . . woe to the man by whom the temptation comes!*), she added: "When one gets involved in a scandalous business like hers . . ."

To what extent was she titillated by the "Bardot scandal" because in her unconscious it reminded her of the "Coco scandal" which she refused consciously to remember? She advised Bardot to employ in her thirties the most effective device for sex appeal: modesty.

Coco accepted being named Companion of Jean Nicot † for outstanding services rendered to the tobacco industry. She showed me her medal, not without pride but a little uneasy because she had sent her managing director to accept it for her. "I ought to have made the effort," she said; "there were ministers there."

It is supposed that she also accepted the Fashion Oscar awarded by Stanley Marcus of Dallas. However, there was no possibility of her accepting the Fashion Oscar, because it had already been awarded to Christian Dior and Hélène Lazareff in previous years. In fact, it was for the fiftieth anniversary of the Neiman-Marcus stores that she agreed to go to Dallas in September 1957. It was a journey which both amused and annoyed her. She said:

"I didn't know Mr. Marcus's tricks. He had instructed all his *buyers*‡ to gather at his house. The big attraction was *Mademoi-*

* Matt. 18:7. Translator.
† A French diplomat, born in Nîmes (1530–1600), who introduced tobacco into France and gave his name to nicotine. Translator.
‡ She used the English word. Translator.

selle Chanel will be there. The buyers are those people who come to buy for stores. I must have shaken thousands of hands. They were all alike — so many sheep."

How did Stanley Marcus prevail on Coco to visit his home? In the spring of 1957 Marcus was lunching with Mademoiselle Chanel at the Château de Lagrange, which René de Chambrun (Marcus's lawyer as well as hers) had turned into a museum of French-American friendship dedicated to Lafayette, Washington and all the other heroes of the American Revolution. In one of the rooms there hung, among other banners of the same period, one in silk announcing a production of Shakespeare's *Hamlet* starring England's great tragic actor Macready. Above his name, and even above Shakespeare's name, the banner said in huge capitals:

GENERAL LAFAYETTE WILL ATTEND

"If you want to get Mademoiselle Chanel to Dallas," Chambrun whispered to Marcus, "you must show her this banner and tell her . . ."

"Right!" Marcus said.

He led Coco to look at the banner. "That's how I'm going to announce our fiftieth anniversary:

MADEMOISELLE CHANEL WILL ATTEND."

"I'll come," Coco said.

A real surprise was prepared for her for an evening party given in Marcus's gardens. A pair of unlikely newlyweds suddenly appeared in the converging beams of a number of spotlights: a very young bull stuffed into evening clothes and wearing a top hat between his horns, and an equally young heifer in a white Chanel with a long veil. Coco burst into laughter. She said:

"And all in a hellish heat. The bedrooms were glacial. I caught cold immediately from the air conditioning. It was so thoroughly

complicated that it was impossible to turn it off. I had five television sets. I used the one in the bathroom. They showed movies
and commercials, and one never knew which was which because
the commercials were just like the movies. It's confusing. And
horrible."

She would have liked to meet "that fellow who reads the
Bible" — Billy Graham, presently second only to President
Nixon on the list of men best known to Americans. A director of
the American company, Chanel Incorporated, tried to take her to
one of Graham's revivals, but she had to give it up because of the
blocked traffic all around, Coco said; she was much impressed.
Of Graham she said:

"He's a very intelligent person: he lives in his time and he
helps people to understand it. He tells them: 'Look at me, I'm
smiling, I have good teeth, I've had them worked on to give me a
beautiful smile because you can't teach people anything if you're
homely.' He plays golf for the same reason: 'See, I'm up to date:
I'm not an old fogy just because I talk to you about the Bible.'"
She looked at me: "Why are you laughing?"

On the subject of the Dallas trip, she sighed: "No one will ever
get me to be a star again."

17

Coco's Solitude

She did not like her models, with some rare exceptions. Did she see something of herself in her daily confrontations with them? One more reason to be alone.

She said: "A model is like a watch. The watch tells the time. The model should *tell* the dress that one puts on her."

It was interesting to watch her with her girls, and to listen to her talk about them, for surely she was seeing herself again at their age. "They are beautiful," she murmured; "that's why they can get these jobs. If they were intelligent they'd give them up." Her life, her choice — in two sentences.

Sometimes she grumbled: "That kind is greedy. All they think of is money. They don't care a single damn about you. They come here looking like housemaids on a day off and they leave looking like scrubwomen."

At other times she allowed herself a certain benevolence: "All the same, I think they have a little core of admiration for me — that's their nice side. They lie in wait for my old suits. The more worn the suits are, the more pleased the girls seem to be to get them. Ten times Marie-Hélène said to me: 'You won't sell this suit, mademoiselle; I'd so much like to have it.' And ten times I've had to tell her: 'I can't give it to you, Marie-Hélène; I have no other.'"

For a few years, around 1960, her showroom seemed to have been staffed from the *Almanach de Gotha*. She addressed them all with the familiar *tu* — Mimi, Comtesse d'Arcangues; the princesses; the most serene highnesses like Odile de Croy. She said:

"They're bored. Their mothers and grandmothers had a different occupation: love. The men in their circle didn't work. Those men were always available for love, like Bernstein's* heroes. But what man today could indulge in such absorbing passions? So these girls phone one another to exchange stupidities: 'Shall we go to work for Chanel? Some of the crowd will be there, and besides there are the clothes.'"

Coco added: "They come to see a collection, and then they stay, and it isn't always for love."

Love . . . *it isn't always for love*: one had to hear her say that, the woman who had always been able to put off a lover because her house had precedence.

She was interested in her girls' sentimental entanglements, though she would pretend annoyance with them. A beautiful Spaniard became involved in a complicated affair with a married man ("Well, that was all right") who had no money ("The girl was out of her mind!"). "What would you do if he left you, you fool?"

"Go into a convent, mademoiselle."

A convent, when one is twenty and lovely? That had never entered Coco's mind in Moulins. In the persons of her models she relived Moulins and Compiègne. These girls had the same assets that she had had. They used them badly. They did nothing with them. The idiots wanted happiness, they loved, they wanted to be loved. Deep inside Coco something protested: "Not that!"

* Henri Bernstein (1876–1953), a succesful Parisian author of innumerable drawing-room dramas. Translator.

Surely one must be mad to put happiness ahead of money? Forgive me, correction: ahead of independence? To go on being poor, a prisoner, a slave of happiness when one had that capital to invest: beauty? Happiness or the convent? What fuzzy thinking. "Take rich lovers," she told her models. Oh, she did not press the point too much: she did not like them all. By giving them a prod along the path that she had chosen for herself, she was *wiping out her guilt. Every beautiful girl has done, is doing or will do what I did.* Having prodded them, however, she set herself apart from these lovely girls. *As for me, I went on to something else, I did better; none of them will ever bring off what I've brought off. So!* . . . So she, Coco, had not done quite what she was encouraging her models to do. The poor things, that was the only thing they could do — at best, put themselves on the block for money. She said:

"Women have no ambition anymore. They want to have money. That's not the same thing! The ambition to learn something . . . that doesn't interest them, except the American women, who ask you questions all the time: 'What do you think of this painter?' 'Nothing.' 'Tell me whether you like him.' 'To hell with him.' 'What writers do you like?'

"If they'd only shut up! There's no end to it with an American: she wants to learn; it's painful but it's touching. That's why they still manage to marry Europeans, who enjoy educating them. But even that is dying out. Frenchmen are becoming like Americans — all they care about is their clothes; they go to places where they'll be seen. That's the way the times make them. Why do women stand for all that?

" 'We live together like pals,' a girl told me.

" 'And that's all right with you, to spend your life with a pal?'

"What a sorry existence! This is the end of many things. Women get slapped, and they take it. I would have cried like a baby if anyone had talked to me the way boys talk to girls today.

"And it's always the women who *initiate!* Why run after the men? Why not let them come? Women are going crazy. Men live off them. The women work, the women pay! It makes you almost die laughing. Women are becoming monsters. They want to be men. What miserable men! The girls are victims. And they complain . . . they turn themselves inside out, they stamp their feet, they slam doors. They don't know anymore what it is to be loved. They're with boys who care more about the crease in their trouser legs than they do about their girls. I wouldn't have let such guys shine my shoes. They aren't even capable of making fools of themselves for a woman.

"The women are heading for disaster. Work, work hard, always on the run, have no children because that holds you back in life, chase after money with the idea of doing everything better than the men . . . Soon they'll be asked to do everything because they are stronger than men. The Chinese know this very well. And the Russians! Have you noticed what they're doing? [The first woman cosmonaut had just gone into orbit around the earth.] They've tossed a woman up there, the Russians have. Women can take anything. Imagine a man having a child! He'd never recover from it. A man's an invalid when he has a cold in the head."

Did she recognize that she bore a large share of the responsibility for the change in the status of women? Not at all. To her, her own case seemed not typical but unique. What could those poor things hope for who lifted their eyes to her?

"Do you know any? Any women who aren't chasing after jobs?" she asked me. This was the period of spike heels, and she heard the echo of them in her head. "They come home dog-tired, and they have to make dinner — and those imbecile women think they're happier than their mothers." Conclusion: "The queen bee today is the man."

There were times when, like everyone else, she wondered: Was I right in choosing independence? The House of Chanel? Was it so wise not to become a woman? For she knew she was not one, she had never been one.

Never did she conclude the showing of a collection with a

bridal gown. Perhaps because this was customary with all her competitors and she refused to imitate them: but more probably because she had placed marriage outside her law.

She was the bride of her house, which sometimes seemed empty to her, particularly toward the end of her life, when she was burrowing farther into her loneliness and delivering monologues to the butler who took away the plates from which she had eaten nothing. Once she could not restrain a sigh: "Life with a companion is still better than solitude. How frightening it is to be alone!"

By way of convincing herself that she had not made a mistake in her choice, she threw herself into the job of breaking up the couples of her acquaintance who were still together. Among the infinite reproaches she showered on her closest collaborator, Lilou Grumbach, with whom she quarreled incessantly but without whom she was lost, one thing came up constantly, with increasing acerbity: why had Lilou and her husband adopted two children? Unconsciously Coco felt this to be an insult. A lasting marriage, children . . . everything that she had not had and professed to despise.

André Pallasse, her nephew, was the father of two daughters by his first wife, a beautiful Dutch woman. The elder girl was named for her great-aunt Gabrielle; Coco nicknamed her Tiny and made her her confidante, her friend; it was Tiny to whom she gave her discarded dresses. Married to the painter Labrunie, Tiny was the happy mother of two children whom Coco adored even though she grumbled: "I said to Tiny: 'Dear, you'll bring your children to show me when they're clean, when they can walk, because you know how I am about nursing and burping and drooling . . .'" She continued: "I saw them when they were three and two — two real little gentlemen with short hair and American pants, no nonsense at all, and I really enjoyed it."

All such remarks, to which no one offered any particular reaction, would obviously have been much more moving if those who heard them had known that Coco had done everything possible to have a child herself by the Duke of Westminster. Perhaps even by someone else?

She could hardly have been expected to admit openly that she had wasted her life because she had been unable to keep any companion with her to combat her loneliness, or that at times she missed companionship. She said: "Men are not *strong*, as people suppose. Women are smarter and more resourceful; they can take anything. They're capable of meanness, too; and even of kindness at times. Men are much more ingenuous than women, and more vulnerable."

I ought to have questioned her further on this subject — men. But she would not have answered my questions.

"I'm going to have an optimistic collection," she said one evening. "People are uneasy and worried. I'm having things done with flowers; I'm using everything I can find that's as gay and amusing as possible. Unfortunately not everyone in the house cooperates with me. I work in the middle of poor discipline and with tired models. The way people answer me! I never would have thought the day would come when I'd tolerate that, being spoken to in that tone. But I take it, with a patience I didn't know I possessed. I don't like living with bad discipline. Ever since I began working, no one has ever gone over my head."

She was concerned over a quarrel with Marie-Hélène Arnaud, who was very beautiful, a reincarnation of the lovely Davelli, whose face was still associated with Coco's first successes. "They were destroying her when I began to take an interest in her," Coco said, alluding to Marie-Hélène's early days as a cover girl. "Magazines use you and spit you out. So I was a good angel for her. I became rather attached to her."

Coco must have learned the art of understatement from the English; in fact, she could not do without Marie-Hélène. It was quite natural for people to begin to suppose that Coco thought of the girl as her successor. Marie-Hélène's father was made a director of the House of Chanel. Among the Wertheimers, at the top level of Parfums Chanel, thought had to be given to the succession. This was in 1960 and 1961, when Coco was close to eighty.

"Marie-Hélène has had it with being a model," Coco said one evening. "I understand her. But she may be wrong." She had said it all in two sentences: *So that kid thinks she can take my place. Wishing doesn't make one Chanel.* Now that one of her models for once was displaying the ambition that Coco demanded of beauty, Coco viewed it as defiance.

"My daughter is capable of better things than she's doing," Arnaud said to Coco.

"I am Mademoiselle Chanel," Coco growled, "and when I see lights on in the toilets I open the door to see whether they've been flushed, and I don't feel that that's beneath me."

If Coco had needed Marie-Hélène for the House of Chanel, she would have given in. But what did the girl contribute to the house? Everything she had she got from it. "She's invited everywhere to please me," Coco said.

Her quarrel with Marie-Hélène Arnaud, a trivial thing in itself, acquires importance as an insight into Mademoiselle Chanel to the extent to which it shows the defense processes that went into action when Coco thought her rule was threatened.

She was perpetually on trial before her own tribunal — not for conviction and sentence but for self-justification (which nonetheless implied a certain condemnation). When she went into her monologues she was speaking for the prosecutor, for the defense attorney and for the presiding judge.

What could the prosecutor adduce against the charming Marie-Hélène? Before going off on a winter sports vacation, Marie-Hélène had bent over Coco and said: "What are you going to do without me, mademoiselle?"

The crime was lèse-majesté: *Do you suppose, my poor darling, that you are so important that your absence can handicap Mademoiselle Chanel? She'll get along without you very nicely.*

The prosecuting Chanel continued the interrogation: "What do *they* think? That I exist through *her*?"

"They" were the two Arnauds, father and daughter, who lusted after her throne (Coco thought), and "she" was the bait, the indispensable Marie-Hélène.

"That kind of nonsense doesn't work with me," Coco muttered. "Marie-Hélène wasn't important enough in my life for her departure to mean a disaster."

Whereupon she turned over the floor to the defending Chanel — not to defend Marie-Hélène but to defend herself. For the break with Marie-Hélène was painful to her, and she forced it on herself for the sake of the house.

"I taught her a great many things," the defense pleaded. "It worried me when she had to go back to her parents' house at the other end of Neuilly late at night. 'Move into my house in rue Cambon,' I told her. 'And it bothers me that you eat alone, too, in your little restaurant; that doesn't seem like any fun at all. Come to me; I'm always alone, or lunching with friends who'd be happy to see you.'

"I like to teach people," the defense emphasized. "I love explaining things. I don't get impatient when people don't understand right away. I'd make a good teacher. Furthermore, Marie-Hélène used to listen, to be interested when I talked. I think she felt a bit of affection for me."

Judge Chanel interrupted: "For some time, because people had been working on her, she'd been very undependable, and just before the collection."

Just before the collection! Here, clearly, was her guilt, and there were no extenuating circumstances. Just when she was needed.

The prosecutor took advantage of the judge's annoyance to renew the attack: "She said to me: 'Mademoiselle, I'd really like to have dinner with you tonight but I'll have to leave right afterward because I want to go out.'" Did the poor thing think, then, that Mademoiselle Chanel needed her?

"I told her: 'My dear, certainly you mustn't come simply to

please me. I invited you so you wouldn't be bored. Actually I'd rather you didn't come, because I could go back to the hotel and have dinner in bed. I'd eat porridge; it's the only thing I like.' "

She was trying to convince herself that she had been right in breaking off with Marie-Hélène; but she could not succeed — any more than she could approve her behavior toward other friends whom also she had unjustly turned away. She did it each time because she could reign only in a certain loneliness, without standards of comparison. The importance that she ascribed to herself required the perspective of the void. But the void chilled her.

No one must threaten the House of Chanel: it was to her what his bone is to a bulldog. Nor was she capable of accepting anything from anyone. To convince herself that she was not alone in the world, she demanded that others be dependent on her. "If Marie-Hélène doesn't want to model anymore, we'll find someone else. Everyone can always be replaced." Everyone except Mademoiselle Chanel.

She had already found Marie-Hélène's successor: "A seventeen-year-old kid, and anyone can see she's a walking vitamin capsule. She's so happy to be working for Chanel that she smiles all the time, and that makes people laugh. People had made too much of the other one [Marie-Hélène], in large part to please me. This one in a year will put all the others in the shade. Right now she's still dying of shyness. She didn't know how to walk. She wiggled her behind and pulled in her belly. 'Walk as if you were dancing,' I told her; 'you don't pull in your belly when you're dancing.' I'll show her how to walk."

Coco paraded as if she were showing the suit that she was wearing with black boots.

"I've already transformed her. She makes the gestures she ought to make. I'm the one who teaches the girls all that. And I tell them: 'Above all, be gay!' American women are marvelous: they smile all the time. In New York I heard a young woman radio announcer tell of a poliomyelitis epidemic with a smile that showed every tooth in her head. They have good dentists over there."

She was still on her feet. "I'd be as tired as everyone else if I let my feet do all the work. I support myself with my pelvis — that's all the trick there is to it. I'll teach that to the kid. If I do it, she can do it too."

After her "blue-blood" period, when her showroom payroll read like the *Almanach de Gotha,* Coco went over to the Germans. "I like those tall German girls so much," she said, "because they walk well naturally. First they thrust their thighs forward, like animals; the calves and the feet follow. The French and the English girls do the opposite: they put their feet out first, and that's ungraceful."

After one showing of a collection, she invited me into the dressing room, where champagne was being drunk — mournfully, for things were not going well. "Dresses must not be presented like the Holy Sacrament," Coco grumbled. And she got up, glass in her hand, to give a demonstration to her half-undressed models. None of them was fascinated at all: they were completely indifferent.

Her egocentricity made her exaggerate her conflicts with her models and certain rebellions, probably justified, by her other employes.

"Everything went well, though," she said, "because I worked twice as hard. I said to myself: 'If those people have things on their minds, too bad, don't you get into them — you have your collection to finish. Don't let anger carry you away. Have patience.' I'm a bee. That's part of my sign: the lion, the sun. Women born under this sign are faithful, brave and very hardworking. They don't allow themselves to be upset easily. That's my character. I'm a bee born under the sign of the lion."

18

Coco the Musical-Comedy Heroine

Some great men can stroll in streets that bear their names. Others can contemplate their own statues. Coco Chanel could have heard her fabulous life described in song on a Broadway stage — though not her real life. Had she managed to forget what disturbed her? Having learned too late what it was, I could never ask her.

One can imagine the welcome that she would have received in New York if she had agreed to appear at the opening of *Coco*, the musical comedy based on her life.

The idea took shape at the Mille brothers' table in rue de Varenne, a major seat of the international Paris society that was part of the post-Liberation world. That street did not yet belong to the Premier of France; it belonged to the brothers Hervé and Gérard Mille,* through whose home passed everyone who had

---

* For thirty years Hervé Mille was the Richelieu of Jean Prouvost, the French press lord and wool magnate: before the war Prouvost owned *Paris-Soir;* his present properties include *Paris-Match*, a picture magazine; *Marie-Claire, le Figaro* and *Télé Sept Jours* (the French equivalent of *TV Guide*), and he owns a large interest in Radio Luxembourg. Both Mille brothers

talent, reputation, money, everyone who was of any importance, lasting or otherwise, to the newspapers. Theirs was not a *salon* in the sense in which Proust used the word, but in it he would have found a remarkable wealth of characters recognizable not only by the initiate but by everyone; for they included Brigitte Bardot, Marlon Brando, Jean Cocteau, Peter Brook, Juliette Gréco, Marie Bell,* Jean Genêt, Simone Berriau,† all the Italian princes, and a number of politicians, among whom I will mention only Jacques Chaban-Delmas, who was to be Premier of France. In those days Hervé Mille was a kind of gray eminence of the press without whom it was impossible to set up an editorial board.

Between the Mille brothers' rue de Varenne after the Liberation and Coco's rue Cambon after World War I there was no lack of bases for comparison. First of all was the atmosphere created by the physical settings. Gérard Mille, the great decorator, made no secret of his debt to his beloved Coco. The calamander screens; the interplay of mirrors that gave the rooms a magic dimension; the pickled wood of the old chairs; the use, in the magic area created by the mirrors, of objects previously regarded as unsuited to interiors, such as large Chinese vases, Venetian statues of blacks, or even life-size deer — all this, which had been consecrated in rue Cambon, was to be found again in rue de Varenne.

How many press, political, film, musical, theatrical, literary careers began in rue de Varenne? To say nothing of the loves and friendships that were born there. Vadim made it his headquarters when he did not have a penny: that was where he took Brigitte Bardot to dinner, and reassured her parents when they tele-

---

were close friends of Coco; they are leading figures in Paris society. Translator.

   * Marie Bell was the greatest tragic actress in the Comédie Française; she created roles in many of Paul Claudel's plays and was a unique Phèdre. She also introduced Félicien Marceau's *La Bonne soupe*. She is now the director of the Théâtre du Gymnase. Translator.

   † Simone Berriau, who directs the Théâtre Antoine, staged a number of Tennessee Williams's plays in Paris. She was formerly a singer. Translator.

phoned: "Yes, yes, your daughter is here, and we'll send her home to you about midnight." Gérard Mille could be heard choking on his anger when he found that he had no dinner jacket for the evening, even though he owned a half dozen: that same evening Christian Marquand and several friends had to go to a dress rehearsal in black tie, and they had emptied the clothes closet. And Annabel, not yet Buffet, arranged the flowers in the vases.*

Coco felt at home in rue de Varenne. It was there that she met Frederick Brisson, the film producer, who was determined to make her his property in all her forms: autobiography, play or musical comedy, and then a film as the crowning piece. She wanted nothing to do with a book or an autobiographical film. People would have plumbed into the past and uncovered "her truth" that she had so laboriously entombed.

But why not a musical comedy, which by its very nature derives ultimately from fantasy? The theme could be embroidered, and if the musical comedy became a film later, it could be like *My Fair Lady* — an imaginary, almost fairy-tale transposition.

An agreement was made for a musical comedy. Brisson was thinking of his wife for the title part — in which there was nothing surprising: why would stars marry producers if not to prolong their youth? The wife in question was Rosalind Russell, whom Coco considered vulgar. "A big horse," she said. Since she did not keep her opinions to herself, this soon appeared in the American press. Rosalind Russell had already decided against the part, because she felt that there was no affinity between herself and Mademoiselle Chanel. Since, however, she had been in on it at the start, if not at the actual origin of the project, a trace of her connection remained in the program credits. The plot was based on Coco's comeback in 1954, because her age at that time — supposedly in the lower fifties — suited Rosalind Russell.

---

* Marquand became a film director in Hollywood. Annabel, daughter of a rich and aristocratic Jewish family, was an early notable among the existentialists. She married the painter Bernard Buffet. Translator.

Coco would have preferred to have it built around her start in 1913, when, a poor little innocent, she went for the first time to dine at Maxim's. She envisaged herself played by Audrey Hepburn at Deauville, Armenonville, the races, with *cocottes'* gowns and officers' uniforms around her, among rare veteran and vintage automobiles. What she got, however, was an inspired Katharine Hepburn, in whom she no longer recognized herself.

Alan Jay Lerner, the writer of the script, stuck to the theme of a libretto conceived for Rosalind Russell. "Coco," he explained, "is a woman who has sacrificed everything for her independence and who, having gained it, pays the exorbitant price of loneliness for it." It was not a bad insight.

"That is the theme of a tragedy," Hervé Mille observed.

"So it will be a musical tragedy," Lerner laughed.

He began work in 1965 — it had taken almost ten years to persuade Coco and to negotiate with René de Chambrun for the rights that she wanted to retain. Soon it was the spring of 1966, and Brisson arrived in Paris with Lerner and the composer, Andre Previn. They established themselves at the Meurice and invited Coco to a run-through of the musical, Lerner singing all the songs while Previn accompanied him at the piano.

What went on in Coco's mind? Here was a highly schematized review of her life, all in innocent images — but nonetheless they must have recalled many things to her. As a start, she saw her father bending over her cradle and trying to find a nickname for her, ending up with Coco. Whereupon the grandmother repeated the name, announcing in song that she would achieve fame and fortune but would be forever alone.

Alone. Coco's face was flooded with tears. Few people have seen her weep.

She did not go to the opening of the musical. The show added to her celebrity and was useful to her house, but in the depth of her heart she did not approve of it. Furthermore, two things angered her exceedingly.

The first had to do with the libretto. As Lerner had seen the story, after the failure of the first collection in her comeback, Coco had been saved by the talent of an American dress designer who not only put new youth into her creations but also brought her customers from the United States. It would have been enough to give her a stroke if she had had to sit still for that in front of the enchanted Broadway audience.

The second (and secondary) reason for her absence had to do with the costumes designed by Cecil Beaton: more than a hundred "Chanel-type" dresses of which she sometimes spoke with irritation:

"American women I don't know come up to me in the Ritz: 'Are you Mademoiselle Chanel? We saw the musical comedy. Why didn't you do the clothes yourself? At least we would have had something to look at.' "

She summarized the libretto in her own way: "*I* don't do very much — *I* just sit there and everything marches past *me*. They come and sing *me* the songs that *I* liked."

She was planning to launch a new perfume with the musical and thought of calling it, like the musical, Coco. She said: "I made it twenty years ago and I just came on it again." She held her handkerchief under my nose: "What do you think of it?"

"It's refreshing."

"And clinging!" she said. "They don't make perfumes like this anymore. This perfume is mine. Why should I give it to *them?*"

She estimated her profits on a new perfume that would sell as well as No. 5 and for her exclusive enrichment. In the last years of her life the idea that others might make something out of her work became intolerable to her. "I'm exploited, I've been turned into an object," she grumbled. She refused to sign contracts that were brought to her and she made an issue over everything — the musical comedy and other matters. She was suddenly suspicious of everyone; even of her trainer, who suggested buying a half ownership in her stable. Why? Surely he had some idea in the back of his head!

"I see it coming," she said. "I sent a mare to England to be bred. She had two colts, one of which must be very beautiful because I've already had an offer for it. Why should I let my trainer have half?"

"He'd win you the Grand Prix."

"He didn't pay anything toward sending the mare to England; she went twice, and it cost me a million francs each time, or rather two million, because I had to pay in sterling.

"I've learned to be cautious. I have to defend myself, all by myself. And life today is so hard! When I see what young people are all wrapped up in today. If I'd been born into this age I think I'd kill myself. No, I don't think so, because I am reasonable. If I'd been born into this age, I'd be different. But the frivolity of it all! In my day one was young but one wasn't frivolous."

Why go to New York? She said: "Traveling is so complicated. There are so many people everywhere. I make my best journeys on my couch."

No one will ever get me to be a star again. In rue Cambon she was the empress of solitude.

19

A Plot Against Coco

*What is a plot against a throne? While ostensibly no one chal-
lenged Coco's sovereignty over her house, secretly her overthrow
was in preparation. The fashion industry was going mad over the
yéyé fad. Because she totally rejected it, the others wanted to get
rid of her. The press never mentioned this conspiracy against
Coco Chanel; and she forced it to an abortive end.*

When Lilou Grumbach was asked precisely what her duties
under Mademoiselle Chanel were, she would reply with a laugh
that she would be delighted if someone would tell her. No one
spent more time with Coco during the last six or seven years of
her life than did Lilou. I knew her through her brother, Christian Marquand, a friend of Vadim and one of the notables in the
existentialist group at the Tabou. I had assisted Marquand in
getting a start in the theater under the iron discipline of Michel
de Ré in a play that I had in part financed.

In theory Lilou Grumbach's job in the House of Chanel was to
handle press and public relations, though always under Coco's
supervision. What this meant was that she did not do very much,

except always be at hand. She had to be there to listen to Coco, to lunch with her, to walk her back to the Ritz in the evening, to fetch her in the morning. Coco could not manage without her. And yet she was constantly firing her.

"This is the end," Coco would say. "I don't want any more novices around me. Work is serious. No one knows how to work anymore. The important thing in the House of Chanel is work."

Lilou herself could not count how many times she had been fired and how many times she had been rehired.

One afternoon in 1968, the winter collection was being shown to some twenty customers when Lilou was stupefied at the sight of a painter, in full working clothes, on the mirrored staircase. He was calmly going up the steps, with a paint bucket in one hand and brushes in the other. What was he doing there?

While Lilou was wondering, the painter went on through the drawing room, brushing against an astonished model, and then headed for the wall in the back and literally vanished, as if he had walked through it.

In fact, a door had just been cut through to make a direct connection with the next building, in which the officers of Parfums Chanel and Parfums Bourjois were establishing a young dressmaker. It was no longer a question of providing for Mademoiselle's successor: it was a matter of short-circuiting her.

This crisis could have been foreseen. From a business point of view, Chanel was still solid. Almost everywhere in the world, women who had money were faithful to the Chanel style. But "We are turning down fewer orders than usual," Coco did concede.

Always the art of understatement. Her workrooms were busy. If one wanted to amuse oneself by pointing out the number of Chanels in the Ritz or the George V in relation to dresses by other couturiers, the figure would not have led a reasonable investor to sell short. Chanel, I repeat, was holding its own; but nevertheless other things were rising in the market. Chanel no longer reigned alone in the world of fashion — a world always famished for newness.

For years Coco had seen nothing but Chanels when she dined out. Now there were fewer. A hostess who had invited Coco would have her maid shorten her old Chanel. But still Coco would have to smile and shake the proffered hand, even as she sighed to herself: "If I had knees like her I wouldn't show them."

She was suffering. No one knew better than she how to tell which way the wind was blowing. It was no longer blowing her way.

But this! To find by sheer chance that your friends, your associates, the people whose fortunes you thought you'd made, not only had lost confidence in you but, worse, were working against you, and in secret.

Coco led me through the hole made in the wall to show me not the underground chambers that soldiers hollow under the enemy's supposedly impregnable trenches but something very nearly the same: a huge workroom with little tables for sewing machines, glassed-in cubicles for the supervisors, an office for the "foreman" hired to take her place in order to supply mini-skirted Chanels to everyone who wanted them. "They've been sweet-talking me for some time now, trying to get me out," she murmured. "They don't realize what a catastrophe that would be. I employ four hundred persons. If I closed, it would be like shutting down an automobile factory." In her mind Renault and Citroën were still the handcrafters' workshops from which the first cars had come.

I looked at her: she was shrinking before my eyes. The iron curtain of age was closing over her face: all that was left of her was her eyes. There were times when I endured her only despite annoyance, if not irritation. So much insensitivity, so much ego-centricity; the chokers, the heavy jewelry, the rings on her thin fingers, the Chanel accessories; the monologues, the Chanel jargon, with the opinions, the judgments without appeal; her armored, insect, pinching side. But that day she was completely calm, seemingly untouched by the blow that was being struck against her; she pulled her glasses down to the end of her nose for still another examination of the work that had been done to bring down Fortress Chanel.

This story has never been told, though it would have made big headlines in many newspapers, and not only in Paris. Is it hard to imagine what Coco felt in her heart? What went on in her mind? They wanted to steal her house, her child! *The only thing I've ever made myself.*

"It's like a detective story," she mumbled.

In reality she was living an episode from Pierre Decourcelle's story *Les Deux Gosses* — the abduction of Fanfan, whom Ramon de Montlaur turned over to the heartless burglar so that the wretch could turn that little angel of aristocracy into a pariah like himself.

She felt real pain, and I understood her all the better because I had suffered the same torments. I too had been deprived of a child that had then been corrupted — a newspaper. It had not belonged to me as the House of Chanel belonged to Coco; and on the other hand she had more defenses than I. These differences did not stop me from suffering with her and for her. After she had won so many battles, could she lose the last?

She had three more years to live — six collections to prove that she was again — as always — right, that she retained her title as champion of the world. They wanted to retire her, to carry on for her, in her name, pitiable harassing operations, whereas she envisaged total victory. She shrugged, and with a smile almost indistinguishable from a grimace, she said: "Let's get to work."

Indomitable, the English say; and that is undoubtedly more appropriate for Mademoiselle Chanel than its French cognate, *indomptable,* unconquerable, for in the English word there is an added element of nobility.

I had had nothing to do with *Marie-Claire* for some years by now. These had been difficult years for Coco Chanel: reversing the traditional pattern of flowing down from the dressmakers' salons *to* the street, fashion now was rising *from* the street (including one called Carnaby) to the salons. None of this kept me from seeing Coco more and more frequently. I was fascinated by her, though I did not quite know why. When she showed me the workroom set up without her knowledge, in opposition to her own workrooms and to her house, beneath a roof that in a sense bore her name, it seemed to me that I discovered her. She was after all vulnerable, like everyone else; she suffered, she felt pain. In short, she was human, a woman, she who seemed so alien to emotion, always armed to the teeth.

I really could not believe that anyone had *dared to do that to her*. I regarded her as unassailable. What could anyone do to her? Cut back her royalties, give her a little less money?

They were angered by her regality, they wanted to snatch away her scepter and her crown. Oh, there could be no denying that her reign had lost its absoluteness. She was also losing importance. She was no longer prominent in the press. I repeat: though Chanel was still a solid investment on the commercial level, though the fashion house, even at its lessened pace, was still a powerful motive force for the promotion and sale of the perfumes, it was nonetheless clear that Chanel no longer made news, as the press says. Why should a fashion reporter go for news, something new (to say nothing of novelty), to rue Cambon? Every six months she would see there the same perfect suits, this time even more perfect; but how could that come through in the pictures or the headlines? The mini-skirt, the almost naked, that was what kept the special issues going, that was what provided the shock element in the collections.

"The knee will not be shown here," Coco repeated. "The knee is a joint." She held up her almost mummified hand and manipulated her index finger, clenching and opening and reclenching it. "Do you think that should be shown, a joint? A knee? A miserable knee?" She added, indeed: "An *old* knee . . . old . . . an old knee."

She was focusing on some unknown invisible object beyond me, or perhaps she saw it in the depths of my eyes. I was quite aware that she was losing ground. Why? And what was she getting into? I did not know her then as well as I do now: now at last I understand what she was telling me.

"Do you think it's fun to keep hearing people tell you you aren't twenty anymore?"

She tugged at the ends of a red scarf tied around her neck. Her *old* neck. "I know only too well I'm not twenty anymore. I'd be happy to be forty."

In two utterances she had revealed her whole self: *Let's get back to work* and *I'm not twenty anymore, unfortunately.* She was taking on the proportions of a character out of Balzac.

To start, an orphan, ashamed, who refused to be one. How many little girls sense at the age of six that they will be Coco Chanel and that when they die their names will be on the front pages of the whole world's newspapers? Why did Coco not retain memories of a single playmate in the orphanage? Every face from those days was erased. Her first victory was gained over her childhood, which she repudiated. *I'm not an orphan!* She built a house, a nice house, for herself, she dreamed herself a father gone off to the Americas, she gave herself harsh but respectable aunts. She did not accumulate all this in an hour of dreaming. She constructed her whole life in order to establish and preserve her fiction. It was a difficult fiction to establish. It had to be superimposed on a reality that had left its traces. What kind of schooling did she have? She said: "Sometimes I wonder whether I learned to read and write."

What a shame that so little is known of her childhood. Coco at ten, at fifteen . . . "I had dreadful taste."

She said it but she did not believe it. In any event, she alone

Photo by Luc Fournol — *Jours de France*

SHE SAID TO ME . . .

This is how I remember her, sitting on her couch, funny and warm. That smile erased her years. It was a joy to listen to her: "When I'm bored I'm a thousand years old, but when I'm comfortable with a friend why should I worry about my age?" Sometimes, however, she would sigh: "Do you think it's amusing to keep hearing that you're not twenty anymore?" Her figure had not changed since girlhood. "Cut off my head," she said, "and I'm still thirteen."

SHE MADE SUMMER IN THE SOUTH FASHIONAB[LE]

The Côte d'Azur had alw[ays] been a winter resort. In sum[mer] one went to Normandy, in [the] vicinity of Deauville; Septem[ber] meant the Côte Basque. O[nly] people as mad as the bohemi[ans] of Montparnasse would r[oast] themselves on the beaches [of] Juan-les-Pins or St.-Tropez. C[oco] reversed this flow. Paris soci[ety] flocked to her villa in Ro[que]brune, La Pausa, set among o[live] trees and jasmine. At lower [left] she is shown in slacks with [the] Duchesse de Gramont and Fr[an]çois Victor-Hugo. On the op[po]site page, Jean Godebski, [a] nephew of Misia Sert, kis[ses] Coco's hand as she takes [her] ease in bed. Behind him is M[.] Blaque-Belair, a former jour[nal]ist.

Photos by Roger Schall

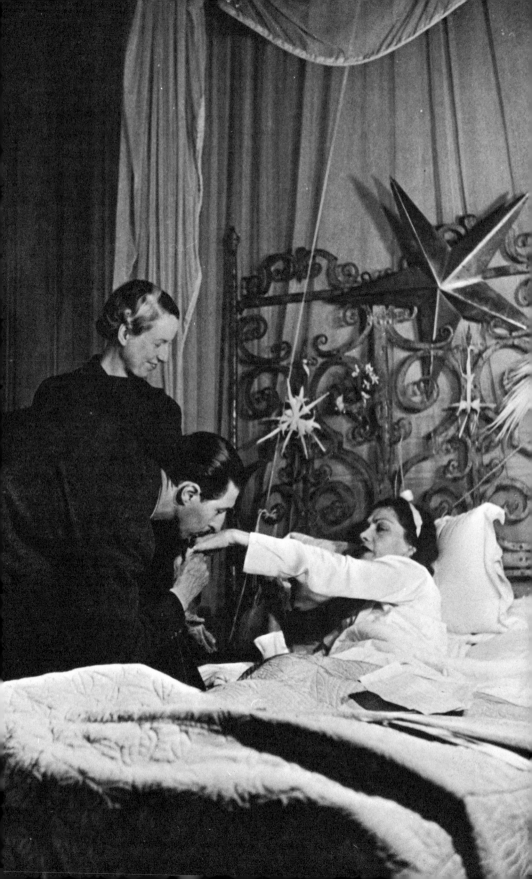

SIGNED "CHANEL"

Coco did not sketch her creations. She com-
posed them on living models. She always refused to buy stylists' drawings. She "authenti-
cated" these five sketches for the Fashion
Documentation Center. They are collectors'
items.

Centre de Documentation de Costume, Paris
Reproductions by Editions Robert Laffont

1954: THE COMEBACK

Photo by Horvat — Magnum

ery few champions have succeeded in what is called a come-
ack, a triumphal return to snatch away the title, the crown from
e younger rivals who had assumed that they had taken over.
'hen Coco Chanel made such an attempt in 1954, she was
venty-one. The victory was a hard one, and therefore the more
lendid. The picture at the left, taken during a fitting, shows the
amility with which *la Grande Mademoiselle* adapted herself to
e exigencies of her work. At top right, her shadow on the stair-
se during the "battle" (the presentation of the collection).

Photos by Willy Rizzo — *Paris-Match*

AT THE PEAK OF HER GLO
THE HUMILITY OF THE WORK

he made her dresses on her models, cutting the fabric with scissors strokes
to make the clothes simpler. She redesigned them with pins. "Who will do
these things when I'm not here anymore?" she wondered. Clothes are old
friends, she said; they must be kept for a long time. One must not change
them frequently. Women make a mistake when they think change means
happiness.

RUE CAMBON, THE MAGIC DRAWING ROOM

"I've made my best journeys on my couch," she said. One evening, after a highly successful collection, I found her sleeping on her couch, her hat over her eyes. "Fame is solitude," she murmured as she sat up. Surrounded by her models in her most brilliant period, when the whole world had been Chanel-ized, sitting in the midst of these dazzling girls she shared, by a kind of magic osmosis, their age, their beauty, their charm.

Photos by Willy Rizzo — *Paris-Match*

SHE DRESSED HISTORY

Photo by Camera Press — Holmès-Leb

If one thing was lacking in her life, it might well have been the fact that she
had not dressed Madame de Gaulle — though she never even hinted at this.
Madame Pompidou, a friend and customer of many years, wore a Chanel at
the religious service in Notre Dame for General de Gaulle. Coco never left
her television set. "I feel reassured when my wife gets her clothes from you,"
President Pompidou told her after a dinner at the Elysée Palace. The Pom-
pidous are shown above. At upper right, Queen Fabiola of Belgium; at lower
right, Princess Paola.

AS SEEN BY . . .

Sem

Don

Cecil Beaton

Christian Bérard

Collection of Boris Kochno

Jean Cocteau

IN HER LIFETIME
THE CHANEL MYTH GOES TO BROADWA

Again the famous staircase, but this time on Bro:
way — built for the stage setting of *Coco*,
musical comedy to which Coco had given
authorization because it was imaginary, a dre
life. Katharine Hepburn as Coco was a smash
success.

Photos by Cecil Beaton — Camera Press London

shaped her imperial taste, beginning by raising herself above her state as a poor orphan in a black apron.

The second victory that she gained came at Royallieu. What was she? A pretty country girl taken up to Paris by an officer who found her amusing. And who kept her — less sumptuously than his official mistress, a celebrated *cocotte*, Emilienne d'Alençon.

What became of the little orphan girls in their black aprons? What became of the pretty seamstresses of Moulins and elsewhere who enjoyed the compliments of dashing officers? What became of the *cocottes?*

Even as the chances of destruction mounted around her, Coco triumphed again, over others and herself, and as she had freed herself from poverty, she pulled herself out of the bondage of being a pretty girl kept for the few years of her springtime.

When she opened her first shop on a mezzanine where she made hats, who would have thought that three years later "everyone who was anyone" in Paris and then in the whole world (the jet set of the time) would throng to her, to her shop in the Faubourg-St.-Honoré and her house in Roquebrune? This was her third victory, which raised her as it were to a throne of fashion that could be seen from the ends of the earth. She became the queen, the acknowledged empress of elegance and taste. With her little face so unlike the others she was the incarnation of Paris. She *was* Paris, as Sarah Bernhardt had been the theater.

This was already a fabulous career, and she had made it on her own, adjusting herself to everything, educating herself. "No one taught me anything," she said. "I always learned everything by myself."

What was there left for her still to conquer? A duke, one of the world's richest men. This was Westminster, her fourth victory, to be followed by a fifth, over money, over business, over the rulers of the French perfume empire, against whom she triumphed by cunning and by her peasant woman's stubbornness, and so becoming the most highly paid company president in the world.

And then she was to carry off one of the most difficult, the more rarely accomplished of undertakings: a comeback. And at seventy-one, when she was thought to be too old, outmoded, left behind, she was to reconquer the scepter of fashion that by her own free will she had temporarily dropped at the start of the war.

And now the glory gained through such long combats was once more at stake by reason of this blow that was about to be struck at her, this conspiracy mounted by her own people, who were seeking to force her into retirement.

The collection that Coco had just shown, in 1968, had had merely the loyal acclaim that now was automatically hers. She thought, however, that it had been smashing.

"One can't do something new every time," she had told me, "but this time I'm revolutionizing everything; and I'm not doing it for a handful of lunatics but for everyone."

The day before the opening I lunched with her. She refused to reveal the smallest detail of her secret. "My dear, I'm very fond of you, but you shall see nothing today. Come back tomorrow with your thingumajig." The thingumajig was a cassette, the kind used by radio reporters. "I'll talk into your box if you want me to."

Lauren Bacall attended the collection, which was shown on a steaming-hot day. What was the revolutionary innovation on which Coco was relying to regain the ground she had lost? When all the other designers were raising hems even more, she was gambling on Chanel modesty: beneath a skirt that ended only slightly above the knee she was proposing pants, a kind of French culotte that went to the knee. It seemed a bit heavy for suits in Scottish tweeds. For evening gowns in delicate fabrics, on the other hand, it was marvelous — garments for Persian princes. "Persian princes?" one of those old war-horses who never miss a collection observed sarcastically.

War-mare would be more accurate: a "nice woman," one of

those Paris monsters who ruin everything because the only thing they know how to do is to be precisely where they ought not to be — those monsters of Paris that are hurled into the social orbit because of their birthright. I can still hear that woman laughing — not maliciously, either, but merely out of the empty-headedness that had brought her there to the House of Chanel where gowns for women were being shown. "Can you see me in that?" she asked me in her gravelly voice. "I'd look like a Persian war veteran."

Another monster of the same genus but the New York species commented that I had been "completely *brain-washed* by Coco." She used the English word in her Franglais, keeping herself cool with a tiny battery-powered electric fan. "I came here because Coco is an old lady," she told me.

Out of respect. One hears things in Paris that leave one stunned. The opening of a high-fashion collection has to be seen. From the ambush of a half-opened window through which I caught an occasional breath of air from the street, I observed the highly specialized fauna that congregate twice a year at these showings. The striking thing is the absence of young people; one would think that in order to qualify for the assignment a fashion reporter would have to be a thousand years old. But, to tell the truth, these creatures, these Vestals of fashion, are no older than other women of their age: it is simply that they have no age, no sex, nothing of what — sometimes — interests men. Entrenched in their importance, these important persons have a way of recognizing one another without seeing one another: they know the hierarchy of the seating — why, *she* wasn't so far front last year. The smaller fry are wheedling, grasping, peevish, and dressed like no other women anywhere in the world, still showing bare thigh above the tops of their stockings when every schoolchild in Podunk is wearing panty-hose.

What could these creatures know of Mademoiselle Chanel? A few actresses were watching Lauren Bacall. There were also a number of Courrèges- and Cardin-clothed ladies who knew everyone, shaking their long hair everywhere. Later Coco said to me of one of them: "Rich, yes; she's very rich; but all the same she's not happy, because she thinks she's beautiful and behaves as if she were, but she isn't."

But now Coco was at the top of the mirrored staircase, crouched on a step. "I know at once when a collection's a success," she often said. So she must know by now that her revolution had aborted. Trousers below skirts that had barely been shortened, when elsewhere the navel was being shown. She turned her back to the room, but in the mirrors she saw everything: the models coming out of their hiding place and holding up the numbers of the dresses for the spotlights, the Vestals fidgeting on their chairs, and the chairs that had become empty. She sent someone to me to ask me not to applaud any longer.

I knew what she thought of the creatures gathered to sit in judgment on her, whose decrees — and this was astounding — she accepted in advance. From the building next door one could hear the workmen knocking down partitions. In my mind I heard her voice rasp again: "Do you think it's amusing to keep hearing that you're not twenty anymore?"

What was she still hoping for? What victory could she still win? Only this: the proof, before she died, that she was still the youngest of them all. In her work.

I was uncomfortable as I climbed the stairs to her private quarters afterward. What was there to say to her? There was no crowd jostling to congratulate her. She who had rejected false pockets, buttonholes without buttons, was now for the first time offering something that had no practical use whatever: trousers below Scottish tweed skirts, in the age of central heating. Her "revolution" was evidence of her confusion.

She smiled, and kept hold of my hand: "I'm very pleased. As you see, there was no big audience, but the people who did come really understand work done well. No one pays me compliments anymore simply to please me: it's my work that I'm congratulated on, and to me that's the only thing that counts."

20

"I'm Taking a Real Beating . . ."

Difficult times. The house kept going (not quite so well) and the name still dazzled, but the wind of fashion was blowing from a different quarter. Coco was thinking of death more often. She was preparing a refuge in Switzerland. She was consolidating her financial defenses. Like all aging despots, she was looking back to her early successes for the formulas for new triumphs. For, though she talked more and more often of giving up, she was in actuality regrouping her forces in order to hold out to the very end of the storm. It was touching to watch her using all her weapons in order to enable her kingdom to survive to the final victory.

Withdraw, surrender, retire? She talked about it, though not seriously: "Why do I keep on in this lousy business? Very often I'd like to dump it all."

She used to say that even in her most triumphal days, when she was snowed under by compliments. So her friends said: "You've said that before. Fortunately . . ."

She shrugged and smiled. "What would I do if I didn't work

any longer? I'd be so bored." With much stress on the penultimate word: "I'd be *so-o-o* bored."

Yet she referred more often to a house that she had bought in Lausanne. "No, of course not right on the lake, which is appalling, with swans that smell awful. The marsh hens are dying off — the water's polluted. I'll be up the hill, at Le Signal, in a little house that's also called Le Signal. These days one can't live in a house that requires more than two servants. I want something small, a nest, where I can relax until I die. It's a very comfortable house — water and heat are in, I don't have to do anything. I have three bathrooms and a shower, not to mention my own bathroom. Inside I'll do the walls in lacquered things; the outside, since it's Switzerland, I'll do in chalet style."

What about the view? "All I can see is my own garden. Ten yards from the house there's a magnificent landscape. But anyway, one spends one's life in one's room, no?

She showed me a bed and chairs done in wrought iron, miracles created by the brother of the sculptor Alberto Giacometti: "Everything will be very simple — I'm not going in for any *chichi* there. The house will be open only to my friends. I don't intend to amuse myself by giving parties in Switzerland. Though there are some people there who think so: Mademoiselle Chanel will do this, and then she'll do that. They're wrong."

Retirement in Switzerland? The nest where she would wait for death? "I must think of my collection," she said, "because that's the future."

Could she desert high fashion when she was the last remaining repository of its secrets? I was stunned when I heard her invoke the paramount interests of France. If it had been a matter of her alone . . . why fight the whole world? "I could stop. I don't need anything. My royalties on the perfumes are paid in Switzerland. I'm certainly not going to pay ninety per cent in taxes; I'm not working for the state."

Not for the state but for the idea of France. Coco could not understand why no one came to plead with her:

"Stay with us, dear Mademoiselle Chanel. It is impossible that you should no longer spread the glory of French luxury to the ends of the earth. We exhort you to drive into the abyss the wretches who with their little shops take advantage of the follies of the moment, do grave disservice to fashion and impede the conversion of the masses through the Chanel style."

One day she told me: "Three dress houses have been bought up by the Americans. Why doesn't someone go see the minister and tell him: 'Sir, something very important is slipping out of our hands in high fashion'?"

She evidenced the greatest anxiety when she talked about the inroads being made by the Italians in the fashion field. She was not wrong. The light was no longer shining from Paris alone. Because *they* were blacking out the lighthouse in rue Cambon, Coco reasoned, *they* were diminishing her influence. Who were *they*? Her enemies. It never occurred to her that the public might tire of the Chanel style.

"I talked about it with a man who knows these problems very well," she said. "He told me: 'Dear mademoiselle, Italy is very important because the Italians are very practical. They don't close all their factories in August [as the French do] just when everyone needs cloth to fill orders.'"

Coco leafed through American magazines — *Harper's Bazaar, Vogue, Life.* Her lips twisted when she examined the fashion pictures taken in Rome. "The Americans would understand what it meant if Chanel closed." Surrender in the face of the Italian designers? Unthinkable.

For some time, as she climbed her mirrored stairs, she had had to stop for breath, always at the same step. "That step is well known by now," Madame Raymonde, one of her shop supervisors, said.

Coco was now adopting two poses. One was that she no longer ate; the other was that she no longer drank wine. "And yet my liver's never given me any trouble," she said. "I don't even know where it is. But one can die of liver trouble without ever having suffered from it, can't one?"

To the extent to which she acknowledged the (relative) failure of her latest collections, especially the one in which she had shown the trousers below the skirts, she attributed it to the reporters; and to her own publicity department, which, in sober truth, existed simply to suffer her bad moods.

"No one mentioned Chanel," she complained to me. "You ought to work on that with me."

From time to time she came back to "our" book: "I was filing some papers and I came across the letter you wrote me to persuade me to tell the story of my life. I've been asked for it for years. Perhaps we'll do it."

How could I have persuaded her to confess the marvelous truth about her childhood, nothing of which I suspected when we talked about this project? Or how prevail on her to talk about Moulins and Royallieu?

How could I have realized, when I had not yet learned the truth about her, that the project that now consumed her energies was her alibi, bestowing reality on her imaginary life?

Chanel was simplistic about the reasons for the conspiracy against her reign: if Chanel did not hold out, there would be no high fashion left. "The women's magazines have killed fashion," she sighed. "They're just drugstores now. They don't tell one about fashion anymore, they explain how not to have children." She looked at me slyly. "Would people have more now than they ever did?"

Then she added: "I know a young woman who takes the pill. She has swollen up here [her hands were on her bosom] and got fat all over; it hasn't done her any good at all. I asked her: 'How did you manage *before?* You didn't have any children.'"

She sighed. "Well, there it is, they don't want to get up anymore, they just want to stay in bed afterwards. And that's the only thing all the papers write about: the pill, the pill. And they stultify people with their comic strips, too. My maid reads all those things. Do you think that makes her brain work?"

(What would Pierre Decourcelle have been like in comic strips? His novels kept Coco's brain working long after she had finished them.)

She was wearing a round light-beige hat; I would have called it a Breton cap if, as she adjusted it on her overblack curls, she had not said: "They say it's a Breton cap." She shrugged. Everything that was written about her was ridiculous. "They say I'm short: I'm five feet five." And judgment was handed down: "Everything's always a lie that's printed about me in the papers."

One was tempted to smile, thinking: "No more a lie than what you said about yourself, and yet it was your own truth that you were inventing."

After our sessions with the tape recorder, I had shown her a manuscript, virtually a literal transcription of what she had said, with, of course, the story of that first dress, the mauve princess model, clinging (*to what?*), with the Parma violet underskirt, the hat with the artificial wisteria:

"No, never, never." She reared like a filly at a hedge that she would not jump.

I brought her back to the obstacle. "It was you yourself, though, who provided all those details. And it's a marvelous story."

Coco was mortally frightened of being found out. "*They*'ll all write things about me," she murmured.

And yet it was precisely in order to have me collect them that she had made me so many confidences, to enable me to rediscover her in her "real truth."

She had another explanation for her temporary difficulties: she was too much alone in her work. She said:

"One can't do anything without help. I'm going to stop. One can't find people anymore. It's paralyzing. People don't recognize anymore what you do for them. And the women are crazy. They hear 'string bean' and they all turn into string beans. Or 'be

Empire,' and they all shout: 'Hurrah for the emperor!' 'Be a tri-
angle,' 'be a diamond' . . . and that's what they turn into. Now
their navels are being shown. It's not exactly their best part. I saw
it in a newspaper: trousers below the navel and a blouse that
stops above it. The navel's so precious, isn't it? It ought to be put
in a glass case to be admired."

She remembered a picture of Jane Fonda. "Why, her navel's a
bomb crater," Coco shrilled. "Who has anything that big? One
would think it was to put a candle in. Soon women'll be showing
their asses."

That was a word that she had never used. She was almost at
the end of her endurance. "All this leaves me paralyzed," she
whimpered. "Oh, I'm taking a real beating these days." She was
pathetic in her admissions. "I can't do everything alone, all
alone. I tell *them:* 'If you don't help me, I won't do anything
anymore.' "

To whom did she say that? She was growing old, her age was
catching up with her. All along the wrinkles that connected her
nostrils with the corners of her mouth there were varyingly
prominent pockets forming, their swelling varying with the
burning of her inner tortures.

"One can do nothing without help," she repeated. "One must
know when to stop. High fashion is done for. I'm surrounded by
people who think of nothing but making money without deserv-
ing it. Yesterday was a holiday [1 May], Labor Day. Thursday
we'll be closed again, for Ascension Day. 'All right,' I said, 'if you
don't want to work, we won't work, but I'll treat you all as loafers.' " She tugged at her fingers. "Even when they don't work I
still have to pay them. And their social security to boot. It runs
into millions."

These problems, of course, were no concern of hers. She had
no slightest occasion to worry about the business end or the accounts payable of the House of Chanel.

"People always used to work on Ascension Day," she went on.

"Friday everyone will be interested only in getting away at six o'clock. People work without pleasure."

She lashed herself with these administrative problems, on top of her own real problems, because she was no longer certain what she was doing. "One has to 'find' a collection," she told me. She thrust her index finger into my chest. "My dear, I have to see everything."

Who could have deputized for her?

"I'm told: 'If you don't talk to stylists, things will go bad.' I say: 'What are stylists?'" She did not wait for an answer. "It seems they're young women who come from America or somewhere else to sell little dressmaking secrets. Can you imagine such a thing? Everyone's going crazy."

In the House of Chanel everything went through her. Nothing could be conceived, let alone carried out, without her. The more ground she lost, the more tenaciously she clung to what was left to her. Increasingly demanding, increasingly authoritarian, she exacted an ill-humored submission that at once recognized and refused to recognize her authority. *The old woman's losing her marbles.* One could read that in everyone's eyes; one might say it was *understood* in every exchange of glances. Coco, of course, unchanged, as sure of herself as ever, though wheezing more, caught none of this. *I know I'm right.* Marshal Joffre slept and ate well before the Marne. Coco, as I have said, ate very little. Her sleep was broken. She began falling out of bed: "I broke four ribs again."

A few days earlier she had fallen in her bathroom and injured her leg. She also had a bruise on her nose. She treated these wounds herself. "If you call a doctor he puts it on the radio. Fortunately I know first aid." She had brought together the fragments of broken skin on her nose to join them again. "With precision," she said, making the same movements: "like this, one bit against the other, almost to the millimeter."

One leg tended to become stiff when she sat for a long time.

She would stand up and flex the knee: "See, there's nothing wrong with the kneecap. I can stand on the leg; I wouldn't be able to do that if there were a fracture. In the Ritz an American friend asked me whether there was something wrong with my hip. That stupid woman thought I'd broken the neck of my thighbone."

She was stoical about pain, like a peasant woman from the days when doctors were called only to write out death certificates, when social security did not yet cover the expenses of every little ailment.

"One must ignore this sort of thing," Coco said of her broken ribs (if indeed they were broken). "I fell out of bed again. To prevent it the table had been moved against the bed, but that's not enough anymore. I'm going to have my mattress put on the floor; that way, at least I won't have so far to fall."

Her arthritis caused her considerable suffering. Sometimes she cried out in her sleep. "Occasionally," she said, "I fall asleep standing up, or sitting, and then I fall out of my chair—bang!"

She rubbed her head and laughed. Her sleepwalking came up again. When she was only six, her father used to put her back into bed when she got out. "Very gently, in order not to waken me," Coco said. "I was very scared. I would stretch out my hand and cry: '*He's* there! in the dark!' My father would say: 'No, no, don't be afraid, *he* isn't bad, *he* won't do anything to you.'"

From time to time she mentioned her father. She said he had hated pork and forbidden her to eat it.

She lingered over her past: "The winters used to be very cold. In the Auvergne, at my aunts', one sometimes went three or four months without going outside."

Months of being housebound in the Auvergne because the snow surrounded the houses . . . From what more or less Russian novel had she borrowed this memory? When she recalled her childhood, it was always in an atmosphere of snow and cold. There was never the slightest mention of spring, the rebirth of nature, the trees and their buds, the streams burbling through the new green of the meadows and the swarms of buttercups. Nor did she ever talk of summer in the Auvergne with its sudden weather changes, when the hay-charged heat gives way to raw rain streaming from the roofs. Nothing about harvests. Never a mention of life, of blackbirds' song, of love of nature. Always the snow-covered countryside and the warm hearth.

What of *the others?* Cardin and Courrèges, and especially Courrèges? Coco sensed the birth of a style closer than her own to the new era. "It seems he admires me," she said.

A friend of hers — a friend? — had complained to Courrèges because she had had to pay five thousand francs for a Chanel suit—a mere *product,* however: is it still high fashion when one does not turn out new styles?

"If you ask me," Courrèges is supposed (according to Coco) to have replied, "you're quite wrong to complain about the price of the suit. For five thousand francs I couldn't give you the same thing as Mademoiselle Chanel, who has talent and experience. Next to her I don't exist."

Listening to Coco tell of these statements by Courrèges, I could not help laughing. She laughed too. "Don't change that," she said.

She turned back the hem of her skirt: "Linings — there's the secret: linings and cut. Courrèges doesn't line anything." She sighed: "Women disguised as aged little girls . . . What can you do, if they like to make themselves ridiculous?"

Money came more and more frequently into her talk. Yet she said: "One doesn't take it with one, and purgatory is the next step." Since she was constantly volunteering that she had no slightest reason for anxiety about her declining years, one wondered why she so often gave the impression of thinking only about money now. I understood only too late: feeling threatened, she had recourse instinctively to the same defenses as in the past. She piled up money in order to assure herself of independence. "It's no one's business what I do with my money," she said.

After Pierre Wertheimer died, she thought that she could bring about advantageous revisions in the remarkable contract that she had made with him. "After forty years," she reckoned, "Chanel perfumes still haven't reached their full sales potential." Would Wertheimer's son be able to push the perfumes as Chanel wanted? Yes . . . no . . . her opinion changed from day to day. She grew impatient. She began to think aloud: "The business has to be sold."

"And you with it?" I asked, to make her laugh.

"You don't understand," she told me. "You don't know anything about making money."

She offered me a job in her perfume business. Once I had left *Marie-Claire,* she often worried about what would become of me. "What are you doing? Talking on the radio?" I was just beginning my broadcasts on 'Europe No. 1,' speaking at nine o'clock every Sunday morning.

"I would have listened to you if you'd told me," she said. "Were you afraid of waking me up? You're always afraid. Aren't we friends? Can I help you out? You aren't going to go right back to Alsace and write another book, are you? One mustn't let oneself be forgotten, one must stay on the toboggan. The toboggan is what the people who are talked about ride on. One must get a front seat and not let oneself be put out of it."

She hoped to lure away Pierre Berger, Yves St.-Laurent's business manager, for her perfumes. That was a fellow who knew how to make money out of them.

"I'd be satisfied with a third, a tenth of what you have," she was told by one businessman who found her sharp.

She looked him up and down. "What's your name? Who are you? I'm Mademoiselle Chanel and I'm known throughout the world."

She hesitated over the introduction of her new perfume, which she was planning to call Coco. For some time she considered putting it on sale, particularly in the United States, simultaneously with the Broadway opening of the musical comedy, *Coco*. "But then," she figured, "I'll be entitled to *more*, because the musical will provide tremendous introductory publicity and the credit for it will all belong to me alone." She had previously followed the same reasoning after the reopening of her fashion house. At that time the perfume sales had very soon tripled. And without paid advertising, because all the newspapers in the world were talking about her, Chanel. And for nothing. Should she not have been rewarded?

I don't give a damn about money. She went on repeating it in good faith. This did not prevent her from seeming greedier with every year, distrusting everyone and everything. Why should she agree to make a film with François Reichenbach, the French director? The Americans would pay her much better for the same thing. And yet in the beginning she had been attracted by the project. What a pity that it could not have been carried through. There would have been a masterpiece on Coco in her lifetime, like Reichenbach's film about Artur Rubinstein, the pianist.

Yves St.-Martin, the jockey — "my jockey," Coco called him — had invited Coco to his wedding. Reichenbach was there with his cameras and sound equipment.

"It was a real country wedding," Coco said. "No one saw anything but me or heard anything but me. Some chap had put one of those things they call a mike, I think? next to me. I talked and talked, saying just anything, and it recorded everything. I was even heard singing."

Then it came: "Reichenbach is very nice, and he does very beautiful things. He wanted to spend three or four weeks with me for his film. The Americans would have offered me a million dollars for the same thing. Why should I have made François Reichenbach a present of a million dollars?"

I repeat this line of argument because she often went back to it: *I'm being turned into an object. People make money out of me. It's money that belongs to me. What would I do with it? That's my business.*

Another fear, besides that of being financially damaged, had induced her to give up the idea of a film with Reichenbach: "I'd have no defenses. The public would see an old woman on the screen, even older than I actually am."

She was establishing, more or less consciously, a connection between her age and her money. The older she grew, the more she needed money to assure her independence. And money, her money, served as a measure of her power and the power of the House of Chanel. As for the rest:

"Money stultifies women," she said. "A poor woman who gets rich becomes a moron at the same time. Money takes away her taste. All she thinks of now is that money." She added: "Money doesn't stultify men."

"Do you really believe that?"

No, she did not. She knew the ravages of money, even in herself. By way of self-defense, strangely, she attacked the middle class, all the members of which agreed that money ought to be saved. "They've always ganged up against me," she said.

She was obviously thinking of her early days, when she forced her way *against* the rich, who were also the custodians of morality. She was still being looked down on then. And who dared to stare her down through a lorgnette that way? Common women who were not even pretty, who would have degenerated into nothings in an orphanage, who would never have got themselves out of Moulins. It was also against *those people* that she wanted to have her money, the weapon of contempt. Trivial recollections came back to her memory. She talked about Jean Cocteau's mother, a *bourgeoise* who did not know how to entertain, Coco hissed; and about his sister, "who was in dry goods."

"You're Jean's friend; couldn't you run me up some originals?" the sister once asked Coco. How long had that stuck in her gullet?

"They'd like to have everything for nothing, those people," she said. "I want what I do to bring me a profit."

She imitated an extremely rich friend who had admired her treasures. "I'll gladly take this," he said, "and this, and —"

"My dear," she interrupted, "you'll take nothing whatever."

She surveyed her things. "I'd much rather give things away in my lifetime," she said, "because *afterward* . . . One can't tell what will be done with all these."

Her glance dropped to her hands, crossed on the edges of her skirt. *Afterward*. Death.

After her return to rue Cambon she went out relatively little. She explained coquettishly that she had nothing to wear.

"I did have a blue suit in which, yes, I could go anywhere," she said. "I gave it to a friend. She couldn't believe it: 'Are you really giving it to me?' I said to her: 'Take it; this way I won't go anywhere anymore,' because I certainly can't go to people's houses for dinner as I am now [in a light-beige Chanel trimmed with red and blue]. It would look as if I were trying to give lessons to the other guests."

Georges Cravenne,* her great friend, tried very hard to drag her into various parties that he organized. "He needs locomotives," she explained. "Locomotives are people who spend their nights in nightclubs, to which I never go. But, if I go to a party, people say to themselves: 'Well, if Mademoiselle Chanel is going, it must be all right.' And if I don't go they say to themselves: 'She knows what it's right to do, so let's stay home.' But I don't allow myself to be pushed around anymore. 'You'll go by plane, you'll stay at such and such a hotel, you'll do this or that'; and I say to Georges: 'And suppose I don't like it? And why do you want me to do everything you ask of me? Like being pleasant to Monsieur Preminger, for whom I doubly don't give a damn?' And then that nice Georges says to me: 'Now, now.'"

It gave her pleasure to act like a kind of bad child who says

* A leading French public-relations practitioner, specializing in "society" events. Translator.

whatever comes into her head. She was interviewed on television, and her remarks brought her a great quantity of mail. There was general commendation for her attacks on the immodesty of current styles and on women's stupidity. To her it was natural to play the oracle. After an interview that she had given to the *New York Herald Tribune* she asked me: "Did I perhaps go too far?" She had said what she thought of the so-called most elegant women, especially the former Jackie Kennedy. "Bah! When one makes up one's mind to tell the truth one has to go all the way."

Did anyone find favor in her eyes? Cravenne begged her to be a member of a committee formed to celebrate Maurice Chevalier's eightieth birthday. She said: "A man who sings '*She had tiny little tootsies*'? What vulgarity."

The young stars were as filthy as pigs to her: "Go wash yourself and I'll see whether I can lend you some pajamas."

I looked at Coco: "And did they go and wash themselves?"

"Of course."

She criticized Cravenne for giving his parties abroad, in Tunisia and Ireland. What about Paris? The Paris season no longer existed. There was only one ball left, given by the Aga Khan, who was not even French. In such circumstances why should women go on concerning themselves about clothes? In the House of Chanel, even though business was good a hundred women would have to be let go.

It was the duty of the rich to provide work for the poor. She must have preserved this idea in her head to the very end. At the same time she reported a remark of hers to a minister:

"I told him: 'Our policy is despicable. It's simply frightful to think of the people who have to relieve themselves in outdoor privies in courtyards shared by several families. Have you seen that in the mornings?' Before we explore the cosmos we ought to wait until everyone has a toilet. I hope the elections will get rid of de Gaulle and his gang." She adduced a vague social basis for her anti-Gaullism:

"The French can't live any longer on what they earn. Everything that goes into taxes is for front, for prestige. My God, what prestige?"

It was seldom that she ventured into this kind of social comment. Her universe was at the opposite pole. For the de Gaulles, Chanel's definition of luxury did not exist. Oh! She did not deny their nobility, their bearing, which ought to have brought them and her together. But was it not Madame de Gaulle's duty to France to be Chanel-ized? If de Gaulle had invited Coco to the Elysée Palace she would have gone with her heart in her mouth, like a little girl. Or if Madame de Gaulle had asked to see her suits she would have done the fittings herself, with as much pleasure (if not more) as for Madame Pompidou.

Madame Pompidou was ordering clothes from Chanel even before her husband became Prime Minister. She and Chanel had already met more than once at the same dinner parties. Quite as a matter of course Coco was invited to Matignon* and later to the Elysée Palace. After a dinner at Matignon she had delivered a prophecy concerning Madame Pompidou: "She is losing her husband. She has no desire to be the wife of the President of France. She doesn't like that."

Cardin was a guest at the same dinner: "He didn't say a word. He looked very gloomy about everything." (After an encounter with one or another of her enemies, the couturiers, Coco would refer to him for a few days as almost charming, modest, admiring; she would even concede him a certain talent. "I think I could give them all good advice," she would say with a laugh.)

At the Elysée Palace President Pompidou asked her to come again. "He's very pleasant," she said afterward, "very intelligent; and he knows what he wants." But to him she replied: "No, I won't come back. I'm very glad I've seen your house, but I don't like it."

She told the story very amusingly, probably mingling what actually happened and what she wished she had said to the Presi-

* The French Premier's official residence, in rue de Varenne. Translator.

dent. In any case her story matched what she had decided to remember. According to her, she explained to the President that there was exquisite furniture available to him in the storerooms; and she told him that before he made his official journey to the United States (from which he had just returned) he should have consulted his ambassador on the climate that was prevailing there.

"*She* [Madame Pompidou], who is very vivacious, would have liked to go out and fight those people [the demonstrators in Chicago], and she urged her husband to go out and fight," Coco reported. "I said to her: 'My dear, he might have picked on a good boxer and that would have been very annoying for you.' "

This rather childish speech illustrates the royal idea of herself that Coco had formulated for Mademoiselle Chanel. When she spoke of her business, she was talking about an empire; and her imperial responsibilities required her to tell persons in high places the truth about themselves.

Of de Gaulle Coco concluded: "One might have accepted him as President in a pinch. He could have given advice. But he should not have been allowed to have power."

She had known Proust: "He held his hands like this, crossed here [on his penis]. A woman's gesture. He was a woman. He made up his eyes."

She briefly described an actress (one who had fallen into disfavor in rue Cambon): "She's changed completely. Her cheekbones stick out. All she knows is money and pleasure. When she does a play, she starts with the author, because she has a certain sense of precedence. She has a great deal of courage."

A dressmaker: ". . . the silhouette of a Spanish beggar shivering in an old jacket."

She appraised herself: "I'm timid. Timid people talk a great deal because they can't stand silence. I'm always ready to bring out any idiocy at all just to fill up a silence. I go on, I go from one thing to another so that there'll be no chance for a silence. When people don't enjoy my company at all, I feel it right away. I have a kind of nervous flow. I talk vehemently. I know I'm unbearable."

"Why don't people want to stay home anymore?" she sighed. "Not even married couples. They have to go out every evening, be seen, run after excitement. Something has to happen to you every day. And yet we're supposed to be civilized? Scampering, running, gulping a sandwich — why do people tolerate that? Because they're bored."

She would offer sketches of Parisian life:

"Monsieur So-and-So, who is a millionaire, warned us that he would no longer pay for his wife's clothes. She had already had four dresses made. Very properly he paid for them, but when she came back I told her: 'My dear, no more.'

" 'You can't do this to a woman like me!'

" 'A woman like you, my dear? What are you? You get a million [old francs] a month for your clothes and you run up debts? You'd be crazy to get a divorce. You told me you had no money of your own.' "

Another sketch: Coco had given two dresses to a temporarily embarrassed lady of the highest society, her millionaire being out of town. Then he returned, "and immediately she came back to order two more dresses, which I thought was very nice. My dear, you have no idea how low some women can be. I give special prices to some who don't have too much money, and then I meet them wearing Balenciagas, because his things are very expensive and everyone knows it, and they want to be seen with the most expensive things on their backs."

A duchess: "She has never paid anyone for a dress. If she asked me to dress her, I'd say: 'All right, provided you don't tell anyone.' "

To a very rich customer who was her good friend: "If you ask the saleswoman the price of a dress again, I won't dress you anymore."

To someone who asked her for money: "Dear, there are plenty of people who live without playing tennis or riding horseback."

On a hostess: "Things are badly managed in her house because she never has to pay for anything herself."

Coco recalled a trip to Italy with a "tall, very beautiful" friend, and with men as well, who invited some Italians to drinks. "I knew those fellows wanted to get us to the beach. My girl friend was big and strong, but I was so small and frail . . . We managed to get back to the hotel without difficulties. My girl friend asked me: 'Would you have died rather than give in?' I really wouldn't have wanted to die."

And Coco told about the time an actress suggested that Coco go with her to London to have her face lifted: "You'll look twenty years younger."

"But," Coco countered, "I'd be so ashamed to look twenty years younger: everyone knows what I've done (not *everyone knows how old I am*). I have enough wrinkles, but I'd rather have more added than have them removed. People would look closely to find the scars. And I'd really need to have a job done to me. As soon as I lose a couple of pounds there's a hole in my neck."

21

Coco at Work

A great token of confidence and great favor: that was how I interpreted Coco Chanel's suggestion that I work with her when she offered it across a table at the end of lunch.

During the difficult years I saw Coco more often. A clipping service sent her an article that I had written on the phenomena that were unsettling the fashion world.

"That doesn't matter anymore," she told me. "I'm going to start my last collection, which will be the synthesis of everything I've done."

She slid the trim of her suit between her thumb and forefinger. "I've been wearing this suit ten years. I love old fabrics that don't get tired."

She caressed the material, in the same way in which she would have stroked a dog. I had a premonition:* *it will really be the last collection this time; she means it.* I saw that she was bewildered. I heard her ask a reporter for *Women's Wear Daily:* "Will it be long or short, in your opinion?"

---

* False, obviously. M.H.

Apparently she attached some importance to the answer. The paper had just published a full-page advertisement paid for by manufacturers of ready-to-wear and consisting only of this sentence across the page: WE LOVE COCO. The o in "love" had been replaced by a heart.

It seemed to me that I would have to follow the last Chanel collection very closely (as Joinville escorted St. Louis!).* After all, this too was a sort of crusade in defense of the Beautiful, of Perfection. "A collection has to be created," Coco told me. "I'm looking for the theme. It will be talked about. You'll see how it *comes to life*. You'll learn many things."

It was a Saturday in rue Cambon. She had summoned all her kingdom. "I always come when I ask them to work. They know I'm here. If they need to ask me something, they have only to come in." There was a short pause. "But no one ever does. I remain alone, and it's annoying, because things get done by being talked over. But how would you have me do things?"

She was apprehensive and uncertain, yet still sure of herself, as a matter of course. "In the time we're living in now," she said, "one must maintain one's calm if one is to create a good collection." A sigh: "Everything's out of date." The beginning of a self-criticism? "No one makes anything but copies anymore."

This theme was to be taken up again in subsequent days: "One must keep to oneself. One must make something very good. *They* want to turn everything upside down, but *they* no longer know what to do. Shortening skirts isn't enough to change fashions." She hesitated, she was thinking out loud, talking to herself:

"I don't think it's possible to go back to long dresses for daytime. [She was thinking of her winter collection.] Nothing anymore fits in with the lives people lead."

She was wearing big pearl earrings. She was dreaming, remembering a trip to California and a night in Monterrey. "It happened in Monterrey." The balcony of her room looked out

---

* Jean, sire de Joinville (1224–1317) was the king's close adviser and the historian of his crusades. Translator.

over the Pacific in the moonlight. A black (she said "nigg*er*")
was singing.

"He kept repeating the same phrase. I asked him to come and
sing for me. He was excellent. The next day I bought loads of
cowboy things in the stores, did them all over better and made a
fortune with them."

Now she was searching for a new silhouette for a new woman.
"Until now," I pointed out, "you felt no need to make something
new."

She frowned. What was I trying to insinuate? I pushed the
point: "You yourself say everything is out of date."

She evaded: "I can't do everything all by myself."

There was a large glass of water on the low table in front of
her couch, next to a saucer with a pill and a white metal box:
"Sweetens the breath, refreshes the mouth."

"I don't know how to sew; I do know where to stick pins in,"
she said. Her hands were at her waist. She brought them slightly
away from her waist, both hands in the same motion. "Suppose I
wanted to make it a little wider?" Was she finding her silhouette? Had inspiration struck? Without answering my questions,
she showed me her hands, her fingers bent: "All the joints are
swollen, do you see?" She counted: "One, two, three . . . seven,
eight, nine." She was flexing the tips of her fingers against her
thumbs, like a reeling-girl at a spinning wheel.

"I take care of the inside of my fingers," she explained. "In my
work I don't need anything else. I was very skillful, I did whatever I wanted with my hands."

She picked up a wallet with a gilt medallion showing a sign of
the zodiac. "A craftsman was supposed to make me a hundred of
these for Christmas. I'll never get them. One can't get anything.
And yet it's easy to make. All this is covered with a little gold
leaf, which is applied with a brush." She made the gestures as if
she were wielding the brush. "I've invented a few things in my
time."

I found her pathetic, divided between the past, when everything was a success, and this collection to come, this new woman to be created. Could she break with Chanel? Create a collection that would no longer be for herself? Join *the others'* game?

"What *they* do I could do better than them." She was examining the medallion, blowing on it, rubbing it with a corner of her jacket. Then: "The silhouette must be changed. I don't want it to be flat and straight anymore. Fashion is the illusion that a new woman has been born who matches her time."

She looked at me as if I were a rather formidable examiner and she a timid candidate for a degree. She looked for clues in my face before she replied to the questions that she was asking herself. "I think too much," she confessed.

She was sleeping badly. She would wake up and her head would be full of *the revolutionary dress* that she was looking for.

Had inspiration come? "One must not move too fast, or one will turn out things that will be outdated immediately."

In the midst of concentrating on her collection alone, she still touched on a dozen related matters, such as vacations: her whole staff wanted to go away in August, just when the house needed its whole staff. She talked of Nasser too: "The Fourth World War has started already, hasn't it?"

And of *Coco*, the musical comedy. Some gossip columnist had written that Rosalind Russell, who was fifty-four, would play Mademoiselle Chanel, who was eighty-four. "It's all the same to me," Coco snapped. "Let them say I'm a hundred, but what fun it must be for that lady [Rosalind Russell] to read that to play me at eighty-four they've picked her, who's only fifty-four."

And this led her to a fresh complaint: "The entire press is against me."

Which in turn brought her back to her one real concern: "That length [the miniskirt] — I heard it was finished?" She was questioning me now not as if I were passing out examination grades but as if I were God the Father, able to decree the end of the miniskirt for whatever good or bad reason. "It's not selling anymore, is it?"

"Oh, yes, one sees it more and more."

"Soon women will be going out naked." She laughed bitterly. "You'll know right away what to go after. What exhibitionism. People will do anything to shock three or four persons." The conclusion came with a snicker: "Men will have the women they deserve."

She was juggling with figures. "A collection costs 350 million. When something like this" — pulling at her suit — "comes down from the workroom, just stitched together, without any fitting, it already costs two hundred thousand. [She always talked in old francs.*] And I could show you a suit that I've sent back thirty-five times to be started over."

But was that not precisely what luxury meant? To have clothes that could never wear out? She showed me a picture of herself taken during the war.

"It could have been taken today," she said. "I wore my hair differently, but I could put the jacket on again now. A customer from the North brought me a suit made before the war for her aunt, from whom she'd inherited it. It looked fine on her. Today [she shrugged] they have to get shock value. So one displays one's navel. The business has gone to hell."

Her lamentation ran through all the usual channels. "And at the same time what a loss of prestige for France. Magazines have killed fashion. People forget that forty-five thousand seamstresses depend on it to keep them alive. This country's policies don't make sense anymore. We make bombs! Do you think that will stop the Chinese? Oh, the women are going to have a fine time. They won't have any more children because of the pill, and all that gang will get jobs and run back and forth clacking their heels."

What of her inspiration? Of the revolutionary design that ab-

---

* The new franc issued in 1960–1961 was the equivalent of one hundred old francs and was pegged internationally at about twenty cents. Translator.

solutely must be found for the rejuvenation of woman? The new style to be shaped? I kept coming back to this incessantly.

"My people don't help me. No one shows any sign of imagination." Would she have accepted any ideas except her own? Which did not appear. Or, rather, which reappeared: the same old ones.

" 'We need perfection,' I tell them. If you no longer contribute perfection, what do you contribute? Nothing. Because you've never invented a thing, not even a plain hem. Everything comes from me. Everything has always come from me. I have two suits and I'm always well dressed. That's what Chanel means."

She was told that Cardin was raising his hemline: "So much the better. It will be a joke. I saw a big galoot showing her legs up to here [all the way]. Not ugly: nonexistent. If you can find some imbecile to marry you, my girl! I thought. If I had a daughter she would have to have damned well-shaped knees before I'd let her show them."

I endeavored timorously to explain to her that this *yéyé* style, as she called it, was in fact that of the first generation of girls without mothers — girls who chose their own clothes and no longer asked mamma's opinion, and who, in addition, insisted on offering visible evidence of their emancipation. She persisted in her own preoccupation: "There isn't one woman in a hundred who has pretty knees."

Then she revised the percentage: "I'm being generous. In America they make plastic knees to wear inside one's stockings. Soon everything will be plastic. I've never seen anything uglier than these short dresses. One would think women had to weep to get a little more cloth."

All this she piled up like so many sandbags on the banks of a flooding river — the torrent of modern bad taste.

"If I hadn't made certain commitments, I'd close the house and go away. But since I always finish everything I've started . . ." A sigh and another shrug: "To hell with what anyone says, I'll have done the best I can."

By now it was July. The collection was progressing well — classic, hyper-Chanel: "Every time I want to do something different, I ask myself: 'Would you wear it?' No, I couldn't wear anything but Chanel."

She appraised her chances. "High fashion is doing badly. Places are being closed. The House of Chanel is doing well, but then fewer orders are being turned down than usual. Molyneux asked me what he ought to do." She advised him to go into ready-to-wear: "What do you want, my dear?" she said to him. "Others have been through all this ahead of you. People decide you're old hat, and you're through."

People decide . . . That applied not only to Molyneux. But she was battling against time as a gladiator caught in the net struggled against death. She tugged at the red-and-blue trim that bordered her suit: "I have this, borders, and I'll put on more of them, because that's me. I'm not going to turn my back on what makes my style when I'm influencing ninety per cent of the ready-to-wear."

The atmosphere of the house was turning bleak. "When Mademoiselle comes downstairs about five o'clock, it sets off a panic," a forewoman confided to me. For her and her coworkers this was the end of the afternoon: they wanted to go home. But Coco was just getting up from a long chatty lunch. "Couldn't she work *normally?*" her associates wondered. Rotation lists began to be drawn up: "Are you staying this evening? Good luck."

"I heard she came down covered with smiles?"

"I hired a new tailor," she told me. "I said to him: 'Make something to show me what you're capable of doing.' I let him alone. He put pockets and things everywhere. He even got a dash of originality into what he wanted to show me. But it had no foundation. Nothing stood on its own feet. I said to him: 'My friend, we have arms, we have to be able to move them.' He didn't understand. Men make dresses in which one can't move. They tell you very calmly that the dresses aren't made for action. I'm frightened when I hear such things. What will happen when no one else thinks as I do anymore? I told my girls [her models]: 'I'm going to die. Listen to me. I'm teaching you something very important. Don't stand there looking like such dopes!' "

Then came the moment when she said to me: "Spend the evening with us, and you can watch us work."

She was wearing a beige suit. "It's a traveling suit," she explained, "but I can't wear anything else right now because I have nothing left but beige shoes."

A young man with a barely visible hint of moustache knelt at her feet as soon as she sat down in the big showroom. He began to open a number of cardboard boxes containing blue shoes for Coco, who refused to try them on: "How awful! It grips much too low, it's ugly, it's clumsy. Take one of my old shoes and have it copied exactly."

"Very well, mademoiselle."

"Make it grip here, and then . . ."

"Very well, mademoiselle."

"Yes, mademoiselle." "Very well, mademoiselle." I was to hear nothing else throughout that long evening of work. The cutters, the forewomen: "Yes, mademoiselle. Very well, mademoiselle." One cutter who had endured much staged a mild rebellion, and Coco disposed of him: "You've brought me a thing to fit that isn't for me: it's for a mending shop. Look: see how that one there's been done. What you have here is a parcel. If you'd done it like that . . ."

Her fleshless hands gripped the cloth. They pulled on it. It split. Her hands placed one end over the other, one layer over the other, and moved over the cloth as if it were a handkerchief to be folded, smoothing and shuttling.

This process of adjustment and revision was done on the model, who did not move. There was a vagueness in her eyes,

which were looking very closely or very far away — there was
no way of knowing. I was reminded of the look of a horse while
it is being shod. Occasionally she smiled, and it was like a quick
movement of light over water on a dark day.

On the floor there were bolts of fabric. Necklaces were hung
over the back of a chair — like the noodles that my Aunt Marie
used to hang out to dry on Sunday morning before a confirma-
tion meal. Ribbons, feathers, buttons, pins were all within reach
of Coco's hands, and everything was shown to her. Now it was
stockings: "These stockings turn red in the wash, your maid said,
mademoiselle. We won't buy any more."

Coco's continued calm was amazing. She spoke in an even
voice in which there was no irritation — apparently. "I don't
come downstairs when I feel nervous," she said. "I would keep
them from working."

She chatted with a smiling, rotund cutter who knew how to
handle her. When his first dress appeared on the podium, he
flung himself at Coco's feet: "I can see! It's too long!"

"Do I frighten you, then?" she asked with a laugh.

She beckoned to the model. Without rising from her chair,
Coco opened seams, tearing. What a sound — crrr! crrr! "Jersey
is very hard to work with; it's a thin fabric. I know, as you can
imagine. I began with jersey."

When she had shifted a hem, lengthened this, shortened that,
and changed a shoulder, she sent the model back to the podium
on which the dressing room opens: "That's where the customers
see the dress."

She returned to torturing the "accursed" cutter. "Why did you
use percaline? To waste time! I've called in experts to find out
why all my costs are so high. I didn't need them; I knew the
answer: it's because you come to my fittings with things that
aren't ready. And you do the same thing with the customers. You
use percaline where you need heavy silk. That means five fittings
when three ought to be enough."

She ran her hand over the model's bosom. "This design is supposed to be flat, and look at it! She has no bosom and yet this gives her one!"

The only word for the model's face during all this is *ruminant*. Did she hear? Her bosom was under discussion. She had no bosom. What did she think about that? Did she think? Not at that moment, it seemed. Surely I was mistaken: she must have been seething inside: *Poor old woman — my bosom my foot. If you'd just pay attention to your own . . . as for mine, I know guys who like it just the way it is . . .*

"I can't bear hips sticking out," Coco said. "And look in back, at the jacket: it's like a shelf." She ran her hands over the model's buttocks, gliding slowly. "It has to drop."

She took a tape measure and checked the width of the bodice: six inches, not quite six, almost six. "You must put *give* into fabric. You can't, because there isn't anything."

"Yes," the cutter protested, "it's there."

"No," she said very curtly, "it isn't."

Bettina, the then famous model, came in, but I did not recognize her, because of her tan. She was modeling an organdy gown for a party planned by Baron de Redé.

"What is essential," Coco explained, "is to make a success of one's entrance. I want you to look like a mature young woman, whereas the other sillies will come in wearing miniskirts, or things with trains."

She added an organdy flounce at the shoulder and blue ribbons on the dress. She tried various jewels, pearls, glittering stones. "People have to learn that jewels are ornaments, not a portable fortune."

"Especially nowadays," Bettina said.

"Since always," Coco emphasized.

How was the weather in St.-Tropez? Bettina had just come back. "Bad," she said.

"All the better," Coco said. "Now that all those people are displaying themselves on the beaches, France is done for."

"I love deserted beaches when everyone's gone," Bettina said.

"Come back tomorrow," Coco told her, and went back to work.

"Go put up your hair," she told another model. The question that followed was rhetorical, though she was looking at me: "Why do they want to hide their faces under their hair? A face is a beautiful thing." And to the girl: "You're very pretty without all that hair: you have a forehead, a nose, a chin." ·

The model smiled: "Thank you, mademoiselle."

Like the grand cross of her own chivalric order, Coco wore a scissors on a ribbon around her neck. In 1964, when there was an exhibit in the Louvre in honor of the bicentenary of Baccarat's glass and crystal works, she agreed (at the suggestion of her lawyer, René de Chambrun) to design a large bowl. She was a lover of crystal. As the theme for the bowl, she chose her scissors. She was overwhelmed by the fidelity of the etching wheel's reproduction of her design.

"The identifying label," she told Chambrun, "must point out that my art, the only art I had, lay in my use of the scissors for cutting, for simplifying, whereas others did much more with it."

She mentioned this bicentenary bowl at her last lunch with Chambrun. "I'd very much like to see it again," she said. He at once arranged for it to be brought to Paris from the Baccarat museum and made an appointment to see it with Coco — for the day after her death.

When I close my eyes, this is the image of Coco I shall always have: using her clothes for a pincushion, and sometimes letting out a cry: "Ouch! what's that?" She would show her hand, with a pin in a knuckle. "I prick myself often, but I don't feel anything, except when it hits a bone."

She decided to convert a purple lining into a coat. "I want a colorful collection. The others are going to extremes with black. The country doesn't deserve being made to wear mourning."

She opened the jacket of her suit: "Smell, it's my new perfume. People don't know how to make perfumes anymore — they don't know how to do anything anymore."

The hours dragged on, and the night progressed. She sipped red wine. She said: "The collection is fundamental, because it's the future."

At that time she was eighty — her birthday was only a few weeks away. But there was no thought of wishing her a happy birthday: she would never know any happiness greater than her work. She said:

"People tell you all about their little happinesses, but what horrors! Little happinesses, little unhappinesses. When one of my models talks to me about her little sorrows, I say to her: 'My poor girl, my dear, I hope you will be struck by a great unhappiness: that would do you so much good, because you don't know what unhappiness is.'"

She did not add *and so you likewise know nothing of happiness,* but that went without saying. How to *dig?* If I had interrupted her, she would not have listened to my questions. Nevertheless she must have put them to herself in her sleepless nights. That was why she, who needed sleep so very much, dreaded the instant when she would surrender herself to it. *One moment more, Mr. Executioner.* She talked and talked. Fear of silence, she explained, the panic of the timid. When she was speaking she existed as she created herself. In the silence of her sleep she became once more *the other,* whom she unceasingly strove to bury alive but who wandered through the night, whimpering over some simple lost happinesses.

SHE SAID . . .

I am opposed to a style that does not last. This is my masculine side. I cannot envisage throwing away one's clothes because spring has come.

I love only old clothes. I never go out in a new dress — I am too afraid something will split. Old clothes are old friends.

I love clothes as I do books — to touch them, to play with them.

Women want to change. They are wrong. I am all for happiness. Happiness is not changing.

Elegance does not consist in putting on a new dress. One is elegant because one is elegant: the new dress has nothing to do with it. One can be elegant with a well-chosen skirt and sweater. It would be a disaster if one had to be dressed by Chanel to be elegant. And so restricted!

In the past every house had its own style. I created mine. I cannot depart from it.

I cannot put on something that I would not have made. And I would not make anything that I could not wear.

I always ask myself the same question: could I honestly wear that? In fact, I no longer need even to formulate the question. It has become an instinct in me.

There is no more fashion. It was created for a few hundred persons. I make a style for the entire world. The stores offer "Chanel style." The others have nothing like this.

Chanel never goes out of date. A style does not go out of style as long as it adapts itself to its period. When there is an incompatibility between the style and a certain state of mind, it is never the style that triumphs.

I look at the suits that go out and I think: "Would those who buy them complain of the tiny flaw that I alone detect?" No. And yet I take apart and remake in order to improve.

I have always done everything with passion.

Dressmaking is not an art, it is a business that is being done to death.

I am doing an optimistic collection because things are going badly.

Why am I so determined to put the shoulder where it belongs? Women have very round shoulders that push forward slightly; this touches me and I say: "One must not hide that!" Then someone tells you: "The shoulder is on the back." I've never seen women with shoulders on their backs.

I consider myself quite limited in what I do. Therefore it must be meticulous, and the material must be beautiful. As much as possible I must show a little taste and not change too much. People would say that I was no longer making my clothes.

One grows used to ugliness but never to slovenliness.

A young style? What does that mean? Dressing like a little girl? I know of nothing that ages one more.

Fashion is architecture: it is a matter of proportions.

A woman of eighty should not wear a dress that would not look well on a girl of twenty.

Innovation! One cannot be forever innovating. I want to create classics. I have a handbag that sells steadily. I am being urged to introduce another. Why? I have had the same one for twenty years, I am familiar with it, I know where to put my money and everything else.

Some women want to be gripped inside their clothes. Never. I want women to enter my dresses and to hell with everything else.

When I have made something in a rough fabric, I let it ripen in a corner without looking at it for days. I have made some strange tweeds without going wrong because I have avoided looking at them. After a little time I discovered them.

Few people have a feeling for color.

Some foolish women seek to dazzle men by dressing eccentrically. They scare them off: men do not like eccentricity. A man is quite pleased to have his wife looked at because she is pretty; but if she is eccentric it upsets him: he is ashamed. No more would I go out with a man in a green dinner jacket. Men who want to attract attention through their clothes are morons.

The opposite of luxury is not necessarily poverty: it is hats and skirt lengths that go out of style.

Short dresses do not become outmoded so easily as long.

Women believe a longer skirt will improve legs that they think are not too pretty. It improves nothing.

Nothing is ugly as long as it is alive. Women tell me: "I

have rather thick legs." I ask them: "Do they support you? That's what matters. The legs carry you, you don't carry them. Stop thinking about it; that is not what will make you happy."

A woman asked me: "What should I do to lose weight?"
"Is your health good?"
"Yes."
"How are things going for your husband?"
"Fine."
"Then why do you want to lose weight?"

People do not know how to live. No one has taught them.

I know how to work. I know how to impose a discipline on myself. But, if I do not want to do a thing, nothing and no one can persuade me to do it.

A woman wearing light colors will not easily fall into a bad mood.

Nothing goes out of fashion sooner than a long dress with a very low neck.

A woman with a very good figure can wear slacks in the country, but never in town in the evening.

The hat is not for the street: it will never be democratized. But there are certain houses that one cannot enter without a hat. And one must always wear a hat when lunching with people whom one does not know well. One appears to one's best advantage.

I like hats that hide half the face.

Nothing is more detrimental to a woman's beauty than hair on her face.

That it is only fools who never change their views applies as well in fashion.

What is the best color? The one that most becomes you.

In order to be irreplaceable one must always be different.

22

Coco Discovers the "Ordinary People"

Her solitude was becoming more oppressive. Why put up with the moods of Coco Chanel when she could no longer impose her decrees on the world of fashion? The shadows around her table did not send back the echoes of her monologues.

It was at this period that her butler was promoted. François Mironet was a Norman, the son of peasants of Cabourg. He was a rotund man with the figure of a Munich monk (the one who invented the strong beer that is sold at *Fasching*). I had observed that she asked him many questions as he was serving in his white coat and gloves. She used him as a memorandum book. But her own memory did not too often betray her.

One day we were served by a new butler. "François is taking care of the jewelry now," Coco explained.

She had given him the job of bringing order to a room left in chaos at an associate's death. Having gone into the room to see whether François was doing his job properly, Coco found him working on three necklaces, and she asked him: "Did you make these?"

She imitated François and his shy, blushing modesty: "Yes, mademoiselle, I enjoy doing that."

"Why, these are excellent, François! Don't stop."

She explained to me: "I knew he had good taste, ever since he'd allowed me to visit his apartment." This was an apartment that she had arranged for him: "The law compelled me to," she said.

One evening — a splendid scene to imagine — she was dining alone in rue Cambon. She was more and more frequently alone. *I can't eat when I'm alone, when there's no one across from me to talk to.*

"François . . ."

"Mademoiselle?"

"Take off your gloves and your white coat and come sit down."

This happened a few years before her death. The musical comedy *Coco* was about to open in New York. She was earning fortunes.

"Take off your gloves, François."

She was alone at the table, she had no appetite, she needed to talk — that was all there was left for her to exist for: to eat while she talked, to talk while she ate. By dint of having buried her life day by day, she had finally trapped herself in the abyss.

"Take off your gloves, François, change your jacket and sit down."

To me she offered this preposterous explanation: "I didn't need two butlers."

From then on François was to be found beside her, ready to help her when she climbed the stairs, sitting behind her in the big showroom when she was preparing her collections, saying nothing, sometimes offering her a glass and a pill to be taken. He was her gentleman in waiting. He went with her to Lausanne. He ate with her when they were traveling, and then at the Ritz.

"Will Monsieur François give us the honor of his company at dinner tonight?"

"Not tonight, mademoiselle, I have work to do." But he said that because I was there for dinner.

He was holding two necklaces, both identical in appearance: but one was made of real rubies and the other of paste. Coco herself confused them. She smiled:

"Then it's the other one that someone gave me, many years ago — someone who didn't have the slightest right to give me such a gift, but he said to me: 'Look, this is special: I bought it to give to you and you can't refuse it.' "

She looked at François. "So I didn't make a fuss — I accepted it."

This episode took place in March 1970. I had not seen her for several weeks and she had upbraided me for it, but she did not nurse a grudge.

"It does me good to chat with you," she said. "Don't desert me for such a long period." She was begging. "Don't drop me again." As if to entice me, she started talking again about her early days, with more detail than ever:

"I had been told about a milliner to do my hats, and I hired her. A week later I knew more about the business than she did, because I wanted to learn. I had a passion for learning. I also like to teach others what I know. I've spent my life doing that, and I do it still with François, who listens to me. Those people *downstairs* don't listen to me, and as a result they've retained nothing of what I wanted so much to teach them."

She spoke of the first dress that she had made: "An old jersey, which I opened down the front so that it wouldn't have to be pulled over the head." She mimed, she cut, she put her arms into the sleeves of the opened jersey, she buttoned it.

"I sewed some ribbon there." She held the edge of her jacket between thumb and forefinger, letting them run from top to bottom, along the braid. It was her life that was slipping between those two fingers. "I put a little collar and a bow there."

She put a straw hat on her head: "I bought the blocks at the Galeries Lafayette: first I bought one, then I bought six, then I bought a dozen. I had a good deal of luck. I went out with well-known people. Everyone was in raptures: 'Where did you find that hat? Who made that dress?'" She laughed: she was reliving her happiness, and without anxiety.

She had said to the other women present: "If you like this dress, I'll sell it to you."

"For how much? What price do you want for it?"

"I don't know. I'll have to find out."

Things had happened as simply as that. She smiled, and adjusted her skirt over her knees. "I sold ten dresses, twenty dresses, right away, and masses of hats. See, my dear, I built my fortune on an old jersey."

François reappeared in shirt sleeves, his collar opened and his necktie askew, a bit of paunch hanging over his belt. He wanted to leave. "Shall I call you tomorrow, mademoiselle? About eleven thirty?"

"Come to the Ritz, François, and if the weather is nice we'll go have lunch near St.-Germain."

He left, smiling, reassuring, and reassured too by my presence: *she* would not be left alone.

"Do you think he's got fat?" Coco asked, sketching on herself the paunch above his belt. "He's going to Switzerland for three days, and he'll lose six pounds. It'll come from here [she touched her face], chiefly here; and only a little from there [the paunch]."

She lent him books. "He reads them; if he didn't, he'd tell me: 'Mademoiselle, I don't need your books, I don't read them.' Ah, how restful they are, these ordinary people who are what they are, natural — not at all like the Parisians, all those liars, all those rotten Parisians."

She did not know François's wife. She would have liked to know his mother: "I've been told he looks so much like her."

One Sunday she went to the track at St.-Cloud with François. To relax. To sit on the grass, on the embankment. The sun was shining and the air was full of spring.

"I didn't want to be seen, I wasn't dressed at all for the races, but people have *things* [glasses] for following their horses, and I was seen and everyone said: 'Mademoiselle Chanel is here!' And then the horses went by! I saw my own colors — and I hadn't even known whether my horse was running. And he won. Naturally everyone thought I'd come for that, when actually I was there for the fresh air. I'd said to François: 'As long as it's a lovely day . . .' "

She had begun playing the lottery. Not heavily — three francs, or a bit more when she experimented with various combinations: "The concierge at the Ritz handles it for me. That's another advantage of living in a hotel."

Racing, horses: Royallieu, Balsan, her twenties: "Probably you don't know this, but horses must walk a great deal. So there were lads* who walked them. They all wanted to grow up to be jockeys. I taught them to ride. One of them was afraid. He was weeping. I said to him: 'Stop crying, I'm going to teach you to get on a horse and you won't be scared at all: you'll learn everything, I'll teach you to gallop and your mamma will be very pleased.' "

I had the feeling that she was talking to a little boy whom she would have liked to have. Her face was very small, her eyes more sunken, glowing, pleading, her voice hoarser:

"What's going to happen to me? What can I do? You know I don't go out at all anymore. Everyone asks me for money; people think I exist to give money. In bed at night I ask myself: 'Why do you put up such a front? Why don't you dump all that? Why don't you get out of this town where you have too much work to do?' "

She was preparing a new collection, of course. "I've almost finished with the dresses, because that goes by itself, one gets it all done with pins. But the suits — that's construction. And *they* call them the *little* Chanel suits. That annoys me!"

* Coco used the English word. Translator.

She redid every design. The seams were pulled out, things were lengthened or shortened by a centimeter — "which changes everything, mademoiselle!"

She raised her eyelids. She was having cloth added. "It looks too poor," she explained. "Like a boutique." So many boutiques were springing up all over Paris.

"There must be fur for the winter," she added. "I don't like to skimp on that. It's expensive, but it's essential."

She was holing up inside her money. "It's better to have too much than not enough. And one must always put aside a little of it for diversion." Once more she was stating the fundamental truth of her existence: one can never have too much money to preserve one's independence. She was proving it again by frustrating those who wanted to overthrow her.

During these lean years she no longer felt protected by her genius: it was her millions in Switzerland that kept her on top. They were her castle: what cannon could dislodge her from it? "As long as I have that money, I'm right." The same conviction feeds the pigheadednesses of many other millionaires.

Her monologues often digressed; but even so I was startled when, one evening, she leaped from money to those women-that-certain-customers-of-the-Ritz-take-up-to-their-rooms. "It's revolting."

She imitated the concierge bursting into customers' rooms to drive those creatures out: "Madame, you must leave: this is the Ritz." What mischance had fed this sudden outburst of temper? "If it were up to me, I'd throw out the men who brought in those women!"

Over that outburst one cannot help dreaming. When she was alone, for real, on whom did she fasten the responsibility for her disguises? Because of whom had she not wanted to remain herself? One thinks of Balsan, of Moulins, of Royallieu. But before that? If, as I expect, Mademoiselle Chanel will long continue to excite the curiosity of those who love mysteries, little by little the circles of darkness that surround her adolescence will shrink. Will they finally yield one truth?

One must remember what she said: "Those on whom legends are built *are* their legends."

As for her legend, she had thrown out of her life those men to whom she once owed something, at one time or another, for one reason or another — sometimes money, sometimes pleasure. She wanted to remember only those to whom she had *given,* and among them the richest of all, the Duke of Westminster, by whom she had been able to let herself be loved without calculation, wholly without ulterior motive, and this even if physically she remained detached. "Her sex was in her head," one of her lovers has said.

One day she said to me: "I like your book about Moses very much because there's no sex in it."

Which made us both laugh.

23

The Final Victory:
Triumph from Beyond the Grave

How many women have plunged the whole world into mourning? Though more tears were certainly shed for Sarah Bernhardt, Coco Chanel will leave a more real, a more concrete remembrance. She will be a suit, and style, and length, and taste, and jewelry, and perfume. She will continue to exist with her period face, the unexpected visage of a rebellious orphan who combined the grace of a fawn with the iron grip of an eagle's talons.

She died on a Sunday night, 10 January 1971, in the Ritz. Her maid had helped her to undress and she was about to get into bed. It was a death in the style of de Gaulle: barely time to utter a cry of protest: "So this is how they let you die."

She had more than one thing in common with de Gaulle, who had died two months to the day ahead of her. She renounced her past as he rejected defeat; and she made of Chanel "a certain concept" to which everything else was subordinated.

Rumors of her illness had been coursing through newspaper

offices for some time. I telephoned her, I saw her even more often. When we lunched there was no sign of approaching death about her. Her appetite was coming back. She drank two or three glasses of Alsatian wine and her eyes sparkled.

"Will you come back tomorrow?" she said. "I'll be on time: I know you can't wait. You can leave whenever you like. And give some more thought to what I've suggested."

This was nothing less than collaboration with her in running the House of Chanel. What could I answer? Actually, she wanted me to help her proclaim her victory. For once again she was scoring a triumph. In addition to the Chanel style there was now the Chanel length. Her sales in Paris had risen thirty per cent above those of the previous year. An ultrasimple little black dress was conquering the world. It was to be photographed on Marlene Dietrich and Catherine Deneuve. A poll hastily organized by *Women's Wear Daily* in New York at the request of the Seventh Avenue manufacturers, who were losing millions of dollars because of the midi style, gave its blessing to the Chanel. "It's Chanel we want!" the American women cried. Coco took out of her bag the *Women's Wear* story on the poll, unfolded it and put on her glasses: "Why don't they tell about this here in France?"

"They" were many people at the same time: her competitors; those associates who had tried to thrust her aside; the newspapers; the magazines that were killing fashion; the boutiques that were polluting her Paris.

She was not liked. Why? Was her triumph not France's — and therefore Frenchwomen's? Did de Gaulle never put the same sort of questions to himself? They cheer me, they hide behind me, they expand on the air that I expel. But affection? Love? Seeing him so remote, so lofty, one might have supposed that he would have laughed at such questions. But is it so certain?

Affection requires exchanges of warmth along constantly replenished circuits, and most often one provides one's own warmth without being aware of it. How cold it is, then, when the circuits are left untended.

"A great career," Napoleon asserted, "and a great success are born of the encounter between a character and chance." What chance? For de Gaulle, the disaster of 1940; for Coco, the defeats of Moulins?

Bending over Coco at her death, her maid saw her face covered with tears.

A Sunday night at the Ritz, utterly alone with her maid. She whose name the next day would be on the front pages of all the great newspapers of the world.

Her two grand-nieces came at once, as well as Lilou and François, who had not been there when she died. Often they played cards together, waiting for Mademoiselle to fall asleep. "It reassured her to know that we were there," François said, "but at the same time it kept her from going to sleep."

What was the Hotel Ritz to Coco? Her home, she said. In fact it was a fortress of figures that preserved her independence. Or a desert island set in a sea of money.

Her apartment consisted of a bedroom, a drawing room and a bathroom, but the whole thing was Lilliputian; perhaps one owed this impression, when one entered it, to comparison with rue Cambon. The Ritz apartment was nothing beside rue Cambon — not even a set of convent cells. It was colorless, nondescript. The day after her death it smelled like a hospital. The family had taken over this no-woman's-land. *Coco hoped that . . . She didn't want this, and that . . .*

"If I die," she had told Lilou and François, "take me to Switzerland. Put me between you in the back of the car. If you're questioned at Customs, say: 'It's Mademoiselle Chanel — she's senile; don't mind her.'"

What did Switzerland represent in such a remark? A kind of paradise of money. Even *afterward*, in Switzerland, money retained its powers, providing solitude, independence, distances. In the Lausanne cemetery she occupies the area of four graves. Always a desert around her, to protect her against regret and remorse.

So she slept behind that forbidden door in the Hotel Ritz, watched over by her two grand-nieces. No one else was to see her in death. "You must be my watchdog," she had told Tiny. "It won't be easy."

She spoke sparingly of her family, but she loved it, because a family exists as God does, or the Church, like an Other Dimension, like a Faith, in which, in those days, one was brought up even in the orphanage.

It is impossible to understand Mademoiselle Chanel unless one situates her in her time, which was still that of Birth conferred by a Name or by Money: the time of Privileges, of the Right That Was Still Divine. Perhaps there is no need to search beyond the conventions of her era for all that she invented about herself in order to conform to it; to establish herself within it; to emerge from it; to become Chanel in the world of Proust. In order to achieve this was it not necessary to wipe out the childhood and the adolescence? None of what is considered moving today was acceptable to her: it was all too humiliating. Newsboys had already worked their way to millions, but that was not yet enthroned as a paradigm.

Did she know her time was near? How else is one to explain the impatience that she displayed for revenge, for triumph? On Christmas Eve, or the day before, she told me that she would present her collection in four days: "Yes, my dear! The Americans insisted, and, since one can refuse them nothing . . . It doesn't matter to me: I'm ready."

She suggested that after my broadcast I should spend the evening looking at her new creations. She was so positive that as I was leaving I questioned her supervisors.

"No," they said, "nothing has been pushed up. The collection will be shown toward the end of January, as usual." They said it with an unspoken comment: *You who know her so well know how she talks nowadays.*

In her mind her triumph was certain. She could celebrate in four days or five weeks.

When I came back that evening, at about seven, the house was shadowed with sleep. Coco, however, was waiting for me — for dinner. François had gone out to shop for toys for his children.

At the Ritz a table was always reserved for Mademoiselle Chanel on the outside, in the lobby, at the entrance to the dining room. She could see who was coming in. And she could be seen, too. And this did not make her at all unhappy. The curiosity that she inspired enriched her house; for the sake of Chanel she was willing to be a monument that the most curious could study close up. "Coco, it's Coco Chanel," they would say in English — and in German, and in Spanish.

The satisfaction that had been refused her by Madame de Gaulle's snubbing of Chanels was given to her by Madame Pompidou when she wore a Chanel to Notre Dame for the general's funeral Mass. Coco savored this triumph in her own way, pride making her modest:

"Eighty important people coming from every part of the world — what a break for Paris, because things are not all that good."

I afforded her another pleasure, two days before her death, by devoting a broadcast editorial to her revenge: "Mademoiselle Chanel is coming out victorious in the war that has been declared against her style. She is also gaining a victory for her hemline, the sensible one that makes it possible to sit down decently." Marc Bohan had just conceded: "In the end it's *she* who is right." For by now one said simply "she" when one meant Coco.

She was working in the big showroom, pinning up clothes on her models, when someone brought her a transistor so that she could listen to my broadcast: she had never heard me before.

When I was asked in the newsroom: "Is *she* dead?" I was certainly not taken aback by the question. At her age . . .

Yet every time I saw her she seemed immortal. Lively and voluble, she expounded her views to me on everything and anything with an intensity that was always exhausting to the same degree. She was shriveling. Her eyes were devouring her face; sometimes I see her in memory as a Jivaro Indian, with a very small head and huge eyes that ask innumerable questions.

She had told Lilou and François: "No nonsense after I'm dead, because I'll still be there beside you, in another dimension."

I have only one curiosity left: death. She had said that. To whom? These are words, lines spoken by the character that all of us play. What becomes of that character when death takes us by the hand?

Coco had a ritual attitude toward the dead. Whether she had loved them or loathed them in life, they became precious to her, and perhaps at last close. She showed them more familiarity, she took a peasant woman's liberties with them. She touched them without aversion, in order to wind a rosary around their hands; or to touch up their cold faces.

Why the cemetery in Lausanne?

I've always needed security. In Switzerland one can have that security.

After the farewell in the Madeleine, the models and the workroom people went slowly back to rue Cambon, where the atmosphere had newly changed: silence and apprehension had taken the place of fear. The tears for Mademoiselle were honestly shed. She had suddenly changed in stature. She was being discovered in the immense emptiness that she had left.

As for me, I was now to learn to know her.

INDEX

Picasso, Pablo, 98, 100, 105, 110, 178; and Reverdy, 134, 135
Poincaré, Raymond, 118
Poiret, 91, 120, 166, 168
Poiret, Rosine, 91
Pompidou, Georges, 18, 81, 235–236
Pompidou, Madame, 169, 235–236, 267
Preminger, Otto, 233
Previn, Andre, 208
Proust, Marcel, 236, 266
Prouvost, Jean, 205n

Quant, Mary, 101

Radiguet, Raymond, 110, 115–116
Raimu, 175
Raymonde, Madame, 223
Reboux, Caroline, 83
Redé, Baron de, 248
Reichenbach, François, 9, 231–232
Renoir, 97–98
Reverdy, Pierre, 22, 23, 105, 115, 133–140; unrecognized genius of, 134–135
Reynaud, Paul, 187
Ribbentrop, Joachim von, 147
Ritz Hotel, Paris, 13, 79, 113, 168, 265–266; with Etienne Balsan, 64; Coco's apartment during World War II, 144, 146
Rostand, Edmond, 96
Rothschild, Baron Guy de, 163
Rothschild, Madame Henri de, 191
Rothschild, Marie-Hélène, 163–164
Rothschild, Maurice de, 190
Russell, Rosalind, 207, 242

Sachs, Maurice, 132, 134
Sagan, Prince de, 66
St.-Laurent, Yves, 230
St.-Martin, Yves, 231
St.-Sauveur, Jules de, 89
St.-Sauveur, Pauline de, 67, 69
Salmon, André, 134
Satie, Erik, 114
Saturday Evening Post, 20
Say, Constant, 89
Schiaparelli, Elsa, 141
Schneider, Romy, 191
Sert, José Maria, 100–101, 111–113, 121

Sert, Misia, 43, 96–108 passim, 121; and artists of postwar Paris, 97–98, 114; her birth, 98–99; introduces Coco to Paris society, 99–102, 107, 123, 124, 134; and Diaghilev's death, 107–108; comforts Coco at Boy Capel's death, 111–113; her death, 113; Reverdy's letters to, 135–136
Seventh Avenue, New York, 168
Seyrig, Delphine, 191
Snow, Carmel, 169, 179
"Spatz," see D, Baron von
Stravinsky, Igor, 98, 100, 104, 105, 110

Toulouse-Lautrec, Henri de, 97
Toulouse-Lautrec, Mapie (Marie-Pierre) de, 169, 170
Trubetzkoy, Princess, 99
t'Serstevens, Albert, 171

Ursula, Duchess of Westminster, 127n

Vadim, Roger, 176, 206–207, 211
Vallotton, 97
van Gogh, Vincent, 98
van Zuylen, Maggie, 14, 24, 163; at reopening of House of Chanel (1954), 174
Vian, Boris, 106, 167
Vichy, 53, 54
Vilmorin, Louise de, 17, 72, 73, 162; her version of Coco's childhood, 39
Vionnet, Madeleine, 186
Vogue magazine, 8, 18, 223; hails Chanel's comeback, 176
Vuillard, Jean Édouard, 97

Wertheimer, Paul, 156–159, 160, 161
Wertheimer, Pierre, 155–159, 160, 161; and American success of Chanel, 179–180; death of, 230
Westminster, Duke of, 4, 38, 43, 107, 108, 121, 134, 140, 148, 153, 217, 262; Coco's affair with, 123–132; background, 124; his wealth, 125, 127, 130; his letters to Coco, 126–127; and question of marriage to Coco, 127; Coco's break with, 131–132; his gifts of jewels to Coco, 184
Women's Wear Daily, 239–240, 264